Mastering Selenium WebDriver

Increase the performance, capability, and reliability
of your automated checks by mastering Selenium
WebDriver

Mark Collin

PACKT PUBLISHING

BIRMINGHAM - MUMBAI

Mastering Selenium WebDriver

First published: August 2015

Production reference: 1240815

Published by Packt Publishing Ltd.
Livery Place
35 Livery Street
Birmingham B3 2PB, UK.

ISBN 978-1-78439-435-6

www.packtpub.com

Credits

Author
Mark Collin

Reviewers
Anuj Chaudhary
David Fotel
Ripon Al Wasim

Acquisition Editor
Usha Iyer

Content Development Editor
Shweta Pant

Technical Editor
Edwin Moses

Copy Editors
Stephen Copestake
Vedangi Narvekar

Project Coordinator
Shipra Chawhan

Proofreader
Safis Editing

Indexer
Hemangini Bari

Graphics
Sheetal Aute
Jason Monteiro
Abhinash Sahu

Production Coordinator
Komal Ramchandani

Cover Work
Komal Ramchandani

About the Author

Mark Collin is a professional software tester who has been working in the software testing industry since 2001. He started his career in the financial sector before moving in consultancy. As a consultant, he has had the privilege of working on numerous projects in many different sectors for various large and well-known companies. This has allowed him to gain an eclectic range of skills and proficiencies, which include test automation, security and penetration testing, and performance testing.

He loves technology and is always exploring new and exciting technology stacks to see how they can enhance the capability and reliability of automated checks. He is fully aware that though automation is good, at the moment, nothing can replace the human mind when it comes to having a well-rounded test solution.

He is a great believer in open source technology and spends a lot of time contributing towards open source projects. He is the creator and maintainer of the driver-binary-downloader-maven-plugin, which allows Maven to download ChromeDriver, OperaDriver, the IE driver, and PhantomJS to your machine as a part of a standard Maven build. He is also a core contributor to the jmeter-maven-plugin, a tool that allows you to run JMeter tests through Maven. Mark has also contributed code to the core Selenium code base.

A big thank you to all the core Selenium committers, especially David Burns, Jim Evans, and Luke Inman Semerau. Without these determined individuals, the Selenium project would not be where it is today.

Thank you Raúl Ireneo García Suárez for being a sounding board and pointing me in the right direction many times.

Finally, I'd like to thank my wife and family for giving me the time to put all of this together.

About the Reviewers

Anuj Chaudhary is a software engineer who enjoys working on projects pertaining to software testing and automation. He has vast experience of working on different testing methodologies such as manual testing, automated testing, performance testing, and security testing. He has worked as an individual contributor and a technical lead on various software projects that dealt with all the stages of the application development lifecycle.

He was a recipient of the Microsoft MVP award twice in a row. He blogs at www.anujchaudhary.com.

He has also reviewed books on Selenium by Packt Publishing, such as *Selenium WebDriver Practical Guide* (http://www.packtpub.com/selenium-webdriver-practical-guide/book) and *Selenium Design Patterns and Best Practices* (https://www.packtpub.com/web-development/selenium-design-patterns-and-best-practices).

I would like to thank my wife, Renu, and my son, Arjun, for always supporting me and letting me spend extra time on reviewing this book.

David Fotel has worked in various IT-related fields as a developer, system administrator, and an instructor. The technologies he has worked on include .NET and Linux. He has worked as a test manager, managing tests for an e-learning company. The broad knowledge that he has acquired gives him the ability to choose the right solution for a problem.

Prior to this, David has worked on *Selenium WebDriver Practical Guide, Packt Publishing*, as a technical reviewer.

Ripon Al Wasim has over 13 years of experience in the software industry. His professional experience includes software development and testing (both functional and nonfunctional). He is currently working as a senior software engineer at Cefalo (http://www.cefalo.com/).

He is mainly a Javaist. At present, he is trying to become Rubyist, as he is a fan of Watir (Web Application Testing in Ruby) and Cucumber.

Ripon is an active participant in the professional community of Stack Overflow (http://stackoverflow.com/users/617450/ripon-al-wasim).

He is one of the reviewers of *Selenium WebDriver Practical Guide*, which was his first official effort for Packt Publishing. He also reviewed another book titled *Performance Testing with JMeter, Second Edition*, which was also published by Packt Publishing.

I would like to thank my mother and wife for supporting me. In my spare time, I love to spend time with my wife, Koly, as well as my twin babies, Nawar and Nazif.

Finally, I'd like to thank all my colleagues, friends, and others.

www.PacktPub.com

Support files, eBooks, discount offers, and more

For support files and downloads related to your book, please visit www.PacktPub.com.

Did you know that Packt offers eBook versions of every book published, with PDF and ePub files available? You can upgrade to the eBook version at www.PacktPub.com and as a print book customer, you are entitled to a discount on the eBook copy. Get in touch with us at service@packtpub.com for more details.

At www.PacktPub.com, you can also read a collection of free technical articles, sign up for a range of free newsletters and receive exclusive discounts and offers on Packt books and eBooks.

https://www2.packtpub.com/books/subscription/packtlib

Do you need instant solutions to your IT questions? PacktLib is Packt's online digital book library. Here, you can search, access, and read Packt's entire library of books.

Why subscribe?

- Fully searchable across every book published by Packt
- Copy and paste, print, and bookmark content
- On demand and accessible via a web browser

Free access for Packt account holders

If you have an account with Packt at www.PacktPub.com, you can use this to access PacktLib today and view 9 entirely free books. Simply use your login credentials for immediate access.

Table of Contents

Preface

This book is going to focus on some of the more advanced aspects of Selenium. It will help you develop a greater understanding of Selenium as a test tool and give you a series of strategies to help you create reliable and extensible test frameworks.

In the world of automation, there is rarely only one correct way of doing things. This book will provide you with a series of minimalistic implementations that are flexible enough to be customized to your specific needs.

This book is not going to teach you how to write bloated test frameworks that hide Selenium behind an impenetrable veil of obscurity. Instead, it will show you how to complement Selenium with useful additions that fit seamlessly into the rich and well-crafted API that Selenium already offers you.

What this book covers

Chapter 1, *Creating a Fast Feedback Loop*, shows you how to build a small but powerful Selenium framework that enables you to get started quickly. We will focus on building something that enables people to run Selenium tests quickly and easily without having to download and configure libraries and external binaries themselves.

Chapter 2, *Producing the Right Feedback When Failing*, shows you how to get the framework, which was built in the first chapter, running on a continuous integration server. We will then extend the framework so that it can connect to Sauce Labs (or any other Selenium Grid) and take screenshots when tests fail. We will finish off by looking at stack traces and how we can use the information in them to find out why our tests fail.

Chapter 3, *Exceptions Are Actually Oracles*, examines common exceptions that are thrown by Selenium when running tests. We will work through the exceptions in detail and explore ways to make sure that our tests don't throw them when they shouldn't.

Chapter 4, *The Waiting Game*, explores the most common cause behind test failures in automation. It will explain in detail how waits work in Selenium and how you should use them to ensure that you have stable and reliable tests.

Chapter 5, *Working with Effective Page Objects*, shows you how to use page objects in Selenium. It focuses on proper separation of concerns and also demonstrates how to use the Page Factory classes in the Selenium support package. It finishes off by demonstrating how to build fluent page objects.

Chapter 6, *Utilizing the Advanced User Interactions API*, shows how you can automate challenging scenarios such as hover menus and drag-and-drop controls. It will also highlight some of the problems that you may come across when using the Advanced User Interactions API.

Chapter 7, *JavaScript Execution with Selenium*, introduces the JavaScript executor and shows how you can use it to work around complex automation problems. We will also look at how we can execute asynchronous scripts that use a callback to notify Selenium that they have completed execution.

Chapter 8, *Keeping It Real*, shows you what cannot be done with Selenium. We will then go through a series of scenarios that demonstrate how to extend Selenium to work with external libraries and applications so that we can use the right tool for the job.

Chapter 9, *Hooking Docker into Selenium*, introduces Docker. We will have a look at how we can spin up a Selenium Grid using Docker and start the Docker containers as a part of the build process.

Chapter 10, *Selenium – the Future*, talks about how Selenium is changing as it becomes a W3C specification. You will also find out how you can help shape the future of Selenium by contributing to the project in multiple ways.

What you need for this book

The following software are required for the book:

- Oracle JDK8*
- Maven 3
- IntelliJ IDEA 14**
- JMeter
- Zed Attack Proxy
- boot2docker or Docker***
- Mozilla Firefox
- Google Chrome

Generally, the more the browsers you install, the better. You will be able to perform all the exercises in this book if you have at least Mozilla Firefox and Google Chrome installed.

* You can try using the older versions of Oracle JDK or OpenJDK, but your mileage may vary.

** The community edition of IntelliJ IDEA is free, but it's certainly worth purchasing a license to get access to the full functionality. You can use the older versions of IntelliJ IDEA or another IDE according to your preference. The code for this book has been written in IntelliJ IDEA 14.

*** If you are running Linux, you will be able to install Docker without having to use boot2docker.

Who this book is for

This book is for testers who are interested in automation, have some experience working with Selenium, are competent with Java, and are looking forward to taking the next step in their learning journey.

Java is one of the most widely used languages in the enterprise world. You will often see Java coupled with Maven because of its extremely powerful dependency management and build capabilities. This book will show you how to start using these technologies to their full potential.

The theories in this book are transferable to any language. However, if you are not using Java, the code examples will be of limited use.

Who is this book not for?

This book is not an introduction to basic Selenium functionality. If you have not encountered Selenium before, or if you want to learn the basics of Selenium, you should start out with *Selenium 2 Testing Tools: Beginner's Guide, David Burns*. It is assumed that you will be able to do simple things like finding elements in the DOM with appropriate locators, and that you will have a reasonable level of Java knowledge. This book is not going to teach you how to write Java code.

Conventions

In this book, you will find a number of styles of text that distinguish between different kinds of information. Here are some examples of these styles, and an explanation of their meaning.

Code words in text, database table names, folder names, filenames, file extensions, pathnames, dummy URLs, user input, and Twitter handles are shown as follows: "Start off by creating a src/test/java directory, and then into this directory we will create a file called basicTest.java."

A block of code is set as follows:

```
package com.masteringselenium;

import org.openqa.selenium.WebDriver;
import org.testng.annotations.AfterMethod;
import org.testng.annotations.BeforeSuite;

public class DriverFactory {

    private static ThreadLocal<WebDriverThread> driverThread;

    @BeforeSuite
    public static void instantiateDriverObject() {
        driverThread = new ThreadLocal<WebDriverThread>() {
            @Override
            protected WebDriverThread initialValue() {
                WebDriverThread webDriverThread = new
                WebDriverThread();
                return webDriverThread;
            }
        };
    }
```

When we wish to draw your attention to a particular part of a code block, the relevant lines or items are set in bold:

```
public class DriverFactory {

    private static List<WebDriverThread> webDriverThreadPool =
    Collections.synchronizedList(new
    ArrayList<WebDriverThread>());
    private static ThreadLocal<WebDriverThread> driverThread;

    @BeforeSuite
    public static void instantiateDriverObject() {
        driverThread = new ThreadLocal<WebDriverThread>() {
            @Override
            protected WebDriverThread initialValue() {
```

```
        WebDriverThread webDriverThread = new
        WebDriverThread();
        webDriverThreadPool.add(webDriverThread);
        return webDriverThread;
    }
  };
}
```

Any command-line input or output is written as follows:

```
mvn clean install
```

New terms and **important words** are shown in bold. Words that you see on the screen, in menus or dialog boxes for example, appear in the text like this: "Let's start off by clicking on the **Create New Project** button."

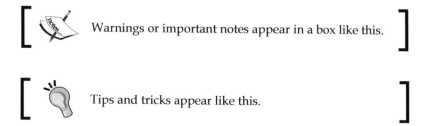

Warnings or important notes appear in a box like this.

Tips and tricks appear like this.

Reader feedback

Feedback from our readers is always welcome. Let us know what you think about this book—what you liked or may have disliked. Reader feedback is important for us to develop titles that you really get the most out of.

To send us general feedback, simply send an e-mail to feedback@packtpub.com, and mention the book title via the subject of your message.

If there is a topic that you have expertise in and you are interested in either writing or contributing to a book, see our author guide on www.packtpub.com/authors.

Customer support

Now that you are the proud owner of a Packt book, we have a number of things to help you to get the most from your purchase.

Downloading the example code

You can download the example code files for all Packt books you have purchased from your account at http://www.packtpub.com. If you purchased this book elsewhere, you can visit http://www.packtpub.com/support and register to have the files e-mailed directly to you.

Errata

Although we have taken every care to ensure the accuracy of our content, mistakes do happen. If you find a mistake in one of our books—maybe a mistake in the text or the code—we would be grateful if you would report this to us. By doing so, you can save other readers from frustration and help us improve subsequent versions of this book. If you find any errata, please report them by visiting http://www.packtpub.com/submit-errata, selecting your book, clicking on the **Errata Submission Form** link, and entering the details of your errata. Once your errata are verified, your submission will be accepted and the errata will be uploaded on our website, or added to any list of existing errata, under the Errata section of that title.

To view the previously submitted errata, go to https://www.packtpub.com/books/content/support and enter the name of the book in the search field. The required information will appear under the **Errata** section.

Piracy

Piracy of copyright material on the Internet is an ongoing problem across all media. At Packt, we take the protection of our copyright and licenses very seriously. If you come across any illegal copies of our works, in any form, on the Internet, please provide us with the location address or website name immediately so that we can pursue a remedy.

Please contact us at copyright@packtpub.com with a link to the suspected pirated material.

We appreciate your help in protecting our authors, and our ability to bring you valuable content.

Questions

You can contact us at questions@packtpub.com if you are having a problem with any aspect of the book, and we will do our best to address it.

1
Creating a Fast Feedback Loop

One of the main problems you hear people talking about with Selenium is how long it takes to run all of their tests. I have heard figures ranging from a couple of hours to a couple of days. In this chapter, we will have a look at how we can speed things up and get the tests that you are writing running both quickly and regularly.

The second problem that you may come across is getting other people to run your tests; this is usually because it is a pain to set up the project to work on their machine and it's too much effort for them. By making things run fast, we are going to make it very easy for others to check out your code and get themselves up and running.

How does this create a fast feedback loop? Well, if your developers are running all of the tests before every check in, they will know if the changes they have made to the code break things before the code leaves their machine.

They can also update the tests as the code changes, transforming the tests into living documentation.

Making it easy for developers to run tests

Ideally, we want our tests to run every time somebody pushes code to the central code repository; part of doing this is ensuring that it's very easy to run our tests. If somebody can just check out our code base, run one command, and have all of the tests just work, it means they are far more likely to run them.

We are going to make this easy by using Apache Maven. To steal a quote from the Maven documentation:

> *"Maven is an attempt to apply patterns to a project's build infrastructure in order to promote comprehension and productivity by providing a clear path in the use of best practices."*

> - https://maven.apache.org/guides/getting-started

Maven is a tool that can be used to build Java projects and manage project dependencies (including downloading any dependencies that you require) and is used in many companies as part of the standard enterprise infrastructure. Maven is not the only solution to this problem (for example Gradle is quickly gaining popularity and traction) but it is one that you are most likely to see on the ground and one that most Java developers will have used at some point in their career.

One of the major plus points is that it encourages developers to use a standardized project structure that makes it easy for people who know Maven to navigate around the source code; it also makes it very easy to plug into a CI system (such as Jenkins, or TeamCity) as all the major ones understand Maven POM files.

How does this make it easy for developers to run tests? Well, when we have set our project up using Maven, they should be able to check out our test code and simply type mvn clean install into a terminal window. This will automatically download all dependencies, set up the class path, and run all of the tests.

It doesn't really get much easier than that.

Building our test project with Apache Maven

Getting a fully working Maven install up-and-running is beyond the scope of this book, but it shouldn't be too hard. Apache has a guide to setting Maven up in 5 minutes at the following link:

http://maven.apache.org/guides/getting-started/maven-in-five-minutes.html

If you are running the Debian derivative of Linux, it is as easy as:

```
sudo apt-get install maven
```

Or, if you are running a Mac with homebrew, it is just:

```
brew install maven
```

Once you have Maven installed and working, we will start our Selenium project with a basic POM file. We are going to start out by creating a basic Maven directory structure and then creating a file called pom.xml in it. The directory structure is displayed here:

There are two main testing frameworks that you will come across in a Java environment: jUnit and TestNG. I personally find TestNG to be easier to get up-and-running out-of-the-box, but I find jUnit to be more extensible. TestNG certainly seems to be popular on the Selenium mailing list with many threads asking questions about it; you don't often see jUnit questions any more.

I'm not going to suggest either one as the right choice as they are both capable frameworks that you will probably come across in the enterprise world. Since TestNG seems to be the more popular option, we will focus on a TestNG implementation in this chapter.

In this chapter, we will implement the same base project, but we will use jUnit instead of TestNG. This means that, instead of worrying about which one is the best, you can have a look at a TestNG implementation and a jUnit implementation. You can then choose which one you prefer and read the relevant section.

So to start off with, let's have a look at a basic POM for a TestNG-based Maven project:

```xml
<?xml version="1.0" encoding="UTF-8"?>
<project xmlns="http://maven.apache.org/POM/4.0.0"
         xmlns:xsi="http://www.w3.org/2001/XMLSchema-instance"
         xsi:schemaLocation="http://maven.apache.org/POM/4.0.0
         http://maven.apache.org/xsd/maven-4.0.0.xsd">

    <groupId>com.masteringselenium.demo</groupId>
    <artifactId>mastering-selenium-testng</artifactId>
    <version>1.0-SNAPSHOT</version>
    <modelVersion>4.0.0</modelVersion>

    <name>Mastering Selenium TestNG</name>
```

```
<description>A basic Selenium POM file</description>
<url>http://www.masteringselenium.com</url>

<properties>
    <project.build.sourceEncoding>UTF-8
    </project.build.sourceEncoding>
    <project.reporting.outputEncoding>UTF-8
    </project.reporting.outputEncoding>
    <!-- Dependency versions -->
    <selenium.version>2.45.0</selenium.version>
</properties>

<dependencies>
    <dependency>
        <groupId>org.seleniumhq.selenium</groupId>
        <artifactId>selenium-java</artifactId>
        <version>${selenium.version}</version>
        <scope>test</scope>
    </dependency>
    <dependency>
        <groupId>org.seleniumhq.selenium</groupId>
        <artifactId>selenium-remote-driver</artifactId>
        <version>${selenium.version}</version>
    </dependency>
    <dependency>
        <groupId>org.testng</groupId>
        <artifactId>testng</artifactId>
        <version>6.8</version>
        <scope>test</scope>
    </dependency>
</dependencies>

</project>
```

What you are seeing here is mainly Maven boilerplate code. The groupId, artifactId, and version properties are subject to the standard naming conventions:

- groupId: This should be a domain that you own/control and is entered in reverse

- artifactId: This is the name that will be allocated to your JAR file, so remember to make it what you want your JAR file to be called

- version: This should always be a number with -SNAPSHOT appended to the end; this shows that it is currently a work in process

The important bits that we have added, and that will be useful to our project, are in the dependencies block. To start off with, we have added a dependency for Selenium and a dependency for TestNG. Note that we have given them a scope of test; this ensures that these dependencies are only loaded into the class path when tests are run.

 We have used a property to set the Selenium version. This is just so that we can quickly update Selenium versions without having to work our way through the POM finding each bit of Selenium that we want to update.

You can now open up this POM file using your IDE. (In this book I'm assuming that you are using IntelliJ IDEA; however, any modern IDE should be able to open up a POM file and create a project from it.)

We now have the basis of our Selenium project. The next step is to create a basic test that we can run using Maven. Start off by creating a src/test/java directory and then in this directory we will create a file called basicTest.java. Into this file we are going to put the following code:

```
package com.masteringselenium;

import org.openqa.selenium.By;
import org.openqa.selenium.WebDriver;
import org.openqa.selenium.WebElement;
import org.openqa.selenium.firefox.FirefoxDriver;
import org.openqa.selenium.support.ui.ExpectedCondition;
import org.openqa.selenium.support.ui.WebDriverWait;
import org.testng.annotations.Test;

public class BasicTest {

    private void googleExampleThatSearchesFor(final String
    searchString) {

        WebDriver driver = new FirefoxDriver();

        driver.get("http://www.google.com");

        WebElement searchField = driver.findElement(By.name("q"));

        searchField.clear();
```

```
        searchField.sendKeys(searchString);

        System.out.println("Page title is: " + driver.getTitle());

        searchField.submit();

        (new WebDriverWait(driver, 10)).until(new
        ExpectedCondition<Boolean>() {
            public Boolean apply(WebDriver driverObject) {
                return driverObject.getTitle().toLowerCase()
                .startsWith(searchString.toLowerCase());
            }
        });

        System.out.println("Page title is: " + driver.getTitle());

        driver.quit();
    }

    @Test
    public void googleCheeseExample() {
        googleExampleThatSearchesFor("Cheese!");
    }

    @Test
    public void googleMilkExample() {
        googleExampleThatSearchesFor("Milk!");
    }
}
```

These two tests should be quite familiar; it's the basic Google cheese scenario with all the main grunt work abstracted out into a method that we are able to call multiple times with different search terms. We now have everything we need to run our tests. To kick them off, just type the following into the terminal:

```
mvn clean install
```

You will now see Maven downloading all of the Java dependencies from Maven central. When this has completed, it will build the project and then run the tests.

 If you have problems downloading the dependencies try adding a -U to the end of the command; this will force Maven to check the Maven central repositories for updated libraries.

Finally, you will see Firefox load up and run through the two basic tests.

 If things don't work it's likely that your versions of Selenium and Firefox are out of sync; check the prerequisites to make sure your environment is set up correctly.

We now have a very basic project set up to run a couple of very basic tests using Maven. Right now this will run very quickly but, as you start adding more and more tests to your project, things are going to start slowing down. To try and mitigate this problem we are going to utilize the full power of your machine by running your tests in parallel.

Running your tests in parallel

Running your tests in parallel means different things to different people, as follows:

- Running all of your tests against multiple browsers at the same time
- Running your tests against multiple instances of the same browser

Should we run our tests in parallel to increase coverage?

I'm sure that, when you are writing automated tests to make sure things work with the website you are testing, you are initially told that your website has to work on all browsers. The reality is that this is just not true. There are many browsers out there and it's just not feasible to support everything. For example, will your AJAX-intensive site that has the odd Flash object work in the Lynx browser?

 Lynx is a text-based web browser that can be used in a Linux terminal window and was still in active development in 2014.

The next thing you will hear is, "OK, we will support every browser supported by Selenium". Again that's great but we have problems. Something that most people don't realize is that the core Selenium team's official browser support is the current browser version, and the previous version at the time of release of a version of Selenium. In practice it may well work on older browsers and the core team does a lot of work to try and make sure they don't break support for older browsers. However if you want to run a series of tests on Internet Explorer 6, Internet Explorer 7, or even Internet Explorer 8, you are actually running tests against browsers that are not officially supported by Selenium.

We then come to our next set of problems. Internet Explorer is only supported on Windows machines, and you can only have one version of Internet Explorer installed on a Windows machine at any time.

> There are hacks to install multiple versions of Internet Explorer on the same machine, but you will not get accurate tests if you do this. It's much better to have multiple operating systems running with just one version of Internet Explorer.

Safari is only supported on OS X machines, and again you can only have one version installed at a time.

> There is an old version of Safari for Windows hidden away in Apple's archives, but it is no longer actively supported and therefore shouldn't be used.

It soon becomes apparent that, even if we do want to run all of our tests against every browser supported by Selenium, we are not going to be able to do it on one machine.

At this point, people tend to modify their test framework so that it can accept a list of browsers to run against. They write some code that detects, or specifies, which browsers are available on a machine. Once they have done this they start running all of their tests over a few machines *in parallel* and end up with a matrix that looks like this:

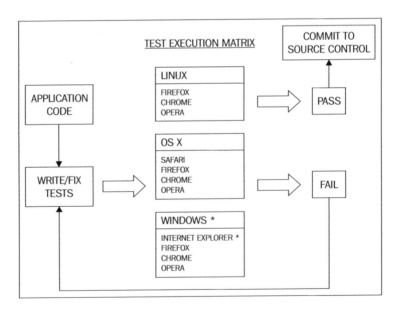

This is great, but it doesn't get around the problem that there's always going to be one or two browsers you can't run against your local machine, so you will never get full cross-browser coverage. Using multiple different driver instances (potentially in multiple threads) to run against different browsers has given us slightly increased coverage. We still don't have full coverage, though.

We also suffer some side effects by doing this. Different browsers run tests at different speeds because JavaScript engines in all browsers are not equal. We have probably drastically slowed down the process of checking that the code works before you push it to a source code repository.

Finally, by doing this we can make it much harder to diagnose issues. When a test fails you have to work out which browser it was running against, as well as why it failed. This may only take a minute of your time, but all those minutes do add up.

So why don't we just run our tests against one type of browser for the moment? Let's make that test run against that browser nice and fast, and then worry about cross-browser compatibility later.

 It's probably a good idea to just pick one browser to run our tests against on our development machines. We can then use a CI server to pick up the slack and worry about browser coverage as part of our build pipeline. It's probably also a good idea to pick a browser with a fast JavaScript engine for our local machines.

Parallel tests with TestNG

The TestNG examples used in this chapter will be using TestNG version 6.9.4 and the Maven failsafe plugin version 2.17. If you use older versions of these components, the functionality that we are going to use may not be available.

To start off, we are going to make some changes to our POM file. We are going to add a `threads` property that will be used to determine the number of parallel threads used to run our checks. Then, we are going to use the maven-failsafe plugin to configure TestNG:

```
<properties>
    <project.build.sourceEncoding>UTF-8
    </project.build.sourceEncoding>
    <project.reporting.outputEncoding>UTF-8
    </project.reporting.outputEncoding>
    <!-- Dependency versions -->
    <selenium.version>2.45.0</selenium.version>
    <!-- Configurable variables -->
    <threads>1</threads>
```

```
            </properties>

    <build>
        <plugins>
            <plugin>
                <groupId>org.apache.maven.plugins</groupId>
                <artifactId>maven-failsafe-plugin</artifactId>
                <version>2.17</version>
                <configuration>
                    <parallel>methods</parallel>
                    <threadCount>${threads}</threadCount>
                    <includes>
                        <include>**/*WD.java</include>
                    </includes>
                </configuration>
                <executions>
                    <execution>
                        <goals>
                            <goal>integration-test</goal>
                            <goal>verify</goal>
                        </goals>
                    </execution>
                </executions>
            </plugin>
        </plugins>
    </build>
```

 When using the `maven-failsafe` plugin, the integration-test goal will ensure that your tests run in the integration test phase. The verify goal ensures that the `failsafe-plugin` checks the results of the checks run in the integration-test phase, and fails the build if something did not pass. If you don't have the verify goal, the build will not fail!

TestNG supports parallel threads out-of-the-box; we just need to tell it how to use them. This is where the maven-failsafe plugin comes in. We are going to use it to configure our parallel execution environment for our tests. This configuration will be applied to TestNG if you have TestNG as a dependency; you don't need to do anything special.

In our case, we are interested in the configuration settings of `parallel` and `threadCount`. We have set `parallel` to `methods`. This will search through our project for methods that have the `@Test` annotation and will collect them all into a great big pool of tests. The failsafe plugin will then take tests out of this pool and run them. The number of tests that will be run concurrently will depend on how many threads are available. We will use the `threadCount` property to control this.

It is important to note that there is no guarantee in which order tests will be run.

We are using the `threadCount` configuration setting to control how many tests we run in parallel but, as you may have noticed, we have not specified a number. Instead, we have used the Maven variable `${threads}`; this will take the value of the Maven property `threads` that we defined in our properties block and pass it into `threadCount`.

Since threads is a Maven property, we are able to override its value on the command line by using the `-D` switch; if we do not override its value, it will use the value we have set in the POM as a default.

So let's run the following command:

```
mvn clean install
```

This command will use the default value of 1 in the POM file. However, if we use this:

```
mvn clean install -Dthreads=2
```

It will now overwrite the value of 1 stored in the POM file and use the value 2 instead. As you can see this gives us the ability to tweak the number of threads that we use to run our tests without making any code changes at all.

So we have used the power of Maven and the `maven-failsafe` plugin to set the number of threads that we want to use when running our tests in parallel. Now we need to modify our code to take advantage of this.

Previously, we were instantiating an instance of `FirefoxDriver` in each of our tests. Let's pull this out of the test, and put browser instantiation into its own class called `WebDriverThread`. We will then add a class called `DriverFactory` that will deal with the marshalling of the threads.

Downloading the example code

You can download the example code files from your account at http://www.packtpub.com for all the Packt Publishing books you have purchased. If you purchased this book elsewhere, you can visit http://www.packtpub.com/support and register to have the files e-mailed directly to you.

We are going to now build a project structure that looks like this:

First of all, we need to create our `WebDriverThread` class:

```
package com.masteringselenium;

import org.openqa.selenium.WebDriver;
import org.openqa.selenium.firefox.FirefoxDriver;
import org.openqa.selenium.remote.DesiredCapabilities;

public class WebDriverThread {

    private WebDriver webdriver;

    private final String operatingSystem =
    System.getProperty("os.name").toUpperCase();
    private final String systemArchitecture =
    System.getProperty("os.arch");

    public WebDriver getDriver() throws Exception {
        if (null == webdriver) {
            System.out.println(" ");
            System.out.println("Current Operating System: " +
            operatingSystem);
            System.out.println("Current Architecture: " +
            systemArchitecture);
            System.out.println("Current Browser Selection:
            Firefox");
            System.out.println(" ");
            webdriver = new
            FirefoxDriver(DesiredCapabilities.firefox());
        }

        return webdriver;
```

```
        }

    public void quitDriver() {
        if (null != webdriver) {
            webdriver.quit();
            webdriver = null;
        }
    }
}
```

This class holds a reference to a `WebDriver` object, and ensures that every time you call `getDriver()` you get a valid instance of `WebDriver` back. If one has been started up, you will get the existing one. If one hasn't been started up, it will start one for you.

It also provides a `quitDriver()` method that will perform a `quit()` on your `WebDriver` object. It also nullifies the `WebDriver` object held in the class. This prevents errors that would be caused by attempting to interact with a `WebDriver` object that has been closed.

> We are using `driver.quit()`, not `driver.close()`. As a general rule of thumb, you should not use `driver.close()` to clean up. It will throw an error if something happened during your test that caused the `WebDriver` instance to close early. The close and clean up command in the WebDriver API is `driver.quit()`. You would normally use `driver.close()` if your test opens multiple windows and you want to shut some of them.

Next, we need to create a class called `DriverFactory.java`:

```
package com.masteringselenium;

import org.openqa.selenium.WebDriver;
import org.testng.annotations.AfterMethod;
import org.testng.annotations.BeforeSuite;

public class DriverFactory {

    private static ThreadLocal<WebDriverThread> driverThread;

    @BeforeSuite
    public static void instantiateDriverObject() {
        driverThread = new ThreadLocal<WebDriverThread>() {
            @Override
```

```
            protected WebDriverThread initialValue() {
                WebDriverThread webDriverThread =
                new WebDriverThread();
                return webDriverThread;
            }
        };
    }

    public static WebDriver getDriver() throws Exception {
        return driverThread.get().getDriver();
    }

    @AfterMethod
    public static void quitDriver() throws Exception {
        driverThread.get().quitDriver();
    }
}
```

This is a small class that will hold a pool of driver objects. We are using a ThreadLocal object to instantiate our WebDriverThread objects in separate threads. We have also created a getDriver() method that uses the getDriver() method on the WebDriverThread object to pass each test a WebDriver instance it can use.

We are doing this to isolate each instance of WebDriver to make sure that there is no cross contamination between tests. When our tests start running in parallel, we don't want different tests to start firing commands to the same browser window. Each instance of WebDriver is now safely locked away in its own thread.

Since we are using this factory class to start up all our browser instances, we need to make sure that we close them down, as well. To do this we have created a method with an @AfterMethod annotation that will destroy the driver after our test has run. This also has the added advantage of cleaning up if our test fails to reach the line where it would normally call driver.quit() — for example, if there was an error in the test that caused it to fail and finish early.

All that is left now is to clean up the code in our basicTest class and change its name to BasicTestWD. You may have noticed that we added an <includes> configuration item to our POM. This is because Maven will use maven-surefire-plugin to run files that have test at the start or end of their name. We don't want maven-surefire-plugin to pick up our tests; we want to use maven-failsafe-plugin instead.

```
public class BasicTestWD extends DriverFactory {
```

```java
private void googleExampleThatSearchesFor(final String
searchString) throws Exception {

    WebDriver driver = DriverFactory.getDriver();

    driver.get("http://www.google.com");

    WebElement searchField = driver.findElement(By.name("q"));

    searchField.clear();
    searchField.sendKeys(searchString);

    System.out.println("Page title is: " + driver.getTitle());

    searchField.submit();

    (new WebDriverWait(driver, 10)).until(new
    ExpectedCondition<Boolean>() {
        public Boolean apply(WebDriver driverObject) {
            return driverObject.getTitle().toLowerCase().
            startsWith(searchString.toLowerCase());
        }
    });

    System.out.println("Page title is: " + driver.getTitle());
}

@Test
public void googleCheeseExample() throws Exception {
    googleExampleThatSearchesFor("Cheese!");
}

@Test
public void googleMilkExample() throws Exception {
    googleExampleThatSearchesFor("Milk!");
}
}
```

We have modified our basic test so that it extends `DriverFactory`. Instead of instantiating a new `FirefoxDriver` instance in the test, we are calling `DriverFactory.getDriver()` to get a valid `WebDriver` instance. Finally we have removed the `driver.quit()` from each test as this is all done by our `DriverFactory` class now.

Let's spin up our test again using the following command:

```
mvn clean install
```

You won't notice any difference. However if you now specify some threads by performing this:

```
mvn clean install -Dthreads=2
```

You will see that this time two Firefox browsers open, both tests run in parallel, and then both browsers are closed again.

 Are you seeing only one browser start up? In the `maven-failsafe-plugin` configuration, we have specified all files that end with `WD.java`. If you use filenames that start or end with `Test`, they will be picked up by the `maven-surefire` plugin and the threading configuration will be ignored. Double-check to make sure that your failsafe configuration is correct.

As you may have noticed, with two very small tests such as the ones we are using in our example, you will not see a massive decrease in the time taken to run the complete suite. This is because most of the time is spent compiling the code and loading up browsers. However, as you add more tests, the decrease in the time taken to run the tests becomes more and more apparent.

 This is probably a good time to tweak your `BasicTest.java` file and start adding some more tests that look for different search terms. Play about with the number of threads and see how many concurrent browsers you can get up-and-running at the same time. Make sure that you note down execution times to see what speed gains you are actually getting (they will also be useful later on in this chapter). There will come a point where you reach the limits of your computer's hardware and adding more threads will actually slow things down rather than making them faster. Tuning your tests to your hardware environment is an important part of running your tests in multiple threads.

So how can we speed things up even more? Well, starting up a web browser is a computationally intensive task, so we could choose not to close the browser after every test. This obviously has some side effects. You may not be at the usual entry page of your application, and you may have some session information that is not wanted.

First of all, we will try and deal with our session problem. WebDriver has a command that will allow you to clear out your cookies, so we will trigger this after every test. We will then add a new `@AfterSuite` annotation to close the browser once all of the tests have finished.

```
package com.masteringselenium;

import org.openqa.selenium.WebDriver;
import org.testng.annotations.AfterMethod;
import org.testng.annotations.AfterSuite;
import org.testng.annotations.BeforeSuite;

import java.util.ArrayList;
import java.util.Collections;
import java.util.List;
public class DriverFactory {

    private static List<WebDriverThread> webDriverThreadPool =
    Collections.synchronizedList(new
    ArrayList<WebDriverThread>());
    private static ThreadLocal<WebDriverThread> driverThread;

    @BeforeSuite
    public static void instantiateDriverObject() {
        driverThread = new ThreadLocal<WebDriverThread>() {
            @Override
            protected WebDriverThread initialValue() {
                WebDriverThread webDriverThread = new
                WebDriverThread();
                webDriverThreadPool.add(webDriverThread);
                return webDriverThread;
            }
        };
    }

    public static WebDriver getDriver() throws Exception {
        return driverThread.get().getDriver();
    }

    @AfterMethod
    public static void clearCookies() throws Exception {
        getDriver().manage().deleteAllCookies();
```

```
        }

    @AfterSuite
    public static void closeDriverObjects() {
        for (WebDriverThread webDriverThread :
        webDriverThreadPool) {
            webDriverThread.quitDriver();
        }
    }
}
```

The first addition to our code is a synchronized list where we can store all our instances of `WebDriverThread`. We then modified our `initialValue()` method to add each instance of `WebDriverThread` that we create to this new synchronized list. This is so that we can keep track of all our threads.

Next we renamed our `@AfterSuite` method, to ensure that the method names stay as descriptive as possible. It is now called `closeDriverObjects()`. This method does not just close down the instance of `WebDriver` that we are using like it did previously. Instead, it iterates through our `webDriverThreadPool`, closing every threaded instance we are keeping track of.

We don't actually know how many threads we are going to have running since this will be controlled by Maven. Thanks to this code, we don't have to know. What we do know is that, when our tests are finished, each `WebDriver` instance will be closed down cleanly, and without errors.

Finally we have added an `@AfterMethod` method called `clearCookies()` that will clear down the browser's cookies after each test. This should reset the browser to a neutral state without closing it so that we can start another test safely.

> Have a go at tweaking your `BasicTest.java` file again by adding some more tests that look for different search terms. Based on your previous experimentation, you will probably have a rough idea of what the sweet spot for your hardware is. Time how long it takes to execute your tests again when you only close all the browsers down when all the tests have finished executing. How much time did you shave off your execution time?

There are no silver bullets

As with everything, keeping your browser windows open while you run all of your tests will not work in every instance.

Sometimes, you may have a site that sets server-side cookies that Selenium is unaware of. In this case, clearing down your cookies may have no effect and you may find that closing down the browser is the only way to ensure a clean environment for each test.

If you use `InternetExplorerDriver`, you will probably find when using slightly older versions of Internet Explorer (for example, Internet Explorer 8 and Internet Explorer 9) that your tests will get slower and slower until they grind to a halt. Unfortunately, older versions of IE are not perfect and they do have some memory leak issues.

Using `InternetExplorerDriver` does exacerbate these issues because it is really stressing the browser. As a result it does get a lot of unfair press. It's an excellent bit of code that deals with an awful lot of crap thrown at it.

This is not to say that you can't use this method; you may not see any issues with your site.

Removing the browser shutdown and start-up time after each test really does make a massive difference to the speed of your test runs. You should always try to keep the browser open whenever realistically possible.

The only way to be sure if it will work for you is experimentation and hard data. Just remember to do that investigation first. Once you are done, you should then tailor your thread usage to each browser/machine combination. Or you should set a baseline that works with everything in your environment.

Multiple browser support

So far, we have parallelized our tests so that we can run multiple browser instances at the same time. However, we are still using only one type of driver, the good old `FirefoxDriver`. I mentioned problems with Internet Explorer in the previous section, but right now we have no obvious way to run our tests using Internet Explorer. Let's have a look at how we can fix this.

To start off with, we will need to create a new Maven property called `browser` and a new configuration setting inside our failsafe plugin configuration called `systemPropertyVariables`. This is pretty much what is says on the tin; everything defined inside `systemPropertyValues` will become a system property, which will be available to your Selenium tests. We are going to use a Maven variable to reference a Maven property so that we can dynamically change this value on the command line.

Here are the changes you need to make to your POM:

```xml
<properties>
    <project.build.sourceEncoding>UTF-8
    </project.build.sourceEncoding>
    <project.reporting.outputEncoding>UTF-8
    </project.reporting.outputEncoding>
    <!-- Dependency versions -->
    <selenium.version>2.45.0</selenium.version>
    <!-- Configurable variables -->
    <threads>1</threads>
    <browser>firefox</browser>
</properties>

<build>
    <plugins>
        <plugin>
            <groupId>org.apache.maven.plugins</groupId>
            <artifactId>maven-failsafe-plugin</artifactId>
            <version>2.17</version>
            <configuration>
                <parallel>methods</parallel>
                <threadCount>${threads}</threadCount>
                <systemProperties>
                    <browser>${browser}</browser>
                </systemProperties>
                <includes>
                    <include>**/*WD.java</include>
                </includes>
            </configuration>
            <executions>
                <execution>
                    <goals>
                        <goal>integration-test</goal>
                        <goal>verify</goal>
                    </goals>
                </execution>
            </executions>
        </plugin>
    </plugins>
</build>
```

We now need to create a package where we are going to store our driver configuration code. We are going to add an interface, and an enum into this package.

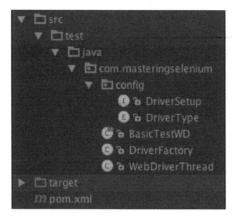

DriverSetup is a very simple interface that DriverType will implement:

```
package com.masteringselenium.config;

import org.openqa.selenium.WebDriver;
import org.openqa.selenium.remote.DesiredCapabilities;

public interface DriverSetup {

    WebDriver getWebDriverObject(DesiredCapabilities
    desiredCapabilities);

    DesiredCapabilities getDesiredCapabilities();
}
```

DriverType is where all the work is done:

```
package com.masteringselenium.config;

import org.openqa.selenium.WebDriver;
import org.openqa.selenium.chrome.ChromeDriver;
import org.openqa.selenium.firefox.FirefoxDriver;
import org.openqa.selenium.ie.InternetExplorerDriver;
import org.openqa.selenium.opera.OperaDriver;
import org.openqa.selenium.remote.CapabilityType;
import org.openqa.selenium.remote.DesiredCapabilities;
import org.openqa.selenium.safari.SafariDriver;

import java.util.Arrays;
```

```java
import java.util.HashMap;

public enum DriverType implements DriverSetup {

    FIREFOX {
        public DesiredCapabilities getDesiredCapabilities() {
            DesiredCapabilities capabilities =
            DesiredCapabilities.firefox();
            return capabilities;
        }

        public WebDriver getWebDriverObject(DesiredCapabilities
        capabilities) {
            return new FirefoxDriver(capabilities);
        }
    },
    CHROME {
        public DesiredCapabilities getDesiredCapabilities() {
            DesiredCapabilities capabilities =
            DesiredCapabilities.chrome();
            capabilities.setCapability("chrome.switches",
            Arrays.asList("--no-default-browser-check"));
            HashMap<String, String> chromePreferences =
            new HashMap<String, String>();
            chromePreferences.put(
            "profile.password_manager_enabled", "false");
            capabilities.setCapability("chrome.prefs",
            chromePreferences);
            return capabilities;
        }

        public WebDriver getWebDriverObject(DesiredCapabilities
        capabilities) {
            return new ChromeDriver(capabilities);
        }
    },
    IE {
        public DesiredCapabilities getDesiredCapabilities() {
            DesiredCapabilities capabilities =
            DesiredCapabilities.internetExplorer();
            capabilities.setCapability(CapabilityType.
            ForSeleniumServer.ENSURING_CLEAN_SESSION, true);
            capabilities.setCapability(InternetExplorerDriver.
            ENABLE_PERSISTENT_HOVERING, true);
            capabilities.setCapability("requireWindowFocus",
            true);
```

```
                return capabilities;
        }

        public WebDriver getWebDriverObject(DesiredCapabilities
        capabilities) {
                return new InternetExplorerDriver(capabilities);
        }
    },
    SAFARI {
        public DesiredCapabilities getDesiredCapabilities() {
                DesiredCapabilities capabilities =
                DesiredCapabilities.safari();
                capabilities.setCapability("safari.cleanSession",
                true);
                return capabilities;
        }

        public WebDriver getWebDriverObject(DesiredCapabilities
        capabilities) {
                return new SafariDriver(capabilities);
        }
    },
    OPERA {
        public DesiredCapabilities getDesiredCapabilities() {
                DesiredCapabilities capabilities =
                DesiredCapabilities.operaBlink();
                return capabilities;
        }

        public WebDriver getWebDriverObject(DesiredCapabilities
        capabilities) {
                return new OperaDriver(capabilities);
        }
    };
}
```

As you can see, our basic enum allows us to choose one of the default browsers supported by Selenium. Each enum entry implements a getDesiredCapabilities() method and a getWebDriverObject() method. This allows us to get a default set of capabilities that we could extend, if required. These desired capabilities can then be used to instantiate a new WebDriver object when calling the getWebDriverObject() method.

Let's have a look at the default desired capabilities we have set for each driver to help things run smoothly.

Firefox

Nothing to see here; the default Firefox profile is normally fine so it's just using all the defaults.

Chrome

We have a couple of options here to try and keep things running smoothly. Chrome has various command-line switches that can be used when starting it up with `ChromeDriver`. When we load up Chrome to run our tests, we don't want it asking us if it can be made the default browser every time it starts, so we have disabled that check. We have also turned off the password manager so that it does not ask if you would like to save your login details every time you have a test that performs a login action.

Internet Explorer

`InternetExplorerDriver` has a lot of challenges; it attempts to work with multiple different versions of Internet Explorer and generally does a very good job. These capabilities are used to try and ensure that sessions are properly cleaned out when reloading the browser (IE8 is particularly bad at clearing its cache), and then trying to fix some issues with hovering. If you have ever tested an application that needs you to hover over an element to trigger some sort of popup, you have probably seen the popup flickering a lot, and had intermittent failures when trying to interact with it. Setting `ENABLE_PERSISTENT_HOVERING` and `requireWindowFocus` should work around these issues.

Safari

Safari used to have some problems clearing down http-only cookies and secure cookies. The `safari.cleanSession` capability is a way to try and force a clear down of settings that `SafariDriver` (a JavaScript-only implementation) has problems with.

Opera

Again, nothing to see here. Opera Blink is relatively new so we are just going to go with the default set of options for now.

You don't need to use any of the desired capabilities described earlier; however, I have found them to be useful in the past, and I now use these as my default set.

If you don't want to use them, just remove the bits you aren't interested in and set up each `getDesiredCapabilities()` method like the `FirefoxDriver` one. Of course the opposite is also true; you can add in any desired capabilities that you find useful in your tests. This is going to be the place that instantiates a driver object so it's the best place to do it.

Now that everything is in place, we need to rewrite our `WebDriverThread` method:

```
package com.masteringselenium;

import com.masteringselenium.config.DriverType;
import org.openqa.selenium.WebDriver;
import org.openqa.selenium.remote.DesiredCapabilities;

import java.net.MalformedURLException;

import static com.masteringselenium.config.DriverType.FIREFOX;
import static com.masteringselenium.config.DriverType.valueOf;

public class WebDriverThread {

    private WebDriver webdriver;
    private DriverType selectedDriverType;

    private final DriverType defaultDriverType = FIREFOX;
    private final String browser =
    System.getProperty("browser").toUpperCase();
    private final String operatingSystem =
    System.getProperty("os.name").toUpperCase();
    private final String systemArchitecture =
    System.getProperty("os.arch");

    public WebDriver getDriver() throws Exception {
        if (null == webdriver) {
            selectedDriverType = determineEffectiveDriverType();
            DesiredCapabilities desiredCapabilities =
            selectedDriverType.getDesiredCapabilities();
            instantiateWebDriver(desiredCapabilities);
        }

        return webdriver;
    }

    public void quitDriver() {
```

```
            if (null != webdriver) {
                webdriver.quit();
            }
        }

    private DriverType determineEffectiveDriverType() {
        DriverType driverType = defaultDriverType;
        try {
            driverType = valueOf(browser);
        } catch (IllegalArgumentException ignored) {
            System.err.println("Unknown driver specified,
            defaulting to '" + driverType + "'...");
        } catch (NullPointerException ignored) {
            System.err.println("No driver specified, defaulting
            to '" + driverType + "'...");
        }
        return driverType;
    }

    private void instantiateWebDriver(DesiredCapabilities
    desiredCapabilities) throws MalformedURLException {
        System.out.println(" ");
        System.out.println("Current Operating System: " +
        operatingSystem);
        System.out.println("Current Architecture: " +
        systemArchitecture);
        System.out.println("Current Browser Selection: " +
        selectedDriverType);
        System.out.println(" ");
        webdriver = selectedDriverType.
        getWebDriverObject(desiredCapabilities);
    }
}
```

There is quite a lot going on here. First of all, we have added some new variables:

- One to read in the browser that we have specified

- One to set a default browser type, in case one has not been specified for any reason

- One to hold the type of driver that is going to be used for our tests after we have decided which browser we are going to use

We have then written a couple of new methods. The method called `instantiateWebDriver()` is basically the code that was previously inside `getDriver()`. We have just moved it out to isolate the function of actually instantiating a `WebDriver` object. The method called `determineEffectiveDriverType()` will take the `browser` variable and then try and work out which enum value maps across to the value it holds. If it cannot map a `DriverType` across to the value of `browser`, it will log an error and then default to our `defaultDriverType`.

The final part is the changes we have made to the `getDriver()` method. It now uses the new methods in `WebDriverThread` and `DriverType` to set up and return a valid `WebDriver` instance for your checks.

Let's try it out. First of all, let's check that everything still works like it used to:

```
mvn clean install -Dthreads=2
```

This time you should have seen no difference from the last time you ran it. Let's check the error handling next:

```
mvn clean install -Dthreads=2 -Dbrowser=iJustMadeThisUp
```

Again, it should have looked exactly the same as the previous run. We couldn't find an enum entry called `IJUSTMADETHISUP`, so we defaulted to `FirefoxDriver`.

Finally, let's try a new browser:

```
mvn clean install -Dthreads=2 -Dbrowser=chrome
```

You have probably had mixed success with this one. You will see that it tried to start up `ChromeDriver`, but if you don't have its executable installed on your system and a system property set up, it most likely threw an error saying that it couldn't find the `ChromeDriver` executable.

You can fix this by downloading the `ChromeDriver` binary and then setting up system properties to provide the path to the binary. This isn't really making our tests easy to run out-of-the-box for developers, though. It looks like we have more work to do.

Downloading the WebDriver binaries automatically

I came across this problem a few years ago, and at the time there wasn't an easy way to get hold of the binaries using Maven. So I did what anybody who is into open source software would do: I wrote a plugin to do it for me.

This plugin will allow you to specify a series of driver binaries to automatically download and remove the manual setup steps. It also means that you can enforce the version of driver binaries that are used, which removes lots of intermittent issues caused by people using different versions of the binaries that can behave differently, on different machines.

We are now going to enhance our project structure so that it looks like this:

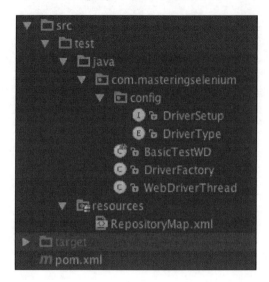

Let's start off by tweaking our POM; we will need a new property that we will call overwrite.binaries.

```
<properties>
    <project.build.sourceEncoding>UTF-8
    </project.build.sourceEncoding>
    <project.reporting.outputEncoding>UTF-8
    </project.reporting.outputEncoding>
    <!-- Dependency versions -->
    <selenium.version>2.45.0</selenium.version>
    <!-- Configurable variables -->
    <threads>1</threads>
    <browser>firefox</browser>
    <overwrite.binaries>false</overwrite.binaries>
</properties>
```

We then need to add the `driver-binary-downloader` plugin:

```
<plugin>
    <groupId>com.lazerycode.selenium</groupId>
    <artifactId>driver-binary-downloader-maven-plugin</artifactId>
    <version>1.0.7</version>
    <configuration>
        <rootStandaloneServerDirectory>${project.basedir}
        /src/test/resources/selenium_standalone_binaries
        </rootStandaloneServerDirectory>
        <downloadedZipFileDirectory>${project.basedir}
        /src/test/resources/selenium_standalone_zips
        </downloadedZipFileDirectory>
        <customRepositoryMap>${project.basedir}
        /src/test/resources/RepositoryMap.xml
        </customRepositoryMap>
        <overwriteFilesThatExist>${
        overwrite.binaries}</overwriteFilesThatExist>
    </configuration>
    <executions>
        <execution>
            <goals>
                <goal>selenium</goal>
            </goals>
        </execution>
    </executions>
</plugin>
```

Finally, we need to add some new system properties to our `maven-failsafe-plugin` configuration:

```
<plugin>
    <groupId>org.apache.maven.plugins</groupId>
    <artifactId>maven-failsafe-plugin</artifactId>
    <version>2.17</version>
    <configuration>
        <parallel>methods</parallel>
        <threadCount>${threads}</threadCount>
        <systemProperties>
            <browser>${browser}</browser>
            <!--Set properties passed in by the driver
            binary downloader-->
```

```
            <webdriver.chrome.driver>${webdriver.chrome.driver}
            </webdriver.chrome.driver>
            <webdriver.ie.driver>${webdriver.ie.driver}
            </webdriver.ie.driver>
            <webdriver.opera.driver>${webdriver.opera.driver}
            </webdriver.opera.driver>
        </systemProperties>
        <includes>
            <include>**/*WD.java</include>
        </includes>
    </configuration>
    <executions>
        <execution>
            <goals>
                <goal>integration-test</goal>
                <goal>verify</goal>
            </goals>
        </execution>
    </executions>
</plugin>
```

The plugin runs in the TEST_COMPILE phase by default. The order in which it is placed in the POM should not matter, as there shouldn't be any tests actually running in this phase. The new overwite.binaries property that we have added allows us to set the overwriteFilesThatExist configuration setting of driver-binary-downloader-maven-plugin. By default it will not overwrite files that already exist. This gives us an option to force the plugin to overwrite existing files if we want to download a new binary version, or just refresh our existing binaries.

We have two more configuration settings that are just specifying file paths. The downloadedZipFileDirectory setting is used to specify the file path that will be used to download the binary zip files. The rootStandaloneServerDirectory setting is the file path where we extract the driver binaries.

Finally, we use customRepositoryMap to point at customRepositoryMap.xml. The customRepositoryMap.xml file is where download locations for all the binaries we want to download are stored.

Finally we have added some system properties variables to maven-failsafe-plugin, to expose the locations of the binaries when they have been downloaded. The plugin, driver-binary-downloader-maven-plugin, will set a Maven variable that will point to the location of the downloaded binaries. Even though it looks like the variables we are using to set our system properties don't exist, it will be fine.

This is where we have been slightly clever; we have set the system properties that Selenium will use automatically to find the location of the driver binaries. This means that we don't need to add any additional code to make things work.

We now need to create a `RepositoryMap.xml` to define the download locations for our binaries; we will probably also need to create the `src/test/resources` directory since we haven't used it before. Here is a basic `RepositoryMap.xml` file using the default download locations for the binaries:

```
<?xml version="1.0" encoding="utf-8" standalone="yes"?>
<root>
    <windows>
        <driver id="internetexplorer">
            <version id="2.45.0">
                <bitrate sixtyfourbit="true">
                    <filelocation>http://selenium-release.storage.
                    googleapis.com/2.45/
                    IEDriverServer_x64_2.45.0.zip</filelocation>
                    <hash>b3cdacc846d7b9c3f8fb8b70af0a9cfc5839bd83
                    </hash>
                    <hashtype>sha1</hashtype>
                </bitrate>
                <bitrate thirtytwobit="true">
                    <filelocation>http://selenium-release.storage.
                    googleapis.com/2.45/IEDriverServer
                    _Win32_2.45.0.zip</filelocation>
                    <hash>cc822d30efe3119b76af9265c47d42fca208f85a
                    </hash>
                    <hashtype>sha1</hashtype>
                </bitrate>
            </version>
        </driver>
        <driver id="googlechrome">
            <version id="2.14">
                <bitrate thirtytwobit="true" sixtyfourbit="true">
                    <filelocation>http://chromedriver.storage.
                    googleapis.com/2.14/chromedriver_
                    win32.zip</filelocation>
                    <hash>4fe4aaf625073c39c29da994d815ffcc2c314c40
                    </hash>
                    <hashtype>sha1</hashtype>
                </bitrate>
            </version>
        </driver>
        <driver id="operachromium">
```

```
            <version id="2.14">
                <bitrate thirtytwobit="true" sixtyfourbit="true">
                    <filelocation>https://github.com/operasoftware
                    /operachromiumdriver/releases/download/v0.1.0/
                    operadriver_win32.zip</filelocation>
                    <hash>4a4ad051c315e4141048f0ae587
                    c05f4c8720c24</hash>
                    <hashtype>sha1</hashtype>
                </bitrate>
            </version>
        </driver>
    </windows>
    <linux>
        <driver id="googlechrome">
            <version id="2.14">
                <bitrate sixtyfourbit="true">
                    <filelocation>http://chromedriver.storage.
                    googleapis.com/2.14/chromedriver_linux64.zip
                    </filelocation>
                    <hash>acb76a3eb2bc94ee96b6a17121980e2662c88650
                    </hash>
                    <hashtype>sha1</hashtype>
                </bitrate>
                <bitrate thirtytwobit="true">
                    <filelocation>http://chromedriver.storage.
                    googleapis.com/2.14/chromedriver_linux32.zip
                    </filelocation>
                    <hash>237a5ed160bb23118a9ea5b84700e8799e897bd4
                    </hash>
                    <hashtype>sha1</hashtype>
                </bitrate>
            </version>
        </driver>
        <driver id="operachromium">
            <version id="2.14">
                <bitrate thirtytwobit="true">
                    <filelocation>https://github.com/
                    operasoftware/operachromiumdriver/releases/
                    download/v0.1.0/operadriver_linux32.zip
                    </filelocation>
                    <hash>feda76d61190161bd9923f8f1613447f722f12fc
                    </hash>
                    <hashtype>sha1</hashtype>
                </bitrate>
                <bitrate sixtyfourbit="true">
```

```
                    <filelocation>https://github.com/operasoftware
                    /operachromiumdriver/releases/download/v0.1.0/
                    operadriver_linux64.zip</filelocation>
                    <hash>c36234222efccc1f874682b2ce2add639d544e9d
                    </hash>
                    <hashtype>sha1</hashtype>
                </bitrate>
            </version>
        </driver>
    </linux>
    <osx>
        <driver id="googlechrome">
            <version id="2.14">
                <bitrate thirtytwobit="true" sixtyfourbit="true">
                    <filelocation>http://chromedriver.storage.
                    googleapis.com/2.14/chromedriver_mac32.zip
                    </filelocation>
                    <hash>64ef44893a87a0e470b60ff8f5fc83a588b78023
                    </hash>
                    <hashtype>sha1</hashtype>
                </bitrate>
            </version>
        </driver>
        <driver id="operachromium">
            <version id="2.14">
                <bitrate thirtytwobit="true">
                    <filelocation>https://github.com/operasoftware
                    /operachromiumdriver/releases/download/v0.1.0/
                    operadriver_mac32.zip</filelocation>
                    <hash>7ab79a1c70bb0f5998b9c5c8d08160ef86b618e9
                    </hash>
                    <hashtype>sha1</hashtype>
                </bitrate>
                <bitrate sixtyfourbit="true">
                    <filelocation>https://github.com/operasoftware
                    /operachromiumdriver/releases/download/v0.1.0/
                    operadriver_mac64.zip</filelocation>
                    <hash>32e5e0fc63bed0f61bb4e8695fd7a8faaebd7b37
                    </hash>
                    <hashtype>sha1</hashtype>
                </bitrate>
            </version>
        </driver>
    </osx>
</root>
```

If you are on a corporate network that does not allow you to access the outside world, you can, of course, download the binaries and put them on a local file server. You can then update your `RepositoryMap.xml` file to point at this local fileserver instead of the Internet. This gives you a great deal of flexibility.

Right, let's run our project again to check that everything works. First of all, let's use this command:

```
mvn clean install -Dthreads=2
```

Everything should still work as normal. Next, let's see if we can now select Chrome and have everything automatically downloaded for us so that it can just run:

```
mvn clean install -Dthreads=2 -Dbrowser=chrome
```

This time you should see two Chrome browsers open up instead of the Firefox ones. The `chromedriver` binary will have been automatically downloaded and the system property that tells Selenium where to find it has been set.

We can now give anybody access to our code, and when they check it out and run it, things should just work.

Going headless

Going headless seems to be all the rage these days, so let's have a look at how we can add `GhostDriver` into the mix. We already have pretty much all of the code we need, so this is just going to be a few minor tweaks. Let's start off by updating our POM to bring in a dependency on `GhostDriver`:

```
<dependency>
    <groupId>com.codeborne</groupId>
    <artifactId>phantomjsdriver</artifactId>
    <version>1.2.1</version>
</dependency>
```

`GhostDriver` depends upon PhantomJS. This is another binary that most people will not have by default, but that's fine; the `driver-binary-downloader` plugin can get it for us.

> This is not the official PhantomJSDriver distribution, but it fixes an error that came in with Selenium 2.44.0. Keep an eye on the group ID `com.github.detro` for official releases, or watch the official phantomjsdriver Github page `https://github.com/detro/`.

Let's update our `RepositoryMap.xml` file as follows:

```xml
<?xml version="1.0" encoding="utf-8" standalone="yes"?>
<root>
    <windows>
        <driver id="internetexplorer">
            <version id="2.45.0">
                <bitrate sixtyfourbit="true">
                    <filelocation>http://selenium-release.
                    storage.googleapis.com/2.45/IEDriverServer
                    _x64_2.45.0.zip</filelocation>
                    <hash>b3cdacc846d7b9c3f8fb8b70af0a9cfc5839bd83
                    </hash>
                    <hashtype>sha1</hashtype>
                </bitrate>
                <bitrate thirtytwobit="true">
                    <filelocation>http://selenium-release.storage.
                    googleapis.com/2.45/IEDriverServer
                    _Win32_2.45.0.zip</filelocation>
                    <hash>cc822d30efe3119b76af9265c47d42fca208f85a
                    </hash>
                    <hashtype>sha1</hashtype>
                </bitrate>
            </version>
        </driver>
        <driver id="googlechrome">
            <version id="2.14">
                <bitrate thirtytwobit="true" sixtyfourbit="true">
                    <filelocation>http://chromedriver.storage.
                    googleapis.com/2.14/chromedriver_win32.zip
                    </filelocation>
                    <hash>4fe4aaf625073c39c29da994d815ffcc2c314c40
                    </hash>
                    <hashtype>sha1</hashtype>
                </bitrate>
            </version>
        </driver>
        <driver id="operachromium">
            <version id="2.14">
                <bitrate thirtytwobit="true" sixtyfourbit="true">
                    <filelocation>https://github.com/operasoftware
                    /operachromiumdriver/releases/download/v0.1.0/
                    operadriver_win32.zip</filelocation>
                    <hash>4a4ad051c315e4141048f0ae587c05f4c8720c24
                    </hash>
```

```
            <hashtype>sha1</hashtype>
        </bitrate>
    </version>
</driver>
<driver id="phantomjs">
    <version id="1.9.8">
        <bitrate thirtytwobit="true" sixtyfourbit="true">
            <filelocation>https://bitbucket.org/ariya/
            phantomjs/downloads/phantomjs-1.9.8-
            windows.zip</filelocation>
            <hash>4531bd64df101a689ac7ac7f3e11bb7e77af8eff
            </hash>
            <hashtype>sha1</hashtype>
        </bitrate>
    </version>
</driver>
</windows>
<linux>
    <driver id="googlechrome">
        <version id="2.14">
            <bitrate sixtyfourbit="true">
                <filelocation>http://chromedriver.storage.
                googleapis.com/2.14/chromedriver_linux64.zip
                </filelocation>
                <hash>acb76a3eb2bc94ee96b6a17121980e2662c88650
                </hash>
                <hashtype>sha1</hashtype>
            </bitrate>
            <bitrate thirtytwobit="true">
                <filelocation>http://chromedriver.storage.
                googleapis.com/2.14/chromedriver_linux32.zip
                </filelocation>
                <hash>237a5ed160bb23118a9ea5b84700e8799e897bd4
                </hash>
                <hashtype>sha1</hashtype>
            </bitrate>
        </version>
    </driver>
    <driver id="operachromium">
        <version id="2.14">
            <bitrate thirtytwobit="true">
                <filelocation>https://github.com/operasoftware
                /operachromiumdriver/releases/download/v0.1.0/
                operadriver_linux32.zip</filelocation>
                <hash>feda76d61190161bd9923f8f1613447f722f12fc
                </hash>
```

```xml
                    <hashtype>sha1</hashtype>
                </bitrate>
                <bitrate sixtyfourbit="true">
                    <filelocation>https://github.com/operasoftware
                    /operachromiumdriver/releases/download/v0.1.0/
                    operadriver_linux64.zip</filelocation>
                    <hash>c36234222efccc1f874682b2ce2add639d544e9d
                    </hash>
                    <hashtype>sha1</hashtype>
                </bitrate>
            </version>
        </driver>
        <driver id="phantomjs">
            <version id="1.9.8">
                <bitrate sixtyfourbit="true">
                    <filelocation>https://bitbucket.org/ariya/
                    phantomjs/downloads/phantomjs-1.9.8-linux-
                    x86_64.tar.bz2</filelocation>
                    <hash>d29487b2701bcbe3c0a52bc176247ceda4d09d2d
                    </hash>
                    <hashtype>sha1</hashtype>
                </bitrate>
                <bitrate thirtytwobit="true">
                    <filelocation>https://bitbucket.org/ariya/
                    phantomjs/downloads/phantomjs-1.9.8-linux-
                    i686.tar.bz2</filelocation>
                    <hash>efac5ae5b84a4b2b3fa845e8390fca39e6e637f2
                    </hash>
                    <hashtype>sha1</hashtype>
                </bitrate>
            </version>
        </driver>
    </linux>
    <osx>
        <driver id="googlechrome">
            <version id="2.14">
                <bitrate thirtytwobit="true" sixtyfourbit="true">
                    <filelocation>http://chromedriver.storage.
                    googleapis.com/2.14/chromedriver_mac32.zip
                    </filelocation>
                    <hash>64ef44893a87a0e470b60ff8f5fc83a588b78023
                    </hash>
                    <hashtype>sha1</hashtype>
                </bitrate>
            </version>
        </driver>
```

```xml
        <driver id="operachromium">
            <version id="2.14">
                <bitrate thirtytwobit="true">
                    <filelocation>https://github.com/operasoftware
                    /operachromiumdriver/releases/download/v0.1.0
                    /operadriver_mac32.zip</filelocation>
                    <hash>7ab79a1c70bb0f5998b9c5c8d08160ef86b618e9
                    </hash>
                    <hashtype>sha1</hashtype>
                </bitrate>
                <bitrate sixtyfourbit="true">
                    <filelocation>https://github.com/operasoftware
                    /operachromiumdriver/releases/download/v0.1.0/
                    operadriver_mac64.zip</filelocation>
                    <hash>32e5e0fc63bed0f61bb4e8695fd7a8faaebd7b37
                    </hash>
                    <hashtype>sha1</hashtype>
                </bitrate>
            </version>
        </driver>
        <driver id="phantomjs">
            <version id="1.9.8">
                <bitrate thirtytwobit="true" sixtyfourbit="true">
                    <filelocation>https://bitbucket.org/ariya/
                    phantomjs/downloads/phantomjs-1.9.8-
                    macosx.zip</filelocation>
                    <hash>d70bbefd857f21104c5961b9dd081781cb4d999a
                    </hash>
                    <hashtype>sha1</hashtype>
                </bitrate>
            </version>
        </driver>
    </osx>
</root>
```

We will then need to update the system properties that we are setting in our POM so that Selenium knows where it needs to look for the PhantomJS binary:

```xml
<systemProperties>
    <browser>${browser}</browser>
    <!--Set properties passed in by the driver
    binary downloader-->
    <phantomjs.binary.path>${phantomjs.binary.path}
    </phantomjs.binary.path>
```

```
    <webdriver.chrome.driver>${webdriver.chrome.driver}
    </webdriver.chrome.driver>
    <webdriver.ie.driver>${webdriver.ie.driver}
    </webdriver.ie.driver>
    <webdriver.opera.driver>${webdriver.opera.driver}
    </webdriver.opera.driver>
</systemProperties>
```

Finally, we need to add a PhantomJS option into `DriverType`:

```
PHANTOMJS {
    public DesiredCapabilities getDesiredCapabilities() {
        DesiredCapabilities capabilities =
        DesiredCapabilities.phantomjs();
        final List<String> cliArguments = new ArrayList<String>();
        cliArguments.add("--web-security=false");
        cliArguments.add("--ssl-protocol=any");
        cliArguments.add("--ignore-ssl-errors=true");
        capabilities.setCapability("phantomjs.cli.args",
        cliArguments);
        capabilities.setCapability("takesScreenshot", true);

        return capabilities;
    }

    public WebDriver getWebDriverObject(DesiredCapabilities
    capabilities) {
        return new PhantomJSDriver(capabilities);
    }
}
```

As you can see, we have set some new capabilities. We are turning off any Web security or SSL error checking and enabling all SSL protocols. Most test environments don't have valid certificates set up; this will allow us to bypass the majority of certificate problems. We can then set a capability to allow us to take screenshots, as it's really quite useful.

We can now run our project again, but this time we are going to specify `phantomjs` as the browser:

`mvn clean install -Dthreads=2 -Dbrowser=phantomjs`

PhantomJS will automatically download, and all of the tests will run again. This time it will be slightly different, you won't see any browsers open up.

The really nice thing about this addition is that it is effectively downloading the browser that is required to run the tests. So a machine with no browsers installed will be able to run our tests and everything that is needed will be automatically downloaded. You can't really make your tests more accessible than that! Don't forget that you can easily change the default browser with a minor tweak to the `defaultDriverType` variable set in `WebDriverThread`. You may decide that PhantomJS is a better option for your default test runs.

Summary

After reading through this chapter, you should:

- Be able to set up a basic project using Maven to download your dependencies, configure your class path, and build your code.

- Know what advantages you gain by running your tests in parallel with multiple instances of the same browser in TestNG.

- Know how to automatically download the driver binaries using a Maven plugin, making your test code very portable.

- Be able to determine the correct number of threads to use as a default value when running your tests. You should also know how to override this, if required.

- Know how to add `GhostDriver` into the mix so that you can run your tests heedlessly.

In the next chapter, we are going to have a look at how to cope when things go wrong. We will also examine how we can keep track of things, now that we have lots of tests all running at the same time.

2
Producing the Right Feedback When Failing

In this chapter, we are going to have a look at how we can make life easier for you when tests start failing. We will:

- Discuss where our tests should live and examine why
- Have a look at test reliability
- Have a look at ways we can force our tests to be run regularly
- Talk about continuous integration and continuous delivery
- Extend the project we started in the previous chapter so that it can run against a Selenium Grid
- Have a look at ways to diagnose problems with our tests

Location, location, location

Many companies still have discrete test and development teams. This is obviously not an ideal situation as the test team is usually not completely aware of what the development team is building. This also provides us with additional challenges if the test team is tasked with writing automated functional tests using the web frontend.

The usual problem is that the test team is behind the development team; how far behind depends upon how frequent development releases are. The thing is, it doesn't really matter how far behind the development team you are. If you are behind them you will always be playing catch-up. When you are playing catch-up, you are constantly updating your scripts to make them work with a new software release.

> Some people may call fixing their scripts to work with new functionality refactoring; they are wrong! Refactoring is rewriting your code to make it cleaner and more efficient. The actual code, or in our case test script, functionality does not change. If you are changing the way your code works, you are not refactoring.

While constantly updating your scripts is not necessarily a bad thing, having your tests break every time there is a new release of code *is* a bad thing. If your tests continually stop working for no good reason, people are going to stop trusting them. When they see a failing build they will assume that it's another problem with the tests, and not an issue with the website you are testing.

So we need to find a way to stop our tests from failing all of the time for no good reason. Let's start off with something easy that shouldn't be too controversial; let's make sure that the test code always lives in the same code repository as the application code.

How does this help?

Well, if the test code lives in the same repository as the application code it is accessible to all the developers. In the previous chapter, we had a look at how we could make it really easy for developers to just check out our tests and run them. If we make sure that our test code is in the same code base as the application code, we have also ensured that any developers who are working on the application will automatically have a copy of our tests. This means that all you have to do now is give your developers a command to run and then they can run the tests themselves against their local copy of code and see if any break.

Another advantage of having your test code in the same repository as the application code is that developers have full access to it. They can see how things work, and they can change the tests as they change the functionality of the application. The ideal scenario is that every change made to the system by developers also results in a change to the tests to keep them in sync. This way, the tests don't start failing for no real reason when the next application release happens and your tests become something more than an automated regression check; they become living documentation that describes how the application works.

Tests are living documentation

So what do I mean by living documentation? As the application is built, automated tests are continually being written to ensure that specific criteria are met. These tests come in many different shapes and sizes, ranging from unit tests to integration tests and leading up to end-to-end functional tests and beyond. All of these tests describe, in some way, how the application works. You have to admit that this sounds just like documentation.

This documentation may not be perfect, but that doesn't stop it from being documentation. Think of an application that has some unit tests, and maybe one badly written end-to-end test. I would equate that with the sort of documentation that you would get with a cheap electrical product, from somewhere like China. It comes with a manual that will undoubtedly include a small, badly written English section which doesn't really tell you very much. It will also have lots of documentation in a language that you probably don't understand, in this case Chinese, which is very useful for somebody who speaks that language. This doesn't mean that the product is bad; it's just hard to work out what to do with it. Most of the time, you can work out what to do without the manual. If it's really complex you will probably go and find somebody who either speaks Chinese, or knows how the product works, and get them to explain it to you.

When I talk about tests as documentation, I usually think of different test phases as being documentation for different people. Let's take the unit tests; these are highly technical in nature and explain how tiny bits of the system work in extreme detail. If you compared this to the manual of an electrical product, these would probably be the tech specs in the appendix that provide lots of in-depth information that most consumers don't care about. Integration tests would probably be the part of the manual that explains how to connect your electrical appliance to other electrical appliances. This is very useful if you are going to connect to another electrical appliance, but you probably don't care about it that much if you aren't. Finally the functional end-to-end tests are the bit of the documentation that actually tells you how to use the appliance. This is the part of the manual that will be read the most by the average user (they probably don't care about the technical nitty-gritty).

I think one of the most important things that you can do when writing automated tests is make sure that they are good documentation. This means: make sure that you describe how all the parts of the application you are testing work (or, to put it another way, have a high level of test coverage). The hardest part though is making the tests understandable for people who are not technical. This is where **domain-specific languages (DSLs)** come in where you can hide the inner workings of the tests behind human-readable language. Good tests are like good documentation; if they are really good they will use plain English and describe things so well that the person reading them will not need to go anywhere else to ask for help.

So why is it living documentation, rather than just normal documentation? Well, it's living because every time the application you are testing changes, the automated tests change as well. They evolve with the product and continue to explain how it works in its current state. If our build is successful, our documentation describes how the system currently works.

Do not think of automated tests as regression tests that are there to detect changes in behavior. Think of them as living documentation that describes how the product works. If somebody comes and asks you how something works, you should ideally be able to open a test that can answer their question. If you can't, you probably have some missing documentation.

So where does regression testing come into this? Well it doesn't. We don't need a regression-testing phase. Our test documentation tells us how the product works. When the functionality of our product changes, the tests are updated to tell us how the new functionality works. Our existing documentation for the old functionality doesn't change unless the functionality changes.

Our test documentation covers regression and new functionality.

Reliability

When it comes to automation, reliability of tests is the key. If your tests are not reliable they will not be trusted, which can have far-reaching consequences. I'm sure you have all worked in environments where test reliability has been hard for one of many reasons; let's have a look at a couple of scenarios.

The test automation team that works in isolation

One of the more common reasons that tests are not reliable is having a dedicated test automation team who work in isolation from the team that develops the application. This should really be avoided if possible as the test automation team is always playing catch-up. The development team rolls out new features that the test automation teams have to automate, but they are never sure what is coming next. They usually find out that existing features have changed when their tests break and as well as fixing them they need to work out what the new functionality is and whether it is behaving as expected.

Something that normally happens in situations like these is that the test manager realizes that they don't have enough time to do everything and they look for ways to reduce the workload. Do you fix the existing failing tests and not automate new tests, instead getting some manual regression scripts put together to cover the gap? Do you continue automating the new functionality and accept that some of your old tests will fail? If you do, how do you deal with failing tests? Maybe put aside some time to fix failing tests and accept that your tests will never be green?

This is where you usually start to hear suggestions that it is time to lower the bar for the automated tests. "It should be fine as long as 95 percent of the automated tests pass; we know we have high coverage and those failing 5 percent are probably due to changes to the system that we haven't yet had the time to deal with." Everybody is happy at first; they continue to automate things and make sure that 95 percent of tests are always passing. Soon though the pass mark starts to dip below 95 percent. A couple of weeks later a pragmatic decision is taken to lower the bar to 90 percent, then 85 percent, then 80 percent. Before you know it tests are failing all over the place and you have no idea which failures are legitimate problems with the application, which ones are expected failures, and which ones are intermittent failures.

When tests go red nobody really pays attention any more, they just talk about that magic 80-percent line: It's a high number—we must have a decent product if that many tests are still passing, right? If things dip below that line we massage a few failing tests and make them pass, usually the low hanging fruit because we don't have time to spend trying to tackle the really thorny issues.

I hate to break it to you, but if you are in this situation your automation experiment has failed and nobody trusts your tests. Instead of looking at that 80 percent number you need to look at the other side of the coin; 20 percent of the functionality of your site is not working as expected and you don't know why! You need to stop the developers from writing any new code and work out how to fix the massive mess that you are currently in. How did you get here? You didn't think test reliability mattered and that mistake came back to bite you.

Oh that test always flickers, don't worry about it

This scenario is one that can occur in both isolated automation teams and integrated teams where everybody works together. You have probably seen automated tests that are not totally reliable; you know that one flickering test that occasionally fails for no obvious reason. Somebody once had a look at it and said that there was no reason for it to fail so it got ignored; and now, whenever it fails again, somebody says, "Oh, it's that flickering test again, don't worry about it. It will be green again soon".

A flickering test is one that intermittently fails for no obvious reason and then passes when you run it again. There are various phrases used to describe tests like this; you may have heard of them described as flaky tests, random failures, unstable tests, or some other name unique to your company.

The thing is that we now have a problem; tests do not flicker for no reason. This test is desperately trying to tell you something and you are ignoring it. What is it trying to tell you? Well you can't be sure until you have found out why it is flickering; it could be one of many things. Among the many possibilities a few are:

- The test is not actually checking what you think it is checking
- The test may be badly written
- There may be an intermittent fault in the application that is under test (for example, there may be a race condition nobody has identified yet)
- Maybe you have some problems with a date/time implementation (it's something that is notoriously hard to get right and the cause of many bugs in many systems)
- Network problems—is there a proxy getting in the way?

The point is that while your test is flickering we don't know what the problem is, but don't fool yourself; there is a problem. It's a problem that will at some point come back and bite you if you don't fix it.

Let's imagine for a moment that the software you are testing is something that buys and sells shares and you are pushing new releases out daily because your company has to stay ahead of the game. You have a test that has been flickering for as long as you can remember. Somebody once had a look at it, said they couldn't find any problems with the code, and that the test was just unreliable; this has been accepted and now everybody just does a quick manual check if it goes red. A new cut of code goes in and that test that keeps flickering goes red again. You are used to that test flickering and everything seems to work normally when you perform a quick manual test, so you ignore it. The release goes ahead, but there is a problem; suddenly your trading software starts selling when it should be buying, and buying when it should be selling. It isn't picked up instantly because the software has been through testing and must be good so no problems are expected. An hour later all hell has broken loose, the software has sold all the wrong stock and bought a load of rubbish. In the space of an hour the company has lost half its value and there is nothing that can be done to rectify the situation. There is an investigation and it's found that the flickering test wasn't actually flickering this time; it failed for a good reason, one that wasn't instantly obvious when performing a quick manual check. All eyes turn to you; it was you who validated the code that should never have been released and they need somebody to blame; if only that stupid test hadn't been flickering for as long as you can remember...

The preceding scenario is an extreme, but hopefully you get the point: flickering tests are dangerous and something that should not be tolerated.

We ideally want to be in a state where every test failure means that there is an undocumented change to the system. What do we do about undocumented changes? Well, that depends. If we didn't mean to make the change, we revert it. If we did mean to make the change, we update the documentation (our automated tests) to support it.

Baking in reliability

How can we try to enforce reliability and make sure that these changes are picked up early?

We could ask our developers to run the tests before every push, but sometimes people forget. Maybe they didn't forget, but it's a small change and it doesn't seem worth going through a full test run for something so minor. (Have you ever heard somebody say, "It's only a CSS change"?) Making sure that the tests are run and passed before every push to the centralized source code repository takes discipline.

What do we do if our team lacks discipline? What if we still keep getting failures that should have been easily caught, even after we have asked people to run the tests before they push the code to the central repository? If nothing else works we could have a discussion with the developers about enforcing this rule.

This is actually surprisingly easy; most **source code management** (**SCM**) systems support hooks. These are actions that are automatically triggered when you use a specific SCM function. Let's have a look at how we can implement hooks in some of the most widely used SCM systems.

Git

First of all, we need to go to the SCM root folder (the place where we originally cloned our project). Git creates a hidden folder called `.git` that holds all the information about your project that Git needs to do its job. We are going to go into this folder, and then into the `hooks` sub folder:

```
cd .git/hooks
```

Git has a series of predefined hook names. Whenever you perform a Git command, Git will have a look in the `hooks` folder to see if there are any files that match any predefined hook names that would be triggered as a result of the command. If there are matches Git will run them. We want to make sure that our project can be built, and all of our tests are run, before we push any code to Git. To make this happen we are going to add a file called `pre-push`. When that file is added we are going to populate it with the following content:

```
#!/usr/bin/env bash
mvn clean install
```

This hook will now be triggered every time we use the `git push` command.

> One thing to note about Git hooks is that they are individual for every user; they are not controlled by the repository you push to, or pull from. If you want them automatically installed for developers who use your code base, you need to think outside the box. You could for example write a script that copies them into the `.git/hooks` folder as part of your build.

We could have added a pre-commit hook, but we don't really care if the code doesn't work on the developer's local machine (they may be half way through a big change and committing code to make sure they don't lose anything). What we do care about is that the code works when it is pushed to the central source code repository.

> If you are a Windows user, you may be looking at the preceding script and thinking that it looks very much like something that you would put on a *nix system. Don't worry, Git for Windows installs Git bash, which it will use to interpret this script, so it will work on Windows as well.

SVN

SVN (subversion) hooks are a little more complicated than Git hooks; they will depend upon how your system is configured to a degree. The hooks are stored in your SVN repository in a sub folder called `hooks`. As with Git, they need to have specific names (a full list of which is available in the SVN manual). For our purposes we are only interested in the pre-commit hook, so let's start off with a *nix-based environment. First of all we need to create a file called pre-commit, and then we will populate it with:

```
#!/usr/bin/env bash
mvn clean install
```

As you can see it looks identical to the Git hook script; however there may be problems. SVN hooks are run against an empty environment, so if you are using an environment variable to make `mvn` a recognized command, things may not work. If there is a symlink in `/usr/bin or /usr/local/bin/`, you should be fine; if not, you will probably need to specify the absolute file path location to the `mvn` command.

Now we need to also make this hook work for people using Windows. It will be very similar, but this time the file needs to be called `pre-commit.bat`; this is because SVN looks for different files in different operating systems.

```
mvn clean install
```

Again it's pretty similar; we just don't need to have a Bash shebang. Windows suffers from the same empty environment problems so again you will probably have to supply an absolute file path to your `mvn install` command. Let's hope that everybody developing in Windows has installed Maven to the same place.

> It is worth bearing in mind that hooks like this are not infallible; if you have some local changes on your machine that are not committed the tests may pass, but that code will not be pushed to the central code repository, resulting in a build failure if anybody else tries to run it. As with all things, this is not a silver bullet, but it can certainly help.

We have now made sure that our tests run before the code is pushed to our central code repository so we should have caught the vast majority of errors; however, things are still not perfect. It's possible that one of the developers made a code change that they forgot to commit. In this case the tests will run on their local machine and pass, but an important file that makes this change work will be missing from the source control. This is one of the causes of *works on my machine* problems.

It's also possible that all files have been committed and the tests pass, but the environment that is on the developers' machines is nothing like the production environment where the code will be deployed. This is probably the main cause of *works on my machine* problems.

What do we do to mitigate these risks and ensure that we quickly find out when things do go wrong despite everybody doing their best to ensure everything works?

Continuous integration is the key

Continuous integration is a way to try and mitigate the issues that we come across by only building and testing code on our development machines. Our continuous integration server will monitor our source code repository and then every time it detects a change it will trigger a series of actions. The first action will be to build the code, running any tests that it can as it builds the code (usually unit tests), and then creating a deployable artifact. This artifact will then usually be deployed to a server that is a replica of the live environment. Once this code has been deployed to a server, the rest of our tests will be run against that server to ensure that everything is working as expected. If things do not work as expected, the build fails and the development team is notified so that they can fix the problems. It's important to note that we only build the artifact once; if we rebuild it multiple times, we will be testing artifacts that are potentially different at every step (maybe it was built with a different version of Java, maybe it had different properties applied to it, and so on).

With continuous integration we are looking for a workflow like this:

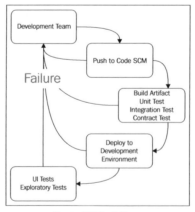

Basic CI Workflow

Most continuous integration systems also have big visible dashboards to let people know the status of the build at all times; if your screen ever goes red, people should stop what they are doing and fix the problem as soon as possible.

Let's have a look at how easily we can get our tests running on a continuous integration server. This is not going to be a fully featured continuous integration setup, just enough for you to run the tests we have built so far. It should be enough to familiarize you with the technologies, though.

The first thing we are going to do is configure a Maven profile. This will enable us to isolate our Selenium tests from the rest of the build if desired, so that we can turn them in a separate UI block of tests on our continuous integration server. This is a very simple change to our POM; we are simply going to wrap our `<build>` and `<dependencies>` blocks with a profile block. It will look like this:

```
<profiles>
    <profile>
        <id>selenium</id>
        <activation>
            <activeByDefault>true</activeByDefault>
        </activation>

        <build>
            <plugins>
                <plugin>
                    ...
                </plugin>
            </plugins>
        </build>

        <dependencies>
            <dependency>
                ...
            </dependency>
        </dependencies>
    </profile>
</profiles>
```

As you can see, we have created a profile called `selenium`. If we want to run this in isolation we can now use the following command:

`mvn clean install -Pselenium`

You will also notice that we have added `<activeByDefault>true</activeByDefault>`; this will ensure that this profile is active if no profiles are specified on the command line, so you will find that the following command still works:

`mvn clean install`

This is to ensure that our tests are still run as part of a normal build, and the SCM hooks that we set up previously still do their job.

We are going to look at two popular continuous integration servers. TeamCity is a personal favorite of mine and Jenkins is one that is prolific; you have probably seen a Jenkins install at some point in your career.

TeamCity

TeamCity (`https://www.jetbrains.com/teamcity/`) is an enterprise-level continuous integration server. It supports a lot of technologies out-of-the-box and is very reliable and capable. One of my favorite features is the ability to spin up **AWS (Amazon Web Services** — `http://aws.amazon.com`) cloud build agents. You will need to create the build agent **AMI (Amazon Machines Image)** but, once you have done this, your TeamCity server can start up, however, many build agents are required and then shut them down again when the build has finished.

A basic TeamCity install should be pretty simple; you just need an application server that can host WAR files. One of the most commonly used application servers is Apache Tomcat, and the install is pretty simple. If you have a working Tomcat install, then all you need to do is drop the WAR into the `webapps` directory. Tomcat will do the rest for you.

Let's have a look at how we can get our build, up-and-running in TeamCity. When you first get into a new install of TeamCity you should see the following screen:

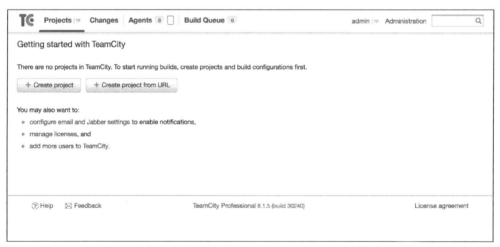

Getting started with TeamCity

Now, follow these steps:

1. Let's start off by clicking on the **Create New Project** button.

Creating a new project

2. We then need to provide a name for our project and we can add a description to let people know what the project does. Bear in mind that this is not an actual build we are creating yet, it is something that will hold all of our builds for this project. Selenium Tests is probably not a great name for a project, but that's all we have at the moment. Click on **Create** and you will see your project created.

3. We then need to scroll down to the **Build Configurations** section:

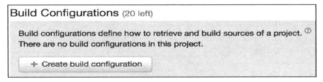

Projects need build configurations

4. When you get there, click on the **Create Build Configuration** button.

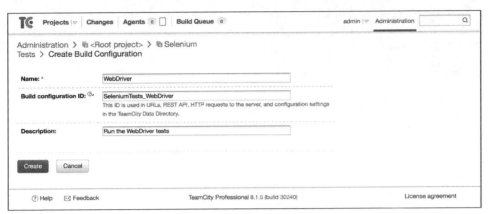

Creating a build configuration

This is where we are going to create our build. I've simply called it `WebDriver` because it is going to run `WebDriver` tests, I'm sure you can come up with a better name for your build configuration.

5. When you are happy with the name for your configuration, click on the **Create** button.

Configuring source control

6. Now we will be asked to configure our source control system so that TeamCity can monitor your source control for changes. I've selected Git and put in some valid values as a guideline; you will obviously need to put in values that relate to your source control system. Once you have created your source control link, it will ask you about the build you want to create.

Configurations need build steps

7. This is where we get into the meat of our build; click on **Add build step** to get started.

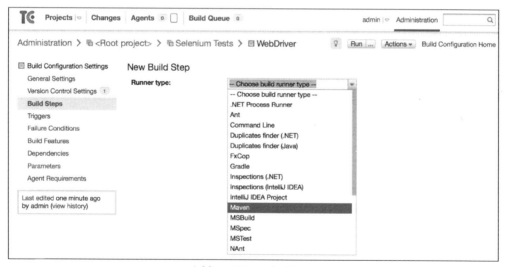

Adding a Maven build step

8. First of all we need to select the type of build; in our case, we have a Maven project so select **Maven**.

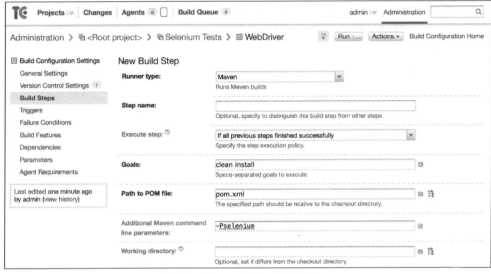

Configuring your Maven build step

9. Finally, we just need to put in the details of our Maven build; you will need to click on the **Show Advanced** options link to display the items in orange. Scroll down and click on **Save** and your TeamCity build is all ready to go. We now just need to make sure that it will trigger every time that you check code into your source code repository. Click on **Triggers**.

Triggers

10. This is where you set up a list of actions that will result in a build being performed. Click on **Add new trigger** and select **VCS Trigger**.

Adding a SCM trigger

11. If you click on **Save** now, a trigger will be set up and will trigger a build every time you push code to your central source code repository.

Jenkins

Jenkins (`http://jenkins-ci.org`) is a firm favorite in the **continuous integration** (CI) world and is the basis for some cloud services (for example: CloudBees—`https://www.cloudbees.com`). It is very widely used and no section on continuous integration would be complete without mentioning it.

A basic Jenkins install should be pretty simple; you just need an application server that can host WAR files. One of the most commonly used application servers is Apache Tomcat, and the install is pretty simple. If you have a working Tomcat install, then all you need to do is drop the WAR into the `webapps` directory. Tomcat will do the rest for you.

Let's have a look at how we can set up a build in Jenkins that will enable us to run our tests.

Welcome to Jenkins

Now, follow these steps:

1. The first thing to do is create a new project:

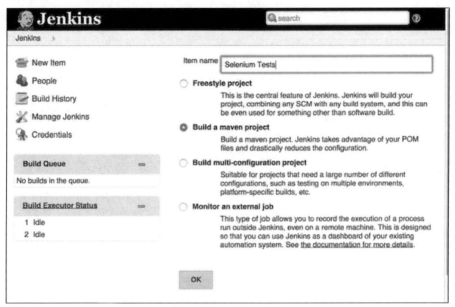

Creating a project

2. Put in the name of your build and then select the **Build a maven project** option.

> Jenkins can do clever things if you have a Maven project. One annoyance is that it will disable `maven-failsafe-plugin` and `maven-surefire-plugin` build failures and let the Maven portion of your build complete. It then checks to see if there were any failures and marks the build as unstable if there were. This means a failed build may well show up as yellow instead of red. To get around this you can always select a freestyle project and add a Maven build step.

Next click on **OK** and you will be taken to a screen that looks like this:

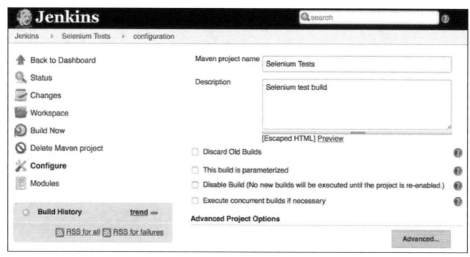

The project configuration

3. You then need to enter two bits of information—first of all the information about your code repository:

 If you want to use Git with Jenkins, you will need to download the Git plugin. Jenkins does not support Git out-of-the-box.

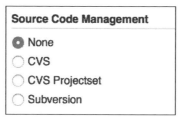

Selecting your SCM

4. Then we need to set up our Maven job:

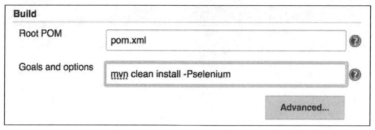

Configuring our Maven build step

5. Using Maven actually makes it very easy, that's all there is to it. You should now be able to run your Jenkins build and it will download all the dependencies and run everything for you.

So far we have looked at how we can set up a very simple continuous integration service; however this is only the tip of the iceberg. We have used continuous integration to give us a fast feedback loop so that we are notified of, and can react to, problems quickly. What if we could extend this to tell us not just whether there are any problems, but whether something is ready to be deployed into production instead? This is the goal of continuous delivery.

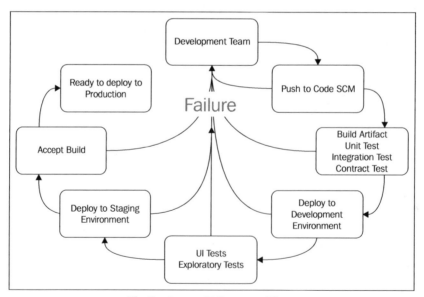

The Continuous Delivery workflow

So what's next after continuous delivery—how about continuous deployment? This is where we get to the point in our pipeline where we are confident that, as soon as every continuous delivery phase has been marked as passed, the code will automatically be deployed to live. Just imagine a new feature being completed and within a matter of hours we have performed enough testing on that functionality to be confident about releasing it, so that the feature is immediately available to your customers.

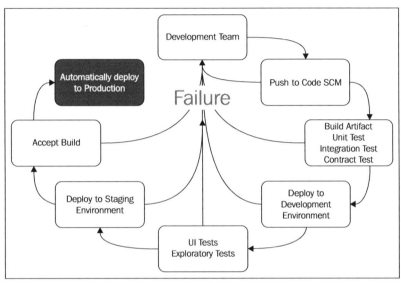

The Continuous Deployment workflow

We haven't got quite that far yet. We now have a basic setup that we can use to run our tests on a CI; however, we still have some pretty big gaps. The basic CI setup that you have so far is running on one operating system and cannot run our tests against all browser/operating system combinations. We can deal with this issue by setting up various build agents that connect to our CI server and run different versions of operating systems/browsers. This does however take time to configure and can be quite fiddly. You could also extend the capabilities of your CI server by setting up a Selenium Grid that your CI server can connect to and run various Selenium test jobs. Again this can be very powerful, but it also does have setup costs. This is where third-party services such as Sauce Labs (`https://saucelabs.com`) can be used. Most third-party grid services have free tiers, which can be very useful when you are getting started and working out what works for you. Remember that getting set up with one third-party service does not lock you into it. One Selenium Grid is pretty much the same as another, so even though you start off using a third-party server, there is nothing to stop you building up your own grid, or configuring your own build agents and moving away from the third-party service in the future.

Extending our capabilities by using a Selenium Grid

Since we already have a working Maven implementation, let's enhance it so that it can connect to a Selenium Grid. These enhancements will enable you to connect to any Selenium Grid, but we are going to specifically look at connecting to a third-party service provided by Sauce Labs since it offers a free tier. Let's have a look at the modifications we need to make to our TestNG code.

We will start off with the modifications to our POM; first of all we are going to add some properties that we can configure on the command line:

```
<properties>
    <project.build.sourceEncoding>UTF-8</project.build.sourceEncoding>
    <project.reporting.outputEncoding>UTF-8</project.reporting.
outputEncoding>
    <!-- Dependency versions -->
    <selenium.version>2.45.0</selenium.version>
    <!-- Configurable variables -->
    <threads>1</threads>
    <browser>firefox</browser>
    <overwrite.binaries>false</overwrite.binaries>
    <remote>false</remote>
    <seleniumGridURL/>
    <platform/>
    <browserVersion/>
</properties>
```

I've left the `seleniumGridURL` element blank because I don't know your Selenium Grid URL, but you can give this a value if you want. The same applies to `platform` and `browserVersion`. Next we need to make sure these properties are read in as system properties so we need to modify our `maven-failsafe-plugin` configuration:

```
<plugin>
    <groupId>org.apache.maven.plugins</groupId>
    <artifactId>maven-failsafe-plugin</artifactId>
    <version>2.17</version>
    <configuration>
        <parallel>methods</parallel>
        <threadCount>${threads}</threadCount>
        <systemProperties>
            <browser>${browser}</browser>
            <remoteDriver>${remote}</remoteDriver>
            <gridURL>${seleniumGridURL}</gridURL>
            <desiredPlatform>${platform}</desiredPlatform>
```

```
            <desiredBrowserVersion>${browserVersion}
            </desiredBrowserVersion>
            <!--Set properties passed in by the driver binary
            downloader-->
            <phantomjs.binary.path>${phantomjs.binary.path}</
phantomjs.binary.path>
            <webdriver.chrome.driver>${webdriver.chrome.driver}</
webdriver.chrome.driver>
            <webdriver.ie.driver>${webdriver.ie.driver}</webdriver.
ie.driver>
            <webdriver.opera.driver>${webdriver.opera.driver}</
webdriver.opera.driver>
        </systemProperties>
        <includes>
            <include>**/*WD.java</include>
        </includes>
    </configuration>
    <executions>
        <execution>
            <goals>
                <goal>integration-test</goal>
                <goal>verify</goal>
            </goals>
        </execution>
    </executions>
</plugin>
```

This will again make our properties available to our test code. Next we need to make some modifications to our `WebDriverThread` class. First of all we are going to add a new class variable called `useRemoteWebdriver`:

```
private final DriverType defaultDriverType = FIREFOX;
private final String browser =
System.getProperty("browser").toUpperCase();
private final String operatingSystem =
System.getProperty("os.name").toUpperCase();
private final String systemArchitecture =
System.getProperty("os.arch");
private final boolean useRemoteWebDriver =
Boolean.getBoolean("remoteDriver");
```

This variable is going to read in the system property that we set in our POM and work out whether we want to use a `RemoteWebDriver` instance or not. Then we need to update our `instantiateWebDriver` method:

```
private void instantiateWebDriver(DesiredCapabilities
desiredCapabilities) throws MalformedURLException {
```

```
System.out.println(" ");
System.out.println("Current Operating System: " +
operatingSystem);
System.out.println("Current Architecture: " +
systemArchitecture);
System.out.println("Current Browser Selection: " +
selectedDriverType);
System.out.println(" ");

if (useRemoteWebDriver) {
    URL seleniumGridURL = new URL(System.getProperty("gridURL"));
    String desiredBrowserVersion =
    System.getProperty("desiredBrowserVersion");
    String desiredPlatform =
    System.getProperty("desiredPlatform");

    if (null != desiredPlatform && !desiredPlatform.isEmpty()) {
        desiredCapabilities.setPlatform(Platform.
        valueOf(desiredPlatform.toUpperCase()));
    }

    if (null != desiredBrowserVersion &&
    !desiredBrowserVersion.isEmpty()) {
        desiredCapabilities.setVersion(desiredBrowserVersion);
    }

    webdriver = new RemoteWebDriver(seleniumGridURL,
    desiredCapabilities);
} else {
    webdriver = selectedDriverType.
    getWebDriverObject(desiredCapabilities);
}
}
```

This is where all of the hard work is done. We are using our useRemoteWebDriver object to work out whether we want to instantiate a normal WebDriver object, or a RemoteWebDriver object. If we want to instantiate a RemoteWebDriver object we start off by reading in the system properties we set in our POM. The most important bit of information is seleniumGridURL. If we don't have this, we don't know where to go to connect to the grid. We are reading in the system property and trying to generate a URL from it. If the URL is not valid an InvalidURLException will be thrown; this is fine because we won't be able to connect to a grid anyway at this point so we may as well end our test run there and then.

The other two bits of information are optional. If we supply a `desiredPlatform` and `desiredBrowserVersion`, the Selenium Grid will use an agent matching these criteria. If we don't supply this information the, Selenium Grid will just grab any free agent and run our test on it. Looking at this code, it's not instantly obvious what browser we are requesting; don't worry, it's covered. Each `DesiredCapabilities` object will set a browser type by default. So if we create `DesiredCapabilities.firefox()`, we will be asking the Selenium Grid to run our test against Firefox. This is one of the reasons we originally kept `getDesiredCapabilities()` separate from `instantiateWebDriver()`.

We are now all done. The easiest way to test this is to set up a free account with a Selenium Grid provider such as Sauce Labs (`https://saucelabs.com`) and run your tests against them. To do that, put the following into your command line (obviously you'll need to supply your own Sauce Labs username and access key for this to work):

```
mvn clean install -Dremote=true -
DseleniumGridURL=http://{username}:{accessKey}@ondemand.saucelabs.
com:80/wd/hub -Dplatform=xp -Dbrowser=firefox -DbrowserVersion=33
```

You should now have a working CI system and the ability to run your tests remotely.

It's great to be able to connect to a third-party grid and see all your tests running without having to do the hard setup work; however this does give us some new challenges. When you are running your tests remotely, it's a lot harder to work out what the problem is when things go wrong, especially if they appear to work locally. We now need to find a way to make it easier to diagnose problems with our tests when we run them remotely.

A picture paints a thousand words

Even if you have made your tests totally reliable, they will fail occasionally. When this happens it is often very hard to describe what the problem is with words alone. If one of your tests fails, wouldn't it be easier to explain what went wrong if you had a picture of what was happening in the browser when the error happened? I know that, when one of my Selenium tests fails, the first thing I want to know is what was on the screen at the time of failure. If I know what was on the screen at the time of failure I will be able to diagnose the vast majority of issues without having to hunt through a stack trace for a specific line number and then looking at the associated code to try and work out what went wrong. Wouldn't it be nice if we got a screenshot showing what was on the screen every time a test failed? Let's take the project that we built in *Chapter 1, Creating a Fast Feedback Loop*, and extend it a bit to take a screenshot every time there is a test failure. Let's have a look at how we can implement this in TestNG.

First of all we are going to create a package called listeners.

Updated project structure

Then we are going to implement a custom listener for TestNG that will detect a test failure and then capture a screenshot for us.

```java
package com.masteringselenium.listeners;

import org.openqa.selenium.OutputType;
import org.openqa.selenium.TakesScreenshot;
import org.openqa.selenium.WebDriver;
import org.openqa.selenium.remote.Augmenter;
import org.testng.ITestResult;
import org.testng.TestListenerAdapter;

import java.io.File;
import java.io.FileOutputStream;
import java.io.IOException;

import static com.masteringselenium.DriverFactory.getDriver;


public class ScreenshotListener extends TestListenerAdapter {

    private boolean createFile(File screenshot) throws IOException {
        boolean fileCreated = false;

        if (screenshot.exists()) {
            fileCreated = true;
        } else {
            File parentDirectory = new
            File(screenshot.getParent());
```

```
            if (parentDirectory.exists() ||
            parentDirectory.mkdirs()) {
                fileCreated = screenshot.createNewFile();
            }
        }

    return fileCreated;
}

private void writeScreenshotToFile(WebDriver driver, File
screenshot) throws IOException {
    FileOutputStream screenshotStream = new
    FileOutputStream(screenshot);
    screenshotStream.write(((TakesScreenshot)
    driver).getScreenshotAs(OutputType.BYTES));
    screenshotStream.close();
}

@Override
public void onTestFailure(ITestResult failingTest) {
    try {
        WebDriver driver = getDriver();
        String screenshotDirectory =
        System.getProperty("screenshotDirectory");
        String screenshotAbsolutePath = screenshotDirectory +
        File.separator + System.currentTimeMillis() + "_" +
        failingTest.getName() + ".png";
        File screenshot = new File(screenshotAbsolutePath);
        if (createFile(screenshot)) {
            try {
                writeScreenshotToFile(driver, screenshot);
            } catch (ClassCastException
            weNeedToAugmentOurDriverObject) {
                writeScreenshotToFile(new
                Augmenter().augment(driver), screenshot);
            }
            System.out.println("Written screenshot to " +
            screenshotAbsolutePath);
        } else {
            System.err.println("Unable to create " +
            screenshotAbsolutePath);
        }
    } catch (Exception ex) {
        System.err.println("Unable to capture screenshot...");
        ex.printStackTrace();
    }
}
}
```

First of all we have the rather imaginatively named `createFile` method that will try to create a file. Next we have the equally imaginatively named `writeScreenShotToFile` method that will try and write the screenshot to a file. Notice that we aren't catching any exceptions in these methods, because we will do that in the listener.

 TestNG can get itself in a twist if exceptions are thrown in listeners. It will generally trap them so that your test run doesn't stop, but it doesn't fail the test when it does this. If your tests are passing but you have failures and stack traces, check to see if it's the listener at fault.

Finally we have the actual listener. The first thing that you will notice is that it has a `try-catch` wrapping the whole method. While we do want a screenshot to show us what has gone wrong, we probably don't want to kill our test run if we are unable to capture it or write a screenshot to disk for some reason. To make sure that we don't disrupt the test run we catch the error, and log it out to the console for future reference. We then carry on with what we were doing before.

You cannot cast all driver implementations in Selenium into a `TakesScreenshot` object. As a result we capture the `ClassCastException` for driver implementations that cannot be cast into a `TakesScreenshot` object and augment them instead. We don't just augment everything because a driver object that doesn't need to be augmented will throw an error if you try. It is usually `RemoteWebDriver` instances that need to be augmented. Apart from augmenting the driver object when required, the main job of this function is to generate a filename for the screenshot. We want to make sure that the filename is unique so that we don't accidentally overwrite any screenshots. To do this we use the current timestamp, and the name of the current test. We could use a randomly generated **GUID (Globally Unique Identifier)** but timestamps make it easier to track what happened at what time. Finally we want to log the absolute path to the screenshot out to console. This will make it easy to find any screenshots that have been created.

As you may have noticed in the preceding code, we are using a system property to get the directory that we save our screenshots in; we need to set this system property in our POM. We need to modify the `maven-failsafe-plugin` section so that it looks like this:

```
<plugin>
    <groupId>org.apache.maven.plugins</groupId>
    <artifactId>maven-failsafe-plugin</artifactId>
    <version>2.17</version>
    <configuration>
        <parallel>methods</parallel>
        <threadCount>${threads}</threadCount>
        <systemProperties>
```

```
            <browser>${browser}</browser>
            <screenshotDirectory>${project.build.
            directory}/screenshots</screenshotDirectory>
            <remoteDriver>${remote}</remoteDriver>
            <gridURL>${seleniumGridURL}</gridURL>
            <desiredPlatform>${platform}</desiredPlatform>
            <desiredBrowserVersion>${browserVersion}
            </desiredBrowserVersion>
            <!--Set properties passed in by the driver
            binary downloader-->
            <phantomjs.binary.path>${phantomjs.binary.path}
            </phantomjs.binary.path>
            <webdriver.chrome.driver>${webdriver.chrome.driver}
            </webdriver.chrome.driver>
            <webdriver.ie.driver>${webdriver.ie.driver}
            </webdriver.ie.driver>
            <webdriver.opera.driver>${webdriver.opera.driver}
            </webdriver.opera.driver>
        </systemProperties>
        <includes>
            <include>**/*WD.java</include>
        </includes>
    </configuration>
    <executions>
        <execution>
            <goals>
                <goal>integration-test</goal>
                <goal>verify</goal>
            </goals>
        </execution>
    </executions>
</plugin>
```

We are only going to add a system property variable; we aren't going to make this a value that you can override on the command line. We have however used a Maven variable to specify the screenshot directory location. Maven has a series of predefined variables that you can use; ${project.build.directory} will provide you with the location of your target directory. Whenever Maven builds your project it will compile all of the files into a temporary directory called target, it will then run all of your tests and store the results in this directory. This directory is basically a little sandbox for Maven to play in while it's doing its stuff. By default this will be created in the folder that holds your POM file.

When performing Maven builds it is generally good practice to use the clean command:

```
mvn clean install
```

The `clean` command deletes the target directory to make sure that when you build your project you don't have anything left over from the previous build that may cause problems. Generally speaking, when we run tests we are only going to be interested in the result of the current test run (any previous results should have been archived for future reference), so we are going to make sure that our screenshots are saved to this directory. To keep things clean we are generating a screenshots' subdirectory that we will store our screenshots in.

Now that our screenshot listener is ready, we just have to tell our tests to use it. This is surprisingly simple; all of our tests extend our `DriverFactory`, so we just add a `@Listeners` annotation to it.

```
import com.masteringselenium.listeners.ScreenshotListener;
import org.testng.annotations.Listeners;

@Listeners(ScreenshotListener.class)
public class DriverFactory
```

From this point onwards if any of our tests fail a screenshot will automatically be taken.

 Why don't you give it a go? Try changing your test to make it fail so that screenshots are generated. Try putting some Windows or OS dialogs in front of your browser while the tests are running and taking screenshots. Does this affect what you see on the screen?

Screenshots are a very useful aid when it comes to diagnosing problems with your tests, but sometimes things go wrong on a page that looks completely normal. How do we go about diagnosing these sorts of problems?

Don't be afraid of the big bad stack trace

It's surprising how many people are intimidated by stack traces. A reaction that I regularly see when a stack trace appears on screen is panic!

"Oh my God, something has gone wrong! There are hundreds of lines of text talking about code I don't recognize and I can't take it all in; what do I do?"

The first thing to do is to relax; stack traces have a lot of information but they are actually really friendly and helpful things. Let's modify our project to produce a stack trace and work through it. We are going to make a small change to the getDriver() method in DriverFactory to force it to always return a null, as follows:

```
public static WebDriver getDriver() {
    return null;
}
```

This is going to make sure that we never return a driver object, something that we would expect to cause errors. Let's run our tests again, but make sure that Maven displays a stack trace by using the –e switch:

mvn clean install -e

This time you should see a couple of stack traces output to the terminal; the first one should look like this:

A stack trace shown when the build fails

It's not too big so let's have a look at it in more detail. The first line tells you the root cause of our problem: we have got a `NullPointerException`. You have probably seen these before. Our code is complaining because it was expecting to have some sort of object at some point and we didn't give it one. Next we have a series of lines of text that tell us where in the application the problem occurred.

We have quite a few lines of code that are referred to in this stack trace, most of them unfamiliar as we didn't write them. Let's start at the bottom and work our way up. We first of all have the line of code that was running when our test failed; this is `Thread.java` line 745. This thread is using a `run` method (on `ThreadPoolExecutor.java` line 617) that is using a `runWorker` method (on `ThreadPoolExecutor.java` line 1142), and this carries on up the stack trace. What we are seeing is a hierarchy of code with all the various methods that are being used. We are also being told which line of code in that method caused a problem.

We are specifically interested in the lines that relate to the code that we have written — in this case, the second and third lines of the stack trace. You can see that it is giving us two very useful bits of information; it's telling us where in our code the problem has occurred and what sort of problem it is. If we have a look at our code, we can see what it was trying to do when the failure occurred so that we can try and work out what the problem is. Let's start with the second line; first of all it tells us which method is causing the problem. In this case it is `com.masteringselenium.DriverFactory.clearCookies`. It then tells us which line of this method is causing us a problem — in this case `DriverFactory.java` line 35. This is where our `clearCookies()` method tries to get a `WebDriver` instance from our `WebDriverThread` class, and then uses it to try and clear all the cookies.

Now, if you remember, we modified `getDriver()` to return a null instead of a valid driver object. This matches up with the first bit of information in our stack trace (the `NullPointerException`). Obviously we cannot call `.manage().deleteAllCookies()` on a null, hence the null pointer error.

So why didn't it fail in `WebDriverThread`; after all, that's where the problem is? Passing a null around is quite valid. It's trying to do something with the null that causes the problem. This is why it also didn't fail on line 30 of `DriverFactory`. The `getDriver()` method just passes on what was returned from `WebDriverThread`, it doesn't actually try to do anything with it. The first time that we tried to do anything with the null is when it failed, which was at line 35 of the `DriverFactory` class.

When it is explained it can seem quite obvious, but it takes a while to get used to reading stack traces. The important thing to remember with stack traces is to read them in full. Don't be scared of them, or skim through them and guess at the problem. Stack traces provide a lot of useful information to help you diagnose problems. They may not take you directly to the problematic bit of code but they give you a great place to start.

 Try causing some more errors in your code and then run your tests again. See if you can work your way back to the problem you put in your code by reading the stack trace.

Summary

After reading through this chapter you should:

- Think of automated tests as living documentation rather than automatic regression
- Have a good understanding of why reliability matters
- Have an understanding of Continuous Integration, Continuous Delivery, and Continuous Deployment
- Be able to configure your tests to run in a Maven profile
- Be able to set up a test build in a Continuous Integration Server
- Be able to connect to a Selenium Grid (both local and third party)
- Be able to take screenshots of test failures
- Be able to read a stack trace and work out what the causes of your test failures are.

In the next chapter, we are going to have a look at exceptions generated by Selenium. We will work through various exceptions that you may see and what they mean.

3
Exceptions Are Actually Oracles

In this chapter, we will have a look at some of the more common exceptions that you may see when working with Selenium. While we look at them we will explore some of the possible causes of these exceptions. Finally we will provide some pointers, that will help you to fix your test code when you see them.

Are exceptions oracles?

So first of all, what is an oracle? An oracle was traditionally seen as a portal that the gods used to talk to people. As with anything, there are various definitions in use. To be clear about what an oracle is in the context of this book, we are going to use the following definition:

> "*A statement believed to be infallible and authoritative*"

Like an oracle, an exception is an infallible statement; it will always tell you why something has gone wrong in your code. It may not always be easy to understand, but it does always tell the truth. Let's have a look at some exceptions that we often see while writing and running Selenium tests and see what they are trying to tell us.

NoSuchElementException

This is probably the most straightforward exception that you will come across. The element that you are trying to find does not exist. There are three common causes for this exception:

- The locator that you are using to find the element is incorrect

- Something has gone wrong and the element has not been rendered
- You tried to find the element before it was rendered

It is quite easy to check for the first cause—an incorrect locator. You can use the Google Chrome development tools to test your locator. To do this, perform the following steps:

1. Open the Google Chrome development tools (*F12*).

2. If your site has multiple frames, or iframes, make sure that you select the correct frame.

3. Type `$("<myLocator>")` into the console.

If the locator finds an element or multiple elements that match the locator, it will display it in the console. You will then be able to examine the element(s) and reveal it in the markup to check whether it is the element that you think you are searching for.

You don't have to use Google Chrome to do this. Most browsers have their own development console. Also, there are other tools available to you. If you use Firebug, there is an additional extension called FirePath, which is very useful for this sort of thing as well.

The second cause is that the element has not been rendered. This is a little harder to diagnose. You will need to go through your code and see what causes the failure. Is it a bug in the application that you are testing, or is a previous step failing (for example, did you use valid login credentials?)?

Screenshots can be a big help in diagnosing the `NoSuchElementException` issues as they give a good view of the state of the application that you are testing when the error occurred. However, they are not infallible. If the cause of the problem is that the element has not yet been rendered, it is possible that the element was not rendered when the error occurred, but it was rendered when the screenshot was taken. In this case, the screenshot will appear to show the element when it was, in actual fact, missing when Selenium tried to find it.

This brings us to the third cause—trying to utilize an element before it has been rendered. Lots of modern websites use technologies such as jQuery or AngularJS, which use JavaScript to manipulate the DOM. Selenium is fast. In many cases, it's ready to start interacting with your website before the JavaScript has finished doing its job. When this happens, things may seem to be missing, when in reality, they just haven't been created yet. There are some tricks that you can use to wait for the JavaScript to finish rendering the page, but the real solution is to know the application that you are automating. You should know what is required for the page to be ready to use and write your code while being aware of these conditions. A good question to ask in many situations is, "What would I do if I were testing this manually?"

Normally, you would wait for the page to load before you could start testing. You have to write your code so that it can do the same thing. When waiting for something to happen, you should never use `Thread.sleep()` to wait for the page to load. If you do this, you are tailoring the test to work on your machine, and your machine alone. If the test is run on a slower machine, the `sleep` method that you have added will most likely not be long enough and the test will fail. If the test is run on a faster machine, it may work, but it will probably be much slower than it could be.

An explicit wait is usually your best friend in this scenario. You can craft an explicit wait to wait for many conditions. In this case, it's likely to be as simple as waiting for an element to become available and then visible. In the Java language bindings, there is an `ExpectedConditions` class that provides lots of example conditions that you can plug into explicit waits.

NoSuchFrameException

It is worth remembering that this exception will be thrown for both errors with frames and errors with iFrames. Frames are not so common in modern web applications, but iFrames are becoming ubiquitous. This exception has a lot in common with a `NoSuchElementException` in that it is usually thrown because the frame doesn't exist when you try to find it. If this is the case, the solutions for a `NoSuchElementException` should also work for a `NoSuchFrameException`. However, working with frames can have its own unique problems. Let's imagine a scenario where you have a page with multiple frames. We will call them frame *A* and frame *B*. We will assume that we first switched to frame *B* to check something in the frame. If we then try to find frame *A*, we will get stuck.

This is because frame *A* does not exist in the context of frame *B*. The way to work around this issue is to always go back to the parent frame before trying to switch to another frame (unless we are trying to switch to a frame that lives inside another frame). Selenium provides a simple way to do this. You just need to use this:

```
driver.switchTo().defaultContent();
```

Don't try to use the following statement:

```
driver.switchTo().frame("relative=top");
```

It will not work. Generally, trying to switch to frames using relative metrics can be confusing, especially if you have a very complex frame structure. When things go wrong, it can be really frustrating to diagnose problems with it, as everything will look like it should work. Ideally, you should use IDs or WebElements to locate frames. Use the frame number as a last resort.

NoSuchWindowException

This exception is caused because the list of windows that you currently have is not up to date. One of the windows that previously existed no longer exists and you can't switch to it. The first thing to do is check your code and make sure that you are not closing a window without refreshing the available list of windows using this:

```
driver.getWindowHandles();
```

The other reason behind why you may get this exception is that you may be trying to switch to a window before calling `driver.getWindowHandles()`. It's not instantly obvious as regards which window handle relates to which window. The best way to track things is to get the handle of the current window before opening up any new windows, using this:

```
String currentWindowHandle = driver.getWindowHandle();
```

When you open a new window and get a list of window handles, you can iterate through the list and ignore the handles for the currently open windows. By the process of elimination, you can figure out which handle is associated with the new window that was just opened.

This can be tricky if your code opens up multiple windows at the same time. If you do this, you will need to switch to each window in turn and search for something in the DOM that will identify the window so that you can keep track of it. That being said, if your site is continually opening up lots of new windows, you probably want to have a chat with the developers to find out why. It may well be the case that it shouldn't do this.

ElementNotVisibleException

This is a very useful exception that you will probably come across on a regular basis. This exception tells you that the WebElement that you are trying to interact with is not visible to the user. It's amazing how many people don't realize how important this exception is. Remember that if the element is not visible to the user, they are not going to be able to interact with it.

Please don't ignore or try to work around this exception. You will probably come across lots of so called solutions to this problem that are really nasty hacks. They usually involve some custom JavaScript to perform the desired action and totally ignore the fact that you really have a legitimate problem.

The Selenium development team has spent a lot of time trying to figure out whether something is visible to the user, and they have done a vey good job. There is code to check whether the element is actually on the screen, or if it has a size that is too small to be seen by a person. There is even code in Selenium that tries to check whether the element is covered by other elements. This is a lot harder than it sounds. CSS can make things extremely hard.

If you see this exception, there is a problem that needs to be fixed with your code. Selenium is very fast and will often try to interact with an element before it has a chance to render the page on the screen. Your code should be aware of what needs to happen for the element to be displayed to the end user. You will need to wait for the page rendering (or at least the part of the page that you are interested in) to complete before trying to interact with the element.

When you see this exception, the best thing to do is walk through the code manually and check whether you can see things that load slowly. The usual fix is to add an explicit wait to wait for the correct conditions to be met before trying to interact with the element in question.

StaleElementReferenceException

This is an exception that you will quite often see when you work with AJAX or JavaScript-heavy websites, where the DOM is continually being manipulated.

You are probably used to seeing code like this:

```
WebElement googleSearchBar = driver.findElement(By.name("q"));
```

The WebElement object that you have created is actually a reference to a specific element in the DOM. Think of it as a phone number that you call to talk to the element.

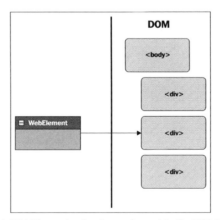

A WebElement refers to an element in the DOM.

When the DOM is manipulated and the old element is destroyed, that reference no longer links to an element in the DOM, and it becomes stale. Using our phone number metaphor, this is where the phone line is disconnected. You can keep calling that number, but it will not ring any more. You'll just get a message telling you that the phone number is not valid.

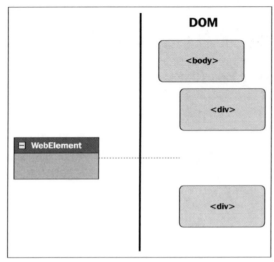

When the element in the DOM is destroyed the WebElement refers to nothing

This can get very confusing when the element that we have a reference to has been destroyed and another identical looking element has replaced it. On the face of it, everything looks identical, but for some reason, it just doesn't work. To finish off with our phone metaphor, think of the situation where one of your friends switches mobile phone networks and gets a new number. Their phone looks the same and they can still make calls on it, but if you try to call them, you get a message telling you that the phone number is not valid.

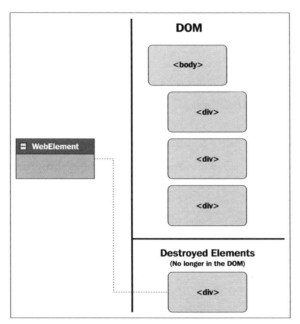

There may be an identical looking element, but the WebElement still refers to the destroyed one that is not in the DOM.

By using the phone metaphor, the solution is simple. Ask your friend for their new number. You can call them again, and everything is back to normal. The Selenium solution is just as simple. Ask Selenium to find that element again, as follows:

```
googleSearchBar = driver.findElement(By.name("q"));
```

The reference is updated, and you can carry on interacting with the WebElement.

It is easy to say that fixing this problem is simple, but how did we get there in the first place?

Well, we did not know what our application was going to do. We did not expect the DOM to be rebuilt and that the original element that we created a reference to would be destroyed.

We now need to start asking questions. Does it matter that the original element was destroyed and then recreated?

If it doesn't matter, maybe we should just find the element every time we want to use it to ensure that we don't get a `StaleElementReferenceException`.

Maybe, we were expecting the element to be destroyed and recreated, and we want to check for that. If so, we could use a conditional wait to wait for the element to become stale before continuing with our test. Let's have a look at some code that will do this for us:

```
WebDriverWait explicitlyWait = new WebDriverWait(driver, 10);
explicitlyWait.until(ExpectedConditions.stalenessOf(
googleSearchBar));
```

It's actually pretty easy to do. Java has some predefined expected conditions that we can use without having to write our own explicit wait condition.

Finally, maybe we're not expecting to get a `StaleElementReferenceException`. If this is the case, it's good news. Your test may have found a bug that needs to be fixed.

InvalidElementStateException

This is an exception that you probably won't see that often, but when it does pop up, it is not always instantly clear what it means. An `InvalidElementStateException` is thrown when the WebElement that you are trying to interact with is not in a state that would allow you to perform the action that you would like to perform.

Think of a `<select>` element that gives you a list of countries to select when filling an address form. This element will allow you to select the country associated with your address.

Now, what if the developers have added some validation that will not let you enter a postcode (or a zip code) until you have selected a country so that they can trigger the correct postcode validation routine? In this case, the postcode `<input>` element, where you enter your postcode, may be disabled until you have selected your country.

If you try to enter a postcode into this disabled `<input>` element, you will get an `InvalidElementStateException`.

The fix is to do whatever a user manually testing the site would do to enable the `<input>` element. In this case, select a country from the `<select>` element.

UnsupportedCommandException

This is one of those exceptions that you may never see or, depending on the driver implementation that you use, or one that you may see all the time. You will find an `UnsupportedCommandException` getting thrown when the WebDriver implementation that you are running does not support one of the core WebDriver API commands.

There are quite a few third-party WebDriver bindings, and these bindings are in various states of completeness. Not all third-party projects have managed to implement the entire WebDriver API yet. When a driver binding that you are using does not support a command that is a part of the WebDriver API, it will throw an `UnsupportedCommandException`.

If this happens to you, there is really not a lot you can do about it. The following are your choices:

- Code around the problem by using a different command
- Switch to a different WebDriver binding
- Write the code required to support the command yourself (and raise a pull request!)

UnreachableBrowserException

To understand an `UnreachableBrowserException` exception, we should first understand how Selenium works. To most people, Selenium is simply an API that you use to write code to drive a browser. Note that I have said code, not tests. The Selenium API is designed to be a browser automation tool, not just a test tool. It is commonly used for testing, but it can be used for any purpose that would require browser automation.

The current API that is in use is the WebDriver API. The old Selenium RC API has been deprecated since Selenium 2 came out and should not be actively used by anybody creating a new project.

Selenium is a bit more than just an API though. It is also a series of plugins, binaries, or native implementations that enable you to talk to the browser. The Selenium API talks to all of these implementation methods using the common wire protocol. This wire protocol is a RESTful web service that uses JSON over HTTP. When we talk about the bit of Selenium that commands are sent to using the wire protocol, we call it the `RemoteWebDriver`.

All browser-specific driver implementations are extensions of the core `RemoteWebDriver` class. The implementation method differs from driver to driver. Some use the client mode, and some use the server mode.

Client mode is where the `RemoteWebDriver` implementation is either loaded as a browser plugin, or natively supported by the browser. The language bindings connect directly to the remote instance and tell it what to do. An example of this implementation method would be `FirefoxDriver`.

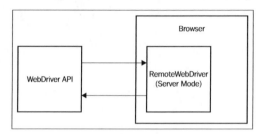

RemoteWebdriver Client Mode

The server mode is where the language binding sets up a server, which acts as a go-between for the language binding and the browser. It basically translates the commands sent by your code into something that the browser can understand. An example of this implementation method would be ChromeDriver.

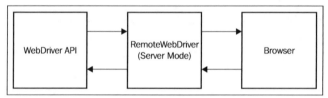

RemoteWebDriver Server Mode

As you can see in the preceding diagram, the code that you have written using the WebDriver API is sent over to the browser via the `RemoteWebDriver` instance using the wire protocol. As you can imagine, this process is problematic if there is no browser available for us to talk to.

If we send out commands but cannot get a response, we get an
`UnreachableBrowserException`. It means that you cannot connect to the
`RemoteWebDriver` instance. There are various problems that could cause this error:

- The browser didn't start because of the following reasons:
  - The browser crashed
  - The version of the `RemoteWebDriver` instance that you are using is
    incompatible with the version of the browser that you are using

- Network issues
  - You could be connected to another machine
  - There could be a firewall involved
  - You could be connecting to the wrong port

- The browser that you are trying to use has not been installed
- The browser is not installed in the default location and Selenium can't find it

Debugging the issue can be frustrating, and you will probably kick yourself when
you find out what the root cause was.

SessionNotFoundException

Occasionally, when you are running your tests, things will go wrong and you will
lose connection with the browser instance that you are driving. When you lose
connection to the browser instance, a `SessionNotFoundException` will be thrown.

This is an error that is similar to the `UnreachableBrowserException`, but in this
case, you have a much smaller list of things to check since you know you were
successfully talking to the `RemoteWebDriver` instance for a while.

The following problems usually cause this error:

- You inadvertently quit the driver instance
- The browser crashed

Summary

After reading this chapter, you should:

- Understand that exceptions are actually trying to tell you something
- Be able to look at some of the more commonly thrown exceptions and quickly diagnose the root cause of the issue
- Have a good understanding of how a WebElement is a reference to an element in the DOM
- Have a decent understanding of the basic architecture of Selenium and how it sends over commands to the browser

In the next chapter, we will have a look at implicit and explicit waits. We will examine the implications of using them in your code and have a look at how we can make them work reliably for you.

4

The Waiting Game

In the previous chapter, we had a look at various exceptions and some of the possible causes behind their occurrence. In this chapter, we will:

- Look at implicit and explicit waits
- Explore the `ExpectedConditions` class in the Selenium support package
- Examine how we can extend `ExpectedConditions` by adding our own customized waits
- Have a look at the core FluentWait functionality that is built into Selenium and the use of functions and predicates

Are we nearly ready yet?

How do we know that the page that we are interested in has loaded and is ready for us to start running our scripts against?

It sounds like a simple question, however, it is one of the things that always catches people out. If you are ever asked why a script doesn't work when the code seems sensible, your usual reply should probably be: it's a wait problem!

Wait problems are probably the most common errors in Selenium scripts. Shockingly, most of the time, people don't even know that they have them. JavaScript-heavy sites are especially prone to wait problems, but you can run into them with sites that don't use much JavaScript as well.

Why are wait problems so prevalent? It's largely due to people not thinking about the consequences of external variables when they write their scripts.

Let's take a made-up scenario. We have a page that waits until it is loaded to make an AJAX request to a server. This page is not ready to be used until the AJAX request is complete, but Selenium thinks that it is ready after the initial page load. How do we let Selenium know that the page has loaded and is ready for us to start our automated script?

I've timed it and I know it takes 5 seconds for the page to load

You would be surprised to know how often people say this. They tend to add something like this to their scripts:

```
Thread.sleep(5000);
```

Code like this will never work reliably. It doesn't take into account any external variables, and it will slow your tests down. What do we mean by external variables? Well, let's look into it.

Machine specifications

Different machines have different specifications. It sounds obvious, yet it is something that many people who write automation scripts do not take into account. A slow machine with very little memory will run your scripts much slower than a fast machine. It will probably take longer to render the page that you are testing. This means that an element that appears instantly on a fast machine may not actually be there for a few hundred milliseconds on a slow machine. This duration is long enough to cause an error in your test, but not long enough for it to be instantly obvious to the human eye.

Server specifications

First of all, let's be clear by what we mean when we say server specification. We mean the machine (virtual or physical) that is hosting the website that you are attempting to test. The effect of the server specification can have varying effects on the site that you are testing, which in a large part is dependent on the design of the site. If your site depends on a lot of server-side processing, it could slow down significantly when under load. If you have a high number of concurrent users, the server may have problems servicing requests, and the responses coming back to the client may take longer than expected. Maybe the site you are using allows the user to download lots of files, but the hard drives in the server are not up to the task, and your request to read data from the disk is being queued up.

There are hundreds of possible reasons behind why a server may not always respond to your request promptly. Don't expect it to be prompt when you write your tests.

The JavaScript engine performance

This can make a massive difference when testing modern JavaScript-heavy sites. Something that is rendered instantly in the latest version of Google Chrome could take seconds to render in Internet Explorer 8. If you are interested in how much variance there is in the various JavaScript engines, have a look at the SunSpider JavaScript benchmark (for more information, visit `http://www.webkit.org/perf/ sunspider/sunspider.html`). Try running the test in various browsers. It's amazing how slow some of the older browsers are.

Networks

If you are testing an AJAX-heavy site, network performance will matter. If your AJAX requests take a long time to resolve, the site that you are testing will take longer to re-render the frontend as a result of the AJAX calls. Something that works fine on your local machine can suddenly start failing all over the place when you run the same tests on a real server.

If you start looking at all of these potential problems, it soon becomes clear that an arbitrary wait of 5 seconds is never going to be reliable. The reaction some people have when they are faced with this problem is that they extend their waits. Before you know it, you will have 10-second waits littered around your test code, and these may stretch out to 15-second waits. Soon enough, your simple test case that wants to load up a page and makes the user to click on a couple of buttons, takes 2 minutes to run.

Simply telling people to not use `Thread.sleep()` is not going to fix the problem either. You need to explain why people should not use `Thread.sleep()`. I worked on a project where we had a member of our team who kept putting `Thread.sleep()` into our code base. We told him not to, but he persisted. Eventually, we added a commit rule to SVN that would reject any code that had `Thread.sleep()` in it. This didn't fix our problem. He changed his code to use `Object.wait()` instead!

The real problem was that we did not sit him down and explain why we didn't want him to use `Thread.sleep()`. We just said that it was something we didn't do. Our assumption was that he would know why it was a bad code pattern. The problem was that he didn't.

So, what do we do?

Let's face it. Figuring out whether something is ready for you to interact with is actually quite a complex process. What would you do if you were testing the site manually?

That's simple. If you were manually testing the site, you would wait for it to be ready before you started testing. The problem is, what does the term *ready* mean?

Well, to me, it means that the page has downloaded and the site has had a chance to render everything that looks like it needs to be rendered and it looks ready to use. Sometimes, I may start using it before it has downloaded all of the images, but I'll usually wait for the main scaffolding to be in a state that looks ready. Unless I'm looking at the network traffic, I won't know whether the AJAX requests have been resolved, but this is where my experience of what the site should look like comes in.

You may have noticed that I used the phrase *looks ready* a couple of times in the preceding lines. So, how do we code *looks ready*? Well, the problem is that you can't. There is a lot of processing that goes on in our brains to come up with *looks ready*.

It's like asking a computer to tell you whether some cream that has been left in the fridge has gone off. How do you define *gone off*? Is it a look or a smell? If there is some mold on the top and we remove it, has the cream still gone off?

I suspect that for the last question, some people will say yes because once it has gone moldy, they will throw it out, whereas others will quite happily remove the mold and continue using it. So, who is right? What should the computer do?

Obviously, building up a mental model in a computer and asking it to interpret the status of something that *looks right* is generally not realistic. So, what can we do?

Well, we can programmatically make sure that specific actions have happened before we start trying to do things, or in other words, we can define what the term *looks right* means in the context of our test. Different tests may have different definitions of *looks right*, or they may share a common understanding of *looks right*.

We are going to use various types of *wait* to help us define *looks right*.

I just want Selenium to do it for me

Well, you do have some options available if you just want Selenium to try and do things for you. Selenium has three built-in waiting mechanisms that you can configure universally by configuring the `Timeouts()` object, which is set on your driver object when you instantiate it.

The following are the available mechanisms:

- The page load timeout
- The script timeout
- The implicit wait timeout

Let's have a look at these mechanisms in some more detail.

The page load timeout

This defines the amount of time that Selenium will wait for a page to load. By default, it is set to 0 (which equates to an infinite timeout). If you want to ensure that an error is thrown if your page takes longer than expected to load, you can modify this by using the following code:

```
driver.manage().timeouts().pageLoadTimeout(15, TimeUnit.SECONDS);
```

If your page does not load within 15 seconds, a `WebDriverException` will be thrown.

You should, of course, be aware that while Selenium does its best to ensure that the page is loaded, you should not rely on it. With a simple website with no JavaScript manipulation of the DOM or AJAX requests firing away in the background, Selenium will be pretty accurate. With modern websites, it isn't that easy.

Selenium will do a variety of things to try and ensure that the page has loaded. The following are a couple of examples:

- Wait for the onload event to be triggered
- Check whether new elements are still being added to the DOM

The exact mechanisms used can differ from driver to driver. It is constantly under review to try and make it as accurate and stable as possible. However, modern websites are a moving target. So, the current revision of code in Selenium may not work for the site that you are testing.

It is also worth noting that various JavaScript frameworks don't actually start doing their DOM manipulation until the onload event has been triggered.

With this in mind, you should always treat the fact that Selenium thinks the page has loaded as a guess. You are going to have to figure out whether the JavaScript manipulation of the DOM or any pending AJAX requests has been completed by yourself. (We will have a look at ways in which we can do this later on in this chapter.)

The script timeout

This one is pretty simple. It sets the amount of time that Selenium will wait for a bit of JavaScript to execute when you use the `executeAsyncScript()` method.

Errors in this area are normally due to callbacks not being invoked or, very occasionally, the script timeout being set to a negative number. It's normally pretty easy to diagnose these problems as you will see an exception that looks like this:

```
org.openqa.selenium.TimeoutException: Script execution failed.
```

The implicit wait timeout

Implicit waits were not originally a part of the WebDriver API. They are actually a hangover from the old Selenium 1 API. It was not going to be put into the WebDriver API, because it encourages people to write tests without thinking, something like this:

> *Why is my test failing when the element should be there? Oh, let's just slap in an arbitrary wait. If it goes green, it must be fine…*

The only reason it made it into the WebDriver API was because of the massive outcry from the community, which was used to the Selenium 1 API and wanted it back.

This is probably the timeout that causes the most confusion, even though on the face of it, it seems very simple. What it does is add a grace period when trying to find an element. So, consider a situation where you set your implicitly wait timeout as follows:

```
driver.manage().timeouts().implicitlyWait(15, TimeUnit.SECONDS);
```

In this case, Selenium will wait for up to 15 seconds for an element to appear in the DOM when trying to find it.

A lot of people have been told not to use implicit waits because they are bad form, but they don't really know why. You may come across code patterns that look like this:

```
public static final int DEFAULT_TIMEOUT_IN_SECONDS = 10;
private static final int POLL_INTERVAL_IN_MILLISECONDS = 300;

public WebElement reliableFindElement(final WebDriver driver,
final By selector) {
    WebDriverWait wait = new WebDriverWait(driver,
    DEFAULT_TIMEOUT_IN_SECONDS, POLL_INTERVAL_IN_MILLISECONDS);
    return wait.until(new ExpectedCondition<WebElement>() {
        public WebElement apply(WebDriver driver) {
            final List<WebElement> elements =
            driver.findElements(selector);
```

```
                for (final WebElement webElement: elements) {
                    if (matches(webElement)) {
                        return webElement;
                    }
                }
                return null;
            }
        });
    }
```

What this is actually doing is re-implementing an implicit wait. That's a lot of code to write and maintain, and it provides no real benefit!

What makes things worse is that once code like this has been written, it's usually used across the project, which means that the problems that it might have fixed will still exist.

So, what are the problems with implicit waits? The following are the two main issues with implicit waits:

- If you want to check whether an element does not exist, implicit waits increase the time for this check to be performed, slowing your tests down
- Implicit waits can break explicit waits

Can it slow my tests down?

This is something that seems very obvious when you stop and think about it, but it is surprising how many people don't.

Something that we all do from time to time in our tests is check whether something doesn't exist. For example, you may have a phone book application and you may want to check whether clicking on the delete link removes a contact from your phone book and no longer displays the contact on screen.

The obvious thing to do is delete the contact and then try to find the elements on screen that were used to display the contact. Let's say that in our example, we have the following four elements that are displayed for a contact:

- Name
- Number
- The type of number
- Address

When we delete a contact, we want to make sure that all four elements have been removed from the screen. So, we check them. The problem is that we have set an implicit wait of 15 seconds. This means that each time we try to find an element, Selenium waits for 15 seconds to allow the element to appear before reporting back that it cannot be found. We have inadvertently added 1 minute to our test runtime, when these checks could have been performed in under a second.

As you can see, the more times you check whether something is not there, the slower your tests get. Before you know it, you'll have a 2-hour test run that nobody bothers to run any more because it takes too much time.

Now, there are ways around this. We could change the implicit wait timeout before each test checks for the nonexistence of an element and then change it back again. The problem is that it doesn't take long for somebody to slip up and forget to do this and then, before you know it, your test execution time has started increasing and you have to go hunting through the code to find out what is wrong. The worst-case scenario is that it happens slowly over a period of time. So, you don't notice the odd 15-second increase in the time it takes to run your tests.

Can it break explicit waits?

This is the other side-effect that people don't always pick up on. Once you have set an implicit wait, it lives for the life of the driver object. This means that when you create your explicit waits, they will use the driver object that already has an implicit wait set on it.

Let's have a look at a couple of scenarios to illustrate the problem.

The explicit wait that never finds an element

You have just started working with a development team that already has a Selenium test framework and a series of tests. The tests are reasonably well-factored, and there is a decent `DriverFactory` class that deals with the driver setup for various browsers. You have been working with this framework for a couple of months and are quite confident with it, but you've never really needed to dig into the internal workings of how the driver object is set up, because it has always worked for you.

You now have a requirement to write a test for a new bit of functionality. This functionality is that when you log into your site, there should now be an animated GIF image displayed while your account details are being loaded. When all the information is ready to show you your home page, the animated GIF image will disappear. Your UX team has spent some time investigating this area of the site, and they have found that if it takes longer than 10 seconds to load your home page, most customers will give up and close the browser. So, we have a hard requirement that this page must load within 10 seconds.

You start writing your test and decide that this is a good candidate for an explicit wait , and so you write some code that looks like this:

```
WebDriverWait wait = new WebDriverWait(getDriver(), 10, 500);
wait.until(not(presenceOfElementLocated(By.
id("loading_image"))));
```

It all looks good. So, you run your test and it fails. You manually check the functionality and it looks like it should work. Looking at it, there is a delay of about 2 seconds, but your explicit wait is waiting for 10 seconds and it is rechecking the page every 500 milliseconds. Why isn't it working?

You decide to step through and debug it. It all looks fine until you get to your explicit wait. When you step into it, you see it perform the initial check. The animated GIF image is still there. So, it loops round. You will see that it keeps looping in your explicit wait while the animated GIF image is being displayed. The animated GIF image disappears and you don't see the breakpoint in your explicit wait hit again, but after 10 seconds, the test fails with a `TimeoutException`.

How did this happen? You double-check your code and you do indeed have a 500 millisecond interval set for your explicit wait. What is going on? The element is there! Maybe it's time to raise a bug report on Selenium, or have a moan on a mailing list about how unreliable Selenium is…

Wait, it's a trap!

What has actually happened is that you have been tricked. In the `DriverFactory` code, somebody has helpfully set a 15-second implicit wait. This means that when the code drops into your explicit wait, a `findElement()` call is made, and this call goes off and tries to find the `<img src="images/loading.gif">` element. This call will wait for up to 15 seconds for the element to appear. However, your explicit wait is going to time out after only 10 seconds. To fix this, you are either going to have to increase your timeout in your explicit wait, or decrease the timeout set in the implicit wait.

The explicit wait that works, but slows your tests down

This scenario is basically the same as the previous scenario, but this time, the UX team has decided that the drop-off point is 15 seconds. So, your explicit wait code now looks like this:

```
WebDriverWait wait = new WebDriverWait(getDriver(), 15, 500);
wait.until(not(presenceOfElementLocated(By.
id("loading_image"))));
```

However, the implicit wait inside the driver factory has helpfully been set to 10 seconds this time.

This time, you don't notice any problems, you run your test and it passes, and everything looks fine. The problem is that the animated GIF image actually disappeared after 2 seconds, but your test waited the whole 10 seconds set by the implicit wait before it realized that the animated GIF image had gone.

You have inadvertently added an 8-second delay to your test for no good reason. The build is reliably green. So, this doesn't get noticed. You are on your first step towards the death of your fast feedback loop by one thousand cuts.

The solution

It is generally safer to not fiddle with the implicit wait timeouts and just deal with the exceptions to the rule (that is, the slow-loading elements) on a case-by-case basis.

You can, of course, use implicit waits if you want to and program around the problems highlighted in the preceding section, but are you sure you want to?

Using explicit waits

The recommended solution for waiting problems is to use explicit waits. There is already a class full of pre-canned examples called `ExpectedConditions` to make your life easy, and it really is not that hard to use them. You can do the simple things, such as find an element once it becomes visible in two lines of code, as follows:

```
WebDriverWait wait = new WebDriverWait(getDriver(), 15, 100);
WebElement myElement = wait.until(ExpectedConditions.
visibilityOfElementLocated(By.id("foo")));
```

Bear in mind that the `ExpectedConditions` class are primarily examples. Though they are helpful, they are actually designed to show you how to set up explicit waits so that you can easily create your own. With these examples, it is trivial to create a new class with conditions that you care about in it. This class can then be reused again and again in your project.

Earlier on, I said that we would have a look at a way to figure out whether your site had finished processing AJAX requests. Let's do this now. First of all, we will create a new class that does let you figure out whether a website using jQuery has finished making AJAX calls, as follows:

```
package com.masteringselenium;

import org.openqa.selenium.JavascriptExecutor;
import org.openqa.selenium.WebDriver;
```

```
import org.openqa.selenium.support.ui.ExpectedCondition;

public class AdditionalConditions {

    public static ExpectedCondition<Boolean>
    jQueryAJAXCallsHaveCompleted() {
        return new ExpectedCondition<Boolean>() {

            @Override
            public Boolean apply(WebDriver driver) {
                return (Boolean) ((JavascriptExecutor)
                driver).executeScript("return (window.jQuery
                != null) && (jQuery.active === 0);");
            }
        };
    }
}
```

What this will do is use a `JavascriptExecutor` to make a request to the page to find out whether jQuery has any outstanding active AJAX requests. There is also some protection that is built in to ensure that if the page does not have jQuery loaded, the JavaScript snippet will not error.

We can now call this condition anywhere in our code by using the following code:

```
WebDriverWait wait = new WebDriverWait(getDriver(), 15, 100);
wait.until(AdditionalConditions.jQueryAJAXCallsHaveCompleted()));
```

We now have an easy way to find out whether jQuery has finished running the AJAX calls in the background before we interact with our jQuery-based site.

Maybe you don't use jQuery. Well, how about AngularJS? Here's the code for that:

```
public static ExpectedCondition
<Boolean> angularHasFinishedProcessing() {
    return new ExpectedCondition<Boolean>() {
        @Override
        public Boolean apply(WebDriver driver) {
            return Boolean.valueOf(((JavascriptExecutor)
            driver).executeScript("return (window.angular !==
            undefined) && (angular.element(document).injector() !==
undefined) && (angular.element(document).injector().
get('$http').pendingRequests.length === 0)").toString());
        }
    };
}
```

This one is a little more complex on the JavaScript side. We have a chain of conditions to ensure that AngularJS is available and it has had time to bootstrap and generate its services. We then hook into the internal `pendingRequests` array and count the number of AJAX requests that still need to complete. We are using some internal knowledge of Angular for this example. So, your mileage may vary, but it should be easy enough to tweak it if Angular does change the way it tracks the pending requests.

As with our previous example, this is now easy to use elsewhere in your code. You just need the following code:

```
WebDriverWait wait = new WebDriverWait(getDriver(), 15, 100);
wait.until(AdditionalConditions.
angularHasFinishedProcessing()));
```

As you can see, it really is quite easy to create new conditions to use in your code. The next question is, how complex can we make these waits?

FluentWaits – the core of explicit waits

At the core of explicit waits is the incredibly powerful fluent wait API. All the `WebDriverWait` objects extend `FluentWait`. So, why would we want to use `FluentWait`?

Well, we get more granular control over the `Wait` object, and we can easily specify specific exceptions to ignore. Let's have a look at an example:

```
Wait<WebDriver> wait = new FluentWait<WebDriver>(driver)
        .withTimeout(15, TimeUnit.SECONDS)
        .pollingEvery(500, TimeUnit.MILLISECONDS)
        .ignoring(NoSuchElementException.class)
        .withMessage("The message you will see in if a
        TimeoutException is thrown");
```

As you can see in the preceding code, we created a wait object with a 15-second timeout that polls every five hundred milliseconds to check whether a condition is met. We have decided that while waiting for our condition to become true, we want to ignore any instances of `NoSuchElementException`. So, we have specified it in the `ignoring` method. We also want to return a custom message if we get a `TimeoutException`. So, we have also added it here.

If you want to ignore multiple exceptions, you have two choices. First of all, you can chain the `ignoring()` method multiple times, as follows:

```
Wait<WebDriver> wait = new FluentWait<WebDriver>(driver)
        .withTimeout(15, TimeUnit.SECONDS)
        .pollingEvery(500, TimeUnit.MILLISECONDS)
        .ignoring(NoSuchElementException.class)
        .ignoring(StaleElementReferenceException.class)
        .withMessage("The message you will see in if a
        TimeoutException is thrown");
```

Alternatively, you can pass multiple types of exception into the `.ignoreAll()` method, as follows:

```
Wait<WebDriver> wait = new FluentWait<WebDriver>(driver)
        .withTimeout(15, TimeUnit.SECONDS)
        .pollingEvery(500, TimeUnit.MILLISECONDS)
        .ignoreAll(Arrays.asList(NoSuchElementException.class,
        StaleElementReferenceException.class))
        .withMessage("The message you will see in if a
        TimeoutException is thrown");
```

If you prefer, you can even pass a collection of exceptions into the `.ignoreAll()` method, as follows:

```
List<Class<? extends Throwable>> exceptionsToIgnore =
new ArrayList<Class<? extends Throwable>>() {
    {
        add(NoSuchElementException.class);
        add(StaleElementReferenceException.class);
    }
};

Wait<WebDriver> wait = new FluentWait<WebDriver>(driver)
        .withTimeout(15, TimeUnit.SECONDS)
        .pollingEvery(500, TimeUnit.MILLISECONDS)
        .ignoreAll(exceptionsToIgnore)
        .withMessage("The message you will see in if
        a TimeoutException is thrown");
```

We now have a `wait` object that is ready to wait for something to happen. So, how do we make it wait for something? We have two options—a function or a predicate. For more information on functions and predicates, have a look at the Guava Libraries documentation by visiting `https://code.google.com/p/guava-libraries/wiki/FunctionalExplained`. Selenium uses the Guava libraries for functions and predicates.

Functions

We are going to create a very basic function that will find and return a `WebElement`, as follows:

```
Function<WebDriver, WebElement> weFindElementFoo =
new Function<WebDriver, WebElement>() {
    public WebElement apply(WebDriver driver) {
        return driver.findElement(By.id("foo"));
    }
};
```

The `Function` may look confusing, but it is actually quite simple. It is simply specifying an input and an output. Let's break it down and take the object definition in isolation, as follows:

```
Function<WebDriver, WebElement> weFindElementFoo
```

What we are saying is that we are going to create a `Function` element named `weFindElementFoo`. We are going to supply this `Function` with an object of `WebDriver` as the input and we will get an object of `WebElement` returned to us as the output.

All functions need to have a single method called `apply`, which takes an input (in this case, a `WebDriver` object) and returns an output (in this case, a `WebElement` object):

```
new Function<WebDriver, WebElement>() {
    public WebElement apply(WebDriver driver) {
        //Do something here
    }
};
```

The code inside the method then just needs to do something with the input to transform it into the output. In this case, we have this code:

```
return driver.findElement(By.id("foo"));
```

Overall, it is very simple once you have broken it down.

The advantage of using a `Function` element is that you can pass in an object of any type as the input and return an object of any type as the output. This gives you a huge amount of flexibility with your waits as you can return all sorts of useful objects when your waiting criteria has been met. Most functions that you will come across in Selenium will probably return a single `WebElement` or a `WebElement` list.

Predicates

Predicates are similar to functions, but you only need to supply them with an input. The output of a predicate will always be a Boolean. Let's create a `Predicate` element based on our original `Function`, as follows:

```
Predicate<WebDriver> didWeFindElementFoo =
new Predicate<WebDriver>() {
    public boolean apply(WebDriver driver) {
        return driver.findElements(By.id("foo")).size() > 0;
    }
};
```

Let's break this down in the same way as we broke down the function. First of all, we have the following code:

```
Predicate<WebDriver> didWeFindElementFoo
```

Here, we are saying that we are going to create a `Predicate` element named `didWeFindElementFoo`. We are going to supply this `Predicate` with an object of `WebDriver`. We don't need to worry about the output as we know that we are going to get a Boolean.

As with functions, all predicates need to have a single method called `apply`, which takes an input (in this case, a `WebDriver` object). As this is a predicate, the `apply()` method will have to return an output of the Boolean type, as follows:

```
new Predicate<WebDriver>() {
    public boolean apply(WebDriver driver) {
        //Do something here
    }
};
```

Finally, we need to add the code inside the method that does something to our input to transform it into the output, which is, of course, an object of the Boolean type, as follows:

```
return driver.findElements(By.id("foo")).size() > 0;
```

Once again, it's pretty simple when you break it down.

> Remember that if you want to return a Boolean, use `Predicate`; if you want to return anything else, use `Function`!

Now that we have something to put into our `wait` object, we can use it to wait for something to happen. Let's start off with the function that we created:

```
wait.until(weFindElementFoo);
```

We are ignoring `NoSuchElementExceptions`. So, we will keep trying to find an element with an ID of foo for 15 seconds. If we do not successfully find the element, we will pause for 500 milliseconds and then try again. If we do not find the element with an ID of foo after 15 seconds, we will throw a `TimeoutException` with the custom message that we specified earlier.

As you can see, we can create nice readable tests that tell us what they are doing. When things go wrong, we can throw exceptions with useful information in the message. Thus, we have a lot of control over timeouts and polling. Also, they are clearly readable for anybody else who starts looking at our code. Finally, we have the ability to do very simple or complex things using functions or predicates that can be given good descriptive names.

Let's have a look at some more predicate examples.

First of all, we have a predicate that uses jQuery to check whether a specific listener has been registered on an element:

```java
public static Predicate<WebDriver> listenerIsRegisteredOnElement
(final String listenerType, final WebElement element) {
    return new Predicate<WebDriver>() {
        public boolean apply(WebDriver driver) {
            Map<String, Object> registeredListeners =
            (Map<String, Object>) ((JavascriptExecutor)
            driver).executeScript("return (window.jQuery
            != null) && (jQuery._data(jQuery(arguments[0]).
            get(0)), 'events')", element);
            for (Map.Entry<String, Object> listener :
            registeredListeners.entrySet()) {
                if (listener.getKey().equals(listenerType)) {
                    return true;
                }
            }
            return false;
        }
    };
}
```

Why is this useful? Well, you may have a requirement that says that when you select an input element, an onfocus event is triggered, which adds a blue border around the element that you are currently editing. This is a hard requirement to test. Checking whether an onfocus event has been registered on an element may be the easiest way to do this.

Next, we have a predicate that will check whether an element is moving on the screen, as follows:

```
public static Predicate<WebDriver> elementHasStoppedMoving(
final WebElement element) {
    return new Predicate<WebDriver>() {
        public boolean apply(WebDriver driver) {
            Point initialLocation = ((Locatable)
            element).getCoordinates().inViewPort();
            try {
                Thread.sleep(50);
            } catch (InterruptedException ignored) {
                //ignored
            }
            Point finalLocation = ((Locatable)
            element).getCoordinates().inViewPort();
            return initialLocation.equals(finalLocation);
        }
    };
}
```

This will be useful if you have some objects that move around the screen for a period of time before stopping so that you can click on them. Trying to click on a moving target is hard, and you will probably get intermittent test failures. This allows you to wait until the object has stopped moving.

You may ask how this could be useful. Type CSS3 games in Google and see what's possible. A site that's worth looking at is http://www.cssplay.co.uk/menu/cssplay-whack-a-rat.html.

Summary

After reading this chapter, you should:

- Understand why using static waits such as Thread.sleep() are bad
- Have a good understanding of the three different types of timeouts that you can set on the driver object
- Know how implicit waits can adversely affect the speed of your tests and understand some of the pitfalls of mixing them with explicit waits
- Know how to use and extend explicit waits
- Have a good understanding of the fluent wait API and how to use functions and predicates

In the next chapter, we will look at page objects and how we can use them effectively without letting them get out of control.

5
Working with Effective Page Objects

In this chapter, we will:

- Study **DRY (Don't Repeat Yourself)** and have a look at how we can apply it to page objects.

- Examine why we should keep our assertions separate from page objects.

- Have a look at the Java `PageFactory` classes that are available in the Selenium Support package.

- Look at how we can build sensible extensible page objects that do the hard work of driving our tests.

- Talk about how we can make a readable **DSL (domain-specific language)** using page objects. We don't need Cucumber to write readable tests.

We are going to work through some examples in this chapter. So, you will need your development IDE set up and ready to start writing some code. You can use the base Selenium implementation that we put together in *Chapter 1, Creating a Fast Feedback Loop*. If you do this, you will probably want to add the following line of code at the beginning of your tests:

```
WebDriver driver = getDriver();
```

This will get a driver object that we can seamlessly use with the examples used in this chapter.

Why do you keep repeating yourself?

After writing automated checks for a while, you tend to see similar patterns emerging. One of the most commonly seen bad patterns is tests that interact with the same page, and the same elements on that page, in different ways.

This normally happens because more than one person automates scenarios in the same area, and as with everything, different people have different ways of doing things.

Let's take as an example a couple of basic HTML pages. First of all, we will have our index page. This is the page that everybody is going to see when they navigate to our website:

```html
<!DOCTYPE html>
<html lang="en">
<head>
    <title>Some generic website</title>
    <link href="http://cdnjs.cloudflare.com/ajax/libs/
    twitter-bootstrap/3.3.2/css/bootstrap.min.css"
    rel="stylesheet">
    <link href="../css/custom.css" rel="stylesheet">
</head>
<body>
<nav class="navbar navbar-inverse navbar-fixed-top"
role="navigation">
    <div class="container">
        <div class="navbar-header">
            <a class="navbar-brand" href="#">
                <img src="http://placehold.it/150x50&text=Logo"
                alt="">
            </a>
        </div>
        <div id="navbar-links">
            <ul class="nav navbar-nav">
                <li><a href="services.html">Services</a></li>
                <li><a href="contact.html">Contact</a></li>
            </ul>
        </div>
    </div>
</nav>
<div class="container">
    <div class="row">
        <div class="col-md-8">
            <img class="img-responsive img-rounded"
            src="http://placehold.it/900x350" alt="">
```

```
        </div>
        <div class="col-md-4">
            <h1>Lorem ipsum dolor</h1>

            <p>Duis in turpis finibus, eleifend nisl et, accumsan
            dolor. Pellentesque sed ex fringilla, gravida tellus
            in, tempus libero. Maecenas mi urna, fermentum et sem
                vitae, congue pellentesque velit.</p>
            <a class="btn btn-primary btn-lg"
            href="#">Nam mattis</a>
        </div>
    </div>
    <hr>
    <footer>
        <div class="row">
            <div class="col-lg-12 left-footer">
                <a href="about.html">About</a>
            </div>
            <div class="col-lg-12 right-footer">
                <p>Copyright &copy; Your Website 2015</p>
            </div>
        </div>
    </footer>
</div>
</body>
</html>
```

Our index page will look like this in a browser:

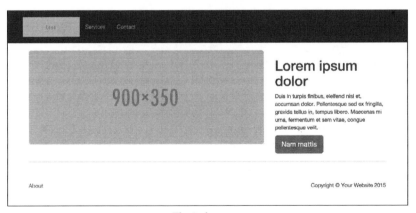

The index page

Next, we will have the about page. This page is going to tell the user a bit about the company's history because people are interested in that sort of thing:

```html
<!DOCTYPE html>
<html lang="en">
<head>
    <title>Some generic website - About us</title>
    <link href="http://cdnjs.cloudflare.com/ajax/libs/
    twitter-bootstrap/3.3.2/css/bootstrap.min.css"
    rel="stylesheet">
    <link href="../css/custom.css" rel="stylesheet">

</head>

<body>
<nav class="navbar navbar-inverse navbar-fixed-top"
role="navigation">
    <div class="container">
        <div class="navbar-header">
            <a class="navbar-brand" href="#">
                <img src="http://placehold.it/150x50&text=Logo"
                alt="">
            </a>
        </div>
        <div id="navbar-links">
            <ul class="nav navbar-nav">
                <ul class="nav navbar-nav">
                    <li><a href="services.html">Services</a></li>
                    <li><a href="contact.html">Contact</a></li>
                </ul>
            </ul>
        </div>
    </div>
</nav>
<div class="container">
    <div class="row">
        <div class="col-md-4">
            <h1>About us!</h1>

            <p>Lorem ipsum dolor sit amet, consectetur adipiscing
            elit. In nec elit feugiat, egestas tortor vel,
            pharetra tellus. Mauris auctor purus sed mi finibus,
            at feugiat
                enim commodo. Nunc sed eros nec libero aliquam
                varius non vel sapien. Cras et nulla non purus
                auctor tincidunt.</p>
        </div>
```

```
    </div>
    <hr>
    <footer>
        <div class="row">
            <div class="col-lg-12 left-footer">
                <a href="about.html">About</a>
            </div>
            <div class="col-lg-12 right-footer">
                <p>Copyright &copy; Your Website 2014</p>
            </div>
        </div>
    </footer>
</div>
</body>
</html>
```

The about page will look like this in a browser:

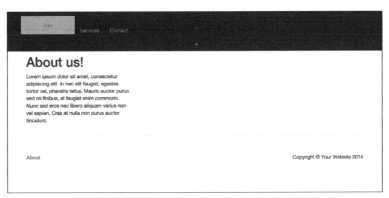

The about page

Both of these pages used a common `custom.css` that contains the following code:

```
body {
    padding-top: 70px;
}

.navbar-fixed-top .nav {
    padding: 15px 0;
}

.navbar-fixed-top .navbar-brand {
    padding: 0 15px;
}

footer {
```

```
        padding: 30px 0;
    }

    .left-footer {
        float: left;
        width: 20%;
    }

    .right-footer {
        text-align: right;
        float: right;
        width: 50%;
    }

    @media (min-width: 768px) {
        body {
            padding-top: 100px
        }

        .navbar-fixed-top .navbar-brand {
            padding: 15px 0;
        }
    }
}
```

There are probably many more pages that make up this site, but we are only interested in these two for our example. We will then assume that when this site was automated, the task was performed by a team of people in an attempt to get the work done really quickly. As a result, we have had two different people working on scripts that interact with these pages in isolation. We will call these scripts goToTheAboutPage() and checkThatAboutPageHasText():

```
@Test
public void goToTheAboutPage() throws Exception {
    driver().get("http://ch5.masteringselenium.com/
    index.html");
    driver().findElement(By.cssSelector(".left-footer >
    a")).click();
    WebElement element = driver().
    findElement(By.cssSelector("h1"));

    assertThat(element.getText(), is(equalTo("About us!")));
}

@Test
public void checkThatAboutPageHasText() throws Exception {
    driver().get("http://ch5.masteringselenium.com/
    index.html");
```

```
driver().findElement(By.cssSelector("footer
div:nth-child(1) > a")).click();
String titleText = driver().findElement(
By.cssSelector(".container > div h1")).getText();

assertThat(titleText, is(equalTo("About us!")));
}
```

If you look closely, you will see that while the scripts initially look different, they are actually doing the same thing. Which one is correct? Well, they both are! They are both reasonably sensible; they just use slightly different locator strategies. In fact, the reason the second one was written is probably because the person writing the second one didn't realize that what they were writing had already been written.

So, how can we get around this problem? How about making it clearer to the person reading the code what each locator is by giving it a sensible name?

Let's refactor goToTheAboutPage() a bit and find out whether we can make it easier to read:

```
@Test
public void goToTheAboutPage() throws Exception {
    driver().get("http://ch5.masteringselenium.com/
    index.html");

    WebElement aboutLink = driver().
    findElement(By.cssSelector(".left-footer > a"));

    aboutLink.click();

    WebElement aboutHeading = driver().
    findElement(By.cssSelector("h1"));

    assertThat(aboutHeading.getText(), is(equalTo("About us!")));
}
```

We have now made goToTheAboutPage() much clearer. A person adding scripts will probably be able to look at this script and realize that some of the locators that they want to use have already been defined. You can then hope that they will use the same locators to save time and ensure consistency. This of course does assume that a person who starts writing scripts looks at the old ones, or somebody who comes back to a set of tests after a period of time remembers what they have done before and checks whether they already have something usable.

Wouldn't it be easier if we could make some explicit definitions for the elements that we are interested in and which everybody knows about in advance? That way, people won't have to keep repeating the work that has already been done.

Well, we can. We can use the DRY principle. We can take some common code that is regularly reused and put it into a centralized location, from where it can be repeatedly called. In the world of Selenium, these definitions are called page objects.

> Page objects are badly named. They do not specifically refer to a page. They actually refer to any group of related objects. In many cases, this will be an entire page, but in other cases, it may be a part of a page or a component that is reused across many pages.
>
> Also remember that if your page objects are hundreds of lines of code in length, you may as well be able to break them up into much smaller and more manageable chunks.

When people start using page objects, they often fall into a few traps. Let's have a look at some common pitfalls.

Starting out with page objects

Let's take goToTheAboutPage(). We have refactored it to make it nice and clear, but we now want to abstract things away into a page object to encourage other people to use all that hard work of finding the correct locators. Let's create two page objects called indexPage and aboutPage and move our element definitions across into in. We will start off with the index page, as follows:

```
package com.masteringselenium.page_objects;

import org.openqa.selenium.By;

public class IndexPage {

    public static By heading = By.cssSelector("h1");
    public static By mainText = By.cssSelector(".col-md-4 > p");
    public static By button = By.cssSelector(".btn");
    public static By aboutLinkLocator = By.cssSelector(".
    left-footer > a");
}
```

Then, we need to create the page object for the about page, as follows:

```
package com.masteringselenium.page_objects;

import org.openqa.selenium.By;

public class AboutPage {

    public static By heading = By.cssSelector("h1");
```

```
    public static By aboutUsText =
    By.cssSelector(".col-md-4 > p");
    public static By aboutHeadingLocator = By.cssSelector("h1");
}
```

You may have noticed that we added a few more locators to the `IndexPage` and `AboutPage` objects. These will be used later on in this chapter. So, don't worry about them for now. Next, we need to modify the `goToTheAboutPage()` test to use the page objects, as follows:

```
@Test
public void goToTheAboutPage()throws Exception {
    driver().get("http://
    ch5.masteringselenium.com/index.html");

    WebElement aboutLink = driver().findElement(
    IndexPage.aboutLinkLocator);

    aboutLink.click();

    WebElement aboutHeading = driver().findElement(
    AboutPage.aboutHeadingLocator);

    assertThat(aboutHeading.getText(), is(equalTo("About us!")));
}
```

Excellent. Now, we are using the page objects, and we have a series of element definitions that can be reused. However, we still have a couple of issues.

First of all, we put our page object in with our tests.

The original test structure

It may seem like a good idea at first, but when you have a mature product with quite a few tests, you will find out that it will be hard to search for the page objects. So what should we do? Well, we are going to keep our page objects separate to ensure that we have a clear separation of concerns.

Let's create a place for our page objects to live that is separate from the tests and has a sensible name that will indicate to people what these pieces of code are.

The improved test structure

Using page objects to ensure good separation of concerns

Our second issue is that while we abstracted away the WebElement creation, we didn't abstract away any of the heavy lifting that was performed by our test script. We are now using a page object, but we are still going to have lots of duplication in our code. Let's illustrate this by looking at a script that would perform a login and how we would do this using our new page objects.

Let's start with a basic login page object and a login test that uses it:

```
package com.masteringselenium.page_objects;

import org.openqa.selenium.By;

public class LoginPage {

    public static By usernameLocator = By.id("username");
    public static By passwordLocator = By.id("password");
    public static By loginButtonLocator = By.id("login");
}

@Test
```

```
public void logInToTheWebsite()throws Exception {
    driver().get("http://
    ch5.masteringselenium.com/index.html");

    WebElement username = driver().
    findElement(LoginPage.usernameLocator);
    WebElement password = driver().
    findElement(LoginPage.passwordLocator);
    WebElement submitButton = driver().
    findElement(LoginPage.loginButtonLocator);

    username.sendKeys("foo");
    password.sendKeys("bar");
    submitButton.click();

    assertThat(driver().getTitle(),
    is(equalTo("Logged in")));
}
```

Our script is quite clean, and we are using a page object to find the elements that we need to use. However, what if we write another script that needs to use the login process? Any other script that performed a login would reuse the first six lines of code that are in this script, which is a lot of code duplication.

We can make this better! We know that the duplicate lines of code are filling in the form fields to perform a login. Let's abstract this action away into the page object, as follows:

```
package com.masteringselenium.page_objects;

import org.openqa.selenium.By;
import org.openqa.selenium.WebDriver;

public class LoginPage {

    public static By usernameLocator = By.id("username");
    public static By passwordLocator = By.id("password");
    public static By loginButtonLocator = By.id("login");

    public static void logInWithUsernameAndPassword(String
    username, String password, WebDriver driver) {

        driver.findElement(loginPage.usernameLocator).
        sendKeys(username);
```

```
        driver.findElement(loginPage.passwordLocator).
        sendKeys(password);
        driver.findElement(loginPage.loginButtonLocator).click();
    }
}
```

We can now use this action, which is in the page object in our tests, as follows:

```
@Test
public void logInToTheWebsite() throws Exception {
    driver().get("http://ch5.masteringselenium.com/
    index.html");
    LoginPage.logInWithUsernameAndPassword("foo",
    "bar", driver());

    assertThat(driver().getTitle(),
    is(equalTo("Logged in")));
}
```

Our test is now much cleaner. It has fewer lines of code, and it is nice and descriptive without being overly verbose. We can now reuse this login function in all of the tests that we write that perform a login.

 We don't want to move too much into our page objects. Remember to keep your assertions in your tests and not in your page objects.

Introducing the Java PageFactory class

Inside the `WebDriver` support library, there is a `PageFactory` class that provides a series of annotations, which can be used when you create page objects.

You can use this class to predefine a series of `WebElement`s, which can be used later in your test. The `PageFactory` class turns these `WebElement` objects into proxied objects using a Java Proxy class. When you try to use them, the annotations that you specify are used to transform these proxied objects into real `WebElement` objects, which can be used in your tests. We need to do the following two things to use the `PageFactory` class:

- Annotate the variables that we want to proxy
- Initialize the proxied objects before we try to use them

Using the PageFactory annotations

We are going to take the existing `LoginPage` class and convert it into one backed by the `DriverFactory` class. Let's start with the most common annotation that is in use, the `@FindBy` annotation. You have a couple of options when it comes to defining them:

```
@FindBy(how = How.ID, using = "username")
private WebElement usernameField;

@FindBy(id = "username")
private WebElement usernameField;
```

The two preceding examples are functionally equivalent, and both are correct. It doesn't matter which one you decide to use.

I personally prefer the first option. I have configured a live template in IntelliJ that creates the annotation and allows me to just press *CMD + J* (or *CTRL + J* if you are not using OS X) and then . (period) to trigger it. I can then press . (period) again, and IntelliJ IDEA then gives me a series of options for the `How` enum. I don't have to remember all the selector options, and it's very quick and easy for me to create annotations.

> The live template that I use in intelliJ IDEA to create the `@FindBy` annotations is `@FindBy(how = How$VAR$, using = "$END$")`.
>
> To learn more about live templates, have a look at `https://www.jetbrains.com/idea/help/creating-and-editing-live-templates.html`.

Other people will prefer the second, less verbose option. Either of the two options is perfectly fine.

So what does the `@FindBy` annotation do? Well, it is a way to pass a `By` object into a `driver.findElement()` call to create a WebElement. This `driver.findElement()` call is completely transparent to you and will be performed in the background whenever you use the `WebElement` that has an annotation applied to it. This also means that you are much less likely to get a `StaleElementReferenceException` because the element will be found every time you try to interact with it.

A good rule of thumb to use when writing page objects using the `PageFactory` implementation is to make all the `WebElement` objects that you define private. This forces you to write functions in your page objects that interact with the `WebElement` objects that you have defined rather than using the page object as a glorified `WebElement` store.

Let's convert the `LoginPage` object into one backed by the `PageFactory` class:

```
package com.masteringselenium.page_factory_objects;

import org.openqa.selenium.WebElement;
import org.openqa.selenium.support.FindBy;
import org.openqa.selenium.support.How;

public class LoginPage {

    @FindBy(how = How.ID, using = "username")
    private WebElement usernameLocator;

    @FindBy(how = How.ID, using = "password")
    private WebElement passwordLocator;

    @FindBy(how = How.ID, using = "login")
    private WebElement loginButtonLocator;

    public void logInWithUsernameAndPassword(String username,
    String password) {
        usernameLocator.sendKeys(username);
        passwordLocator.sendKeys(password);
        loginButtonLocator.click();
    }
}
```

Initializing the proxied objects

For the `PageFactory` annotation to work, you must initialize the class. The `WebElement` objects will not be proxied, and the annotations that you have specified will not be applied if you forget to do this. You can initialize a class using one very simple line of code:

```
LoginPage loginPage = PageFactory.initElements(driver,
    LoginPage.class);
```

While this is easy, it is also quite ugly and not instantly obvious to people who don't know about the `PageFactory` class. Let's make this easier and understandable for the developers who are going to look at our code. What we are going to do is initialize the class in the constructor of our page object, as follows:

```
package com.masteringselenium.page_factory_objects;

import org.openqa.selenium.WebDriver;
```

```
import org.openqa.selenium.WebElement;
import org.openqa.selenium.support.FindBy;
import org.openqa.selenium.support.How;
import org.openqa.selenium.support.PageFactory;

public class LoginPage {

    @FindBy(how = How.ID, using = "username")
    private WebElement usernameLocator;

    @FindBy(how = How.ID, using = "password")
    private WebElement passwordLocator;

    @FindBy(how = How.ID, using = "login")
    private WebElement loginButtonLocator;

    public LoginPage(WebDriver driver) {
        PageFactory.initElements(driver, this);
    }

    public void logInWithUsernameAndPassword(String username,
    String password) {
        usernameLocator.sendKeys(username);
        passwordLocator.sendKeys(password);
        loginButtonLocator.click();
    }
}
```

Now, the code that creates a new page object instance will look like this:

```
LoginPage loginPage = new LoginPage(getDriver());
```

It's much cleaner, and it is a pattern that all Java developers will instantly recognize. We still do have a code smell here though. We are needlessly passing around a driver object all the time. So, how can we go one step further? Well if you are using the Selenium implementation that we put together in *Chapter 1, Creating a Fast Feedback Loop*, there is a solution. The getDriver() method that we are using to pass our driver object into the page object is static. This means that anything can use it to get the driver object associated with the current thread. We can use this in the page objects to eliminate the need to pass around the driver object, as follows:

```
package com.masteringselenium.page_factory_objects;

import com.masteringselenium.DriverFactory;
import org.openqa.selenium.WebElement;
import org.openqa.selenium.support.FindBy;
```

```
import org.openqa.selenium.support.How;
import org.openqa.selenium.support.PageFactory;

public class LoginPage {

    @FindBy(how = How.ID, using = "username")
    private WebElement usernameLocator;

    @FindBy(how = How.ID, using = "password")
    private WebElement passwordLocator;

    @FindBy(how = How.ID, using = "login")
    private WebElement loginButtonLocator;


    public LoginPage() throws Exception {
        PageFactory.initElements(DriverFactory.getDriver(), this);
    }

    public void logInWithUsernameAndPassword(String username,
    String password) {
        usernameLocator.sendKeys(username);
        passwordLocator.sendKeys(password);
        loginButtonLocator.click();
    }
}
}
```

This now means that all we need to do to create a new page object instance is this:

```
LoginPage loginPage = new LoginPage();
```

Our page objects now look like any other object in Java, and the fact that we can just new up a page object without providing any parameters means that it is easy to start using our page objects as building blocks.

One important thing to remember when using page objects is that our page objects are going to abstract away all the heavy work of actually driving the browser. Things that we want to check should be in our tests.

This separation of concerns has two benefits. First of all, it ensures that people do not inadvertently bring assertions into their tests when they don't mean to. Second, it means that your tests do not depend on specific implementations in your page objects. You don't want a test to lose the ability to fail because somebody updated a page object and removed an assertion that shouldn't have been there in the first place.

Remember that a test that cannot fail is worse than no test at all. If there is no test at all, you can see that a specific area of code has no test coverage (or in other words, no documentation) using static analysis tools. Tests that cannot fail are incorrect documentation; they may be lying to the user when they describe how the system works. The problem is that we will also never know when they are going to start lying.

We are going to make sure that our page objects provide some nice, clear, and descriptively named functions for our tests to use. We are not going to use our page objects as a glorified `WebElement` store. If we did do this, we would not be utilizing the full potential of page objects.

Creating extensible page objects

So far, we have only looked at examples where a page object has been used to describe a whole page. Unfortunately, in the real world, web pages that we want to automate are usually much larger and more complicated than the examples that you find in a book. So, how are we going to deal with large, complicated pages while keeping the test code well-factored and readable? We are going to break things down into manageable chunks.

Let's have another look at the HTML page examples that we used earlier in this chapter. We will start with the index page.

If you look carefully, you will see that there are two parts that look particularly generic—the header (the area enclosed in the `<nav>` tag) and the footer (the area enclosed in the `<footer>` tag). It is probably fair to expect a header and footer on every page of the website to share a common set of elements. Let's take these two areas and turn them into reusable components that have their own page objects. First of all, we will create one for the header, as follows:

```
package com.masteringselenium.page_factory_objects;

import com.masteringselenium.DriverFactory;
import org.openqa.selenium.WebElement;
import org.openqa.selenium.support.FindBy;
import org.openqa.selenium.support.How;
import org.openqa.selenium.support.PageFactory;

public class PageHeader {
```

```
@FindBy(how = How.CSS, using = ".nav li:nth-child(1) > a")
private WebElement servicesLink;

@FindBy(how = How.CSS, using = ".nav li:nth-child(2) > a")
private WebElement contactLink;

public PageHeader() throws Exception {
    PageFactory.initElements(DriverFactory.getDriver(), this);
}

public void goToTheServicesPage() {
    servicesLink.click();
}

public void goToTheContactPage() {
    contactLink.click();
}
}
```

Then, we need to create one for the footer, as follows:

```
package com.masteringselenium.page_factory_objects;

import com.masteringselenium.DriverFactory;
import org.openqa.selenium.WebElement;
import org.openqa.selenium.support.FindBy;
import org.openqa.selenium.support.How;
import org.openqa.selenium.support.PageFactory;

public class PageFooter extends PageFactory {

    @FindBy(how = How.CSS, using = ".left-footer > a")
    private WebElement aboutUsLink;

    public PageFooter() throws Exception {
        PageFactory.initElements(DriverFactory.getDriver(), this);
    }

    public void goToTheAboutUsPage() {
        aboutUsLink.click();
    }
}
```

Now, we need to convert the `IndexPage` object into one that uses the `@FindBy` annotations of `PageFactory`, as follows:

```
package com.masteringselenium.page_factory_objects;

import com.masteringselenium.DriverFactory;
import org.openqa.selenium.WebElement;
import org.openqa.selenium.support.FindBy;
import org.openqa.selenium.support.How;
import org.openqa.selenium.support.PageFactory;

import java.util.List;

public class IndexPage {

    @FindBy(how = How.CSS, using = "h1")
    private List<WebElement> heading;

    @FindBy(how = How.CSS, using = ".col-md-4 > p")
    private List<WebElement> mainText;

    @FindBy(how = How.CSS, using = ".btn")
    private List<WebElement> button;

    public IndexPage() throws Exception {
        PageFactory.initElements(DriverFactory.getDriver(), this);
    }

}
```

We now have the reusable components of the page in separate page objects so that we can reuse them when testing other pages that share these reusable components.

Now, look back at the HTML for the about page. The about page has exactly the same HTML code for the header and the footer as that of the last page. This is brilliant. We can now reuse the header and footer page objects without having to duplicate code. Let's convert the `AboutPage` object into one that uses the `PageFactory` `@FindBy` annotations as well, as follows:

```
package com.masteringselenium.page_factory_objects;

import com.masteringselenium.DriverFactory;
import org.openqa.selenium.WebElement;
import org.openqa.selenium.support.FindBy;
import org.openqa.selenium.support.How;
```

```
import org.openqa.selenium.support.PageFactory;

import java.util.List;

public class AboutPage extends PageFactory {

    @FindBy(how = How.CSS, using = "h1")
    private List<WebElement> heading;

    @FindBy(how = How.CSS, using = ".col-md-4 > p")
    private List<WebElement> aboutUsText;

    public AboutPage() throws Exception {
        PageFactory.initElements(DriverFactory.getDriver(), this);
    }

}
```

Next, we will write a quick test that goes to the index page, checks for the existence of some elements, and then goes to the about page and does the same thing. First of all, we need to make some additions to our page objects. For the index page, we need to add the ability to check whether the main block of text and the button on the page are displayed. We will do this by adding the following methods:

```
public boolean mainTextIsDisplayed(){
    return mainText.size() == 1;
}

public boolean mainPageButtonIsDisplayed(){
    return button.size() == 1;
}
```

Then, we need to do something similar on the about page. This time, we are going to add a method to check whether the about text is being displayed:

```
public boolean aboutUsTextIsDisplayed(){
    return aboutUsText.size() == 1;
}
```

You may have noticed that I have not used the Selenium `isDisplayed()` method.

Why haven't I done this?

Well, the `isDisplayed()` method will throw a `NoSuchElementException` if the element does not exist. We are using a `PageFactory` that proxies each element. So, Selenium tries to find it every time we use the proxied `WebElement`. This means that we don't know whether the element has been found or not. We don't want to have any exceptions thrown. Also, we don't want to catch exceptions. So, the easiest thing to do is return a list of elements and then count them. We know that there should only be one of these elements available. So, we check whether the size of the `WebElement` list is equal to one.

Now that we have added the methods to check for elements in page objects, we need to create our test, as follows:

```
@Test
public void checkThatAboutPageHasText() throws Exception {
    driver().get("http://ch5.masteringselenium.com/index.html");
    IndexPage indexPage = new IndexPage();

    assertThat(indexPage.mainTextIsDisplayed(),
    is(equalTo(true)));
    assertThat(indexPage.mainPageButtonIsDisplayed(),
    is(equalTo(true)));

    PageFooter footer = new PageFooter();
    footer.goToTheAboutUsPage();
    AboutPage aboutPage = new AboutPage();

    assertThat(aboutPage.aboutUsTextIsDisplayed(),
    is(equalTo(true)));
}
```

By breaking up the HTML pages into small bite-sized chunks and creating separate page objects for each of these chunks, we ended up with smaller page objects and less code duplication.

There has been an unfortunate side effect of breaking up our page objects though. Our tests are now starting to look a bit untidy, and they are much harder to read. I know that I'm interacting with a header, but I don't really know which page this header is referring to. If my tests were covering multiple pages, it would probably get quite confusing having to switch between various page objects, and it would become hard to keep track of what is going on.

What can we do to clean up the mess that we have made?

Turning your page objects into a readable domain-specific language

Well, it's actually not that hard to make things better. Earlier in this chapter, we moved the page object's initialization into the constructor and had a look at a way of initializing page objects without passing any parameters. Let's use this simplicity to start turning page objects into a fluent, readable **DSL (domain-specific language)**.

We will start off by taking the index page object and creating a reference to the header, the footer, and the page objects inside it, as follows:

```
package com.masteringselenium.page_factory_objects;

import com.masteringselenium.DriverFactory;
import org.openqa.selenium.WebElement;
import org.openqa.selenium.support.FindBy;
import org.openqa.selenium.support.How;
import org.openqa.selenium.support.PageFactory;

import java.util.List;

public class IndexPage {

    @FindBy(how = How.CSS, using = "h1")
    private List<WebElement> heading;

    @FindBy(how = How.CSS, using = ".col-md-4 > p")
    private List<WebElement> mainText;

    @FindBy(how = How.CSS, using = ".btn")
    private List<WebElement> button;

    public PageHeader header = new PageHeader();
    public PageFooter footer = new PageFooter();

    public IndexPage() throws Exception {
        PageFactory.initElements(DriverFactory.getDriver(), this);
    }

    public boolean mainTextIsDisplayed() {
        return mainText.size() == 1;
```

```
    }

    public boolean mainPageButtonIsDisplayed() {
        return button.size() == 1;


    }
}
```

As you can see, we instantiated a page object from a page object. We made this public so that anyone who creates a new instance of the parent page object automatically gets to use all the subpage objects that were defined in the parent as well.

We can now refactor our test to make it much cleaner and easy to read, as follows:

```
@Test
public void checkThatAboutPageHasText() throws Exception {
    driver().get("http://
    ch5.masteringselenium.com/index.html");
    IndexPage indexPage = new IndexPage();

    assertThat(indexPage.mainTextIsDisplayed(),
    is(equalTo(true)));
    assertThat(indexPage.mainPageButtonIsDisplayed(),
    is(equalTo(true)));

    indexPage.footer.goToTheAboutUsPage();
    AboutPage aboutPage = new AboutPage();

    assertThat(aboutPage.aboutUsTextIsDisplayed(),
    is(equalTo(true)));
}
```

It's starting to look cleaner, but let's not stop there. Rather than instantiating a new page object in the test when we need it, we can make page objects return what we want. If you click on a link that takes you to the about us page, you know where you are going. So, why not return the page objects that you are going to use? We can do this. Let's tweak the footer page object to make it return an about page object, as follows:

```
package com.masteringselenium.page_factory_objects;

import com.masteringselenium.DriverFactory;
import org.openqa.selenium.WebElement;
import org.openqa.selenium.support.FindBy;
```

```
import org.openqa.selenium.support.How;
import org.openqa.selenium.support.PageFactory;

public class PageFooter extends PageFactory {

    @FindBy(how = How.CSS, using = ".left-footer > a")
    private WebElement aboutUsLink;

    public PageFooter() throws Exception {
        PageFactory.initElements(DriverFactory.getDriver(), this);
    }

    public AboutPage goToTheAboutUsPage() throws Exception {
        aboutUsLink.click();
        return new AboutPage();
    }
}
```

This will turn our test into the following:

```
@Test
public void checkThatAboutPageHasText() throws Exception {
    driver().get("http://
    ch5.masteringselenium.com/index.html");
    IndexPage indexPage = new IndexPage();

    assertThat(indexPage.mainTextIsDisplayed(),
    is(equalTo(true)));
    assertThat(indexPage.mainPageButtonIsDisplayed(),
    is(equalTo(true)));

    AboutPage aboutPage = indexPage.footer.goToTheAboutUsPage();

    assertThat(aboutPage.aboutUsTextIsDisplayed(),
    is(equalTo(true)));
}
```

It's still a bit messy. So, let's predefine all the page object variables in the DriverFactory class. We don't need to assign anything to the variables. We will be doing this in our tests. In the DriverFactory class, we need to add the following:

```
protected IndexPage indexPage;
protected AboutPage aboutPage;
protected LoginPage loginPage;
```

All of our tests extend `DriverFactory`. So, the variables will be available to them since they have been defined as `protected`. We can now make the test look like this:

```
@Test
public void checkThatAboutPageHasText() throws Exception {
    driver().get("http://
    ch5.masteringselenium.com/index.html");
    indexPage = new IndexPage();

    assertThat(indexPage.mainTextIsDisplayed(),
    is(equalTo(true)));
    assertThat(indexPage.mainPageButtonIsDisplayed(),
    is(equalTo(true)));

    aboutPage = indexPage.footer.goToTheAboutUsPage();

    assertThat(aboutPage.aboutUsTextIsDisplayed(),
    is(equalTo(true)));
}
```

Remember that the naming conventions of the page objects are completely under your control, as are the names of the functions that do the heavy lifting. There is nothing to stop you from using readable method names for all the things that you do.

If you take your time and think about your naming strategies, there is no reason why your tests should not be completely readable by people who are not technical.

In *Chapter 2, Producing the Right Feedback when Failing*, I talked about tests being technical documentation that explained how the system that you are testing works. If you gave the preceding test to a business analyst or a product owner, would they be able to understand it without you needing to explain it to them? The preceding example is contrived, but it illustrates the potential that you have to turn your tests into documentation that describes how the system that you are testing works.

It looks like we are well on our way towards creating readable technical documentation that describes how the application under test works, and we didn't have to pull in another layer to put on top of our tests, which is contrary to what we need to do in Cucumber.

Who needs Cucumber to write tests that can be read and understood by nontechnical people?

So, is there anything else that we can do with our page objects? How about making them use a fluent interface?

Fluent page objects

So, what is a fluent interface?

A fluent interface is an API that uses chains of commands to describe the action(s) that you are performing. Each chained command will return either a reference to itself, a reference to a new method, or a void.

If you want to find out more about fluent interfaces, have a look at `https://en.wikipedia.org/wiki/Fluent_interface`.

The `LoginPage` object that we created earlier in this chapter will provide a good base for a fluent page object. It currently looks like this:

```
package com.masteringselenium.fluent_page_objects;

import com.masteringselenium.DriverFactory;
import org.openqa.selenium.WebElement;
import org.openqa.selenium.support.FindBy;
import org.openqa.selenium.support.How;
import org.openqa.selenium.support.PageFactory;

public class LoginPage {

    @FindBy(how = How.ID, using = "username")
    private WebElement usernameLocator;

    @FindBy(how = How.ID, using = "password")
    private WebElement passwordLocator;

    @FindBy(how = How.ID, using = "login")
    private WebElement loginButtonLocator;

    public LoginPage() throws Exception {
        PageFactory.initElements(DriverFactory.getDriver(),
        this);}

    public void logInWithUsernameAndPassword(String username,
    String password) {
        usernameLocator.sendKeys(username);
        passwordLocator.sendKeys(password);
        loginButtonLocator.click();
    }
}
```

Earlier, we created the `logInWithUsernameAndPassword` method to make it quick and easy to perform a login.

However, this method is not perfect. What if:

- We want to enter only a username? We are stuck sending a null to the `password` field.
- We want to enter a username and a password to trigger some client-side validation but we don't want to click on the login button?
- We have already entered the username and password and we just want to click on the login button? We will end up re-entering data.

Let's rewrite this page object using a fluent interface so that we can easily do all of the aforementioned things. It will look like this:

```
package com.masteringselenium.fluent_page_objects;

import com.masteringselenium.DriverFactory;
import org.openqa.selenium.WebElement;
import org.openqa.selenium.support.FindBy;
import org.openqa.selenium.support.How;
import org.openqa.selenium.support.PageFactory;

public class LoginPage {

    @FindBy(how = How.ID, using = "username")
    private WebElement usernameLocator;

    @FindBy(how = How.ID, using = "password")
    private WebElement passwordLocator;

    @FindBy(how = How.ID, using = "login")
    private WebElement loginButtonLocator;

    public LoginPage() throws Exception {
        PageFactory.initElements(DriverFactory.getDriver(), this);
    }

    public LoginPage enterUsername(String username) {
        usernameLocator.sendKeys(username);

        return this;
```

```
        }

        public LoginPage enterPassword(String password) {
            passwordLocator.sendKeys(password);

            return this;
        }

        public void andLogin() {
            loginButtonLocator.click();
        }
    }
```

We will also need to modify the test to take advantage of the new fluent page object. It will now look like this:

```
@Test
public void logInToTheWebsite() throws Exception {
    driver().get("http://
    ch5.masteringselenium.com/index.html");
    loginPage = new LoginPage();

    loginPage.enterUsername("foo")
            .enterPassword("bar")
            .andLogin();

    assertThat(driver().getTitle(), is(equalTo("Logged in")));
}
```

As you can see, the test is still readable, but by converting it into a fluent page object and making each action a different method, we increased the flexibility massively. Let's have a look at a slightly different scenario where we check some client-side validation. How would we do it with this new fluent page object? Well, it would look like this:

```
@Test
public void logInToTheWebsiteWithClientSideValidationCheck()
   throws Exception {
    driver().get("http://
    ch5.masteringselenium.com/index.html");
    loginPage = new LoginPage();

    loginPage.enterUsername("foo")
            .enterPassword("bar");
```

```
    //TODO Perform client side validation check here

    loginPage.andLogin();

    assertThat(driver().getTitle(), is(equalTo("Logged in")));
}
```

As you can see, we gained lots of flexibility. You may have noted that currently, the `andLogin()` method does not return anything, whereas we were returning page objects earlier when we were clicking on links. This is because the login is not deterministic. There are many places that we could go to when we log in. I've selected the easy option, which is to have a terminating context. You could, if you wanted to, create multiple methods that expected different outcomes. For example, you can create the following methods:

```
public LoginPage andFailLogin() {
    loginButtonLocator.click();

    return this;
}

public IndexPage andSuccessfullyLogin() {
    loginButtonLocator.click();

    return new IndexPage();
}
```

It is up to you to decide which is the least complex and the most understandable implementation for your code. There is no right or wrong answer. That being said, if you end up having 30 different login commands, you're probably unnecessarily overcomplicating things. Remember that you should try to write as little code as possible while still making it readable.

Summary

After reading this chapter, you should:

- Understand that page objects do not need to define actual pages
- Know how to use the `PageFactory` classes in the support package
- Understand how the `PageFactory` classes work under the hood
- Understand how to build page objects that use other page objects

- Know why it is good to have assertions in your tests while you do all the driving of the browser in the page objects
- Think about how you can name page objects to ensure that your tests can be used as documentation for the system that you are testing
- Be able to write page objects using a fluent API

In the next chapter, we will explore the advanced user interactions API inside Selenium.

6
Utilizing the Advanced User Interactions API

This chapter will teach you how to utilize the Advanced User Interactions API. Topics that we will cover include the following:

- Understanding the API
- Performing hover actions
- Using the Advanced Interactions API to drag and drop elements

We are going to work through some examples in this chapter, just like we did in the last chapter. So, you will need your development IDE set up and ready to start writing some code. You can again use the base Selenium implementation that we put together in *Chapter 1, Creating a Fast Feedback Loop*. If you do this, you will probably want to add the following line of code at the beginning of your tests:

```
WebDriver driver = getDriver();
```

This will get a driver object that we can seamlessly use with the examples used in this chapter.

Getting started with the API

The Advanced User Interactions API, more commonly known as the `Actions` object, has been built to enable you to perform complex actions that you may find difficult with the standard Selenium API. The majority of the command set is based around mouse movements and clicks, but it does allow keyboard actions as well. It also allows you to chain a series of commands together.

To get a full list of available actions, you can have a look at the Javadoc for the `Actions` class. It is available at `http://seleniumhq.github.io/selenium/docs/api/java/org/openqa/selenium/interactions/Actions.html`.

Let's start off by creating a basic `Actions` object that we can use to perform a series of actions, as follows:

```
Actions advancedActions = new Actions(driver);
```

It's very simple to create. We just pass in a `driver` object, and we now have an `Actions` object available.

Let's start off by performing a couple of basic commands to give you an idea of what can be done:

```
WebElement anElement = driver.findElement(By.id("anElement"));
advancedActions.moveToElement(anElement).contextClick().perform();
```

We have now created a very basic script that will move the mouse cursor to an element and then right-click on it. The `Actions` object allows us to queue up a series of commands that we want to execute and then perform them all at the same time. With long lists of commands, this can soon get confusing if we keep everything on the same line. We could make each command step clearer by reformatting the code to look like this:

```
WebElement anElement =
driver().findElement(By.id("anElement"));
advancedActions.moveToElement(anElement)
        .contextClick()
        .perform();
```

We have now put each action on a separate line to make it more readable, which is something that I would highly recommend.

You may have noted that there is an extra command on the final line called `perform()`. This tells Selenium that we have no more commands that we want to queue up and it should now go ahead and perform all the commands that we have queued up so far.

If you look at the Javadoc for the `Actions` class (or the various tutorials on the Internet), you may come across a chained command called `.build()` that I have not used before. The `.build()` command is automatically called by `.perform()`. So, there is no benefit in explicitly using it as well. I don't use it, to reduce the code clutter.

Using the API to solve difficult problems

So far, we had a look at the basic API implementation. Now, let's have a look at some day-to-day problems that you will probably come across and how we can use the `Actions` class to solve them.

Working with hover menus

First of all, we need to create a basic HTML page. We are going to use some CSS to style a CSS hover menu. To try and keep it in small, manageable chunks, we will break up the page into a couple of pieces. Let's start by writing the HTML:

```
<!DOCTYPE html>
<html lang="en">
<head>
    <meta charset="utf-8">
    <title>CSS Menu</title>
    <style type="text/css">${TBC}</style>
</head>
<body>
<ul>
    <li id="home">Home</li>
    <li id="about">About</li>
    <li id="services">
        Services
        <ul>
            <li>Web Design</li>
            <li>Web Development</li>
            <li>Illustrations</li>
        </ul>
    </li>
</ul>
</body>
</html>
```

As you can see, it's just a very simple ordered list; you may have also noted that I have added a `<style>` tag, but I've not put anything in it yet. The contents of the `<style>` tag are what make this page work. You can either put the styling inline or put it in a separate file and reference it. The styling that needs to be used to turn this list into a CSS menu is as follows:

```
<style type="text/css">
        body {
            padding: 20px 50px 150px;
```

```
        text-align: center;
        background: white;
    }

    ul {
        text-align: left;
        display: inline;
        margin: 0;
        padding: 15px 4px 17px 0;
        list-style: none;
        box-shadow: 0 0 5px rgba(0, 0, 0, 0.15);
    }

    ul li {
        font: bold 12px/18px sans-serif;
        display: inline-block;
        margin-right: -4px;
        position: relative;
        padding: 15px 20px;
        background: mediumpurple;
        cursor: pointer;
        transition: all 0.3s;
    }

    ul li:hover {
        background: purple;
        color: white;
    }

    ul li ul {
        padding: 0;
        position: absolute;
        top: 48px;
        left: 0;
        width: 150px;
        box-shadow: none;
        display: none;
        opacity: 0;
        visibility: hidden;
        -transition: opacity 0.3s;
    }

    ul li ul li {
```

```
        background: #555;
        display: block;
        color: white;
        text-shadow: 0 -1px 0 black;
    }

    ul li ul li:hover {
        background: dimgrey;
    }

    ul li:hover ul {
        display: block;
        opacity: 1;
        visibility: visible;
    }
</style>
```

If you load this up in a browser, you will see that when you hover your mouse over the **Services** option, another menu will appear and you will be given three new menu options. In this case, we want to try and click on the **Web Development** submenu option.

These sort of menus can be horrible to automate. You can't trigger a CSS :hover event with JavaScript (no matter what some people on the Internet would want you to believe). So, we need to find an alternative option. This is often where people get stuck and then get told on some forum somewhere to use Auto It....

We don't want to do this because the Selenium developers have already come up with a solution! We are going to use the Actions class instead.

So, what actions do we need to perform? Well, we need to make Selenium act like a human would. We need to perform a series of steps that emulate the way a human would use this page:

1. First of all, we are going to move the mouse and make it hover over the **Services** menu option.

2. Once we hover over the **Services** menu option, we need to wait for the submenu to appear.

3. Now that the submenu has appeared, we are going to move the mouse down to the **Web Development** submenu option.

4. When hovering over the **Web Development** submenu option, we are going to click on it.

This may seem like a very verbose way of describing what we want to do, but it is important to be very clear about the actions taken because we need to code each of these steps into our Selenium test.

Let's take a look at some code that does this. First of all, we will need to get the page and set up an `Actions` object and a `WebDriverWait` object, as follows:

```
driver.get("http://ch6.masteringselenium.com/cssMenu.html");
Actions advancedActions = new Actions(driver);
WebDriverWait wait = new WebDriverWait(driver, 5, 100);
```

Then, we need to find the elements on the page that we want to interact with, as follows:

```
WebElement servicesMenuOption =
driver.findElement(By.id("services"));
WebElement webDevelopmentSubMenuOption =
driver.findElement(By.cssSelector("#services > ul >
li:nth-child(2)"));
```

Finally, we will use the `Actions` class to perform the four steps that were outlined in the preceding section, as follows:

```
advancedActions.moveToElement(servicesMenuOption)
        .perform();

wait.until(ExpectedConditions.visibilityOf(
webDevelopmentSubMenuOption));

advancedActions.moveToElement(webDevelopmentSubMenuOption)
        .click()
        .perform();
```

As you can see, the `Actions` class allows you to chain actions. Unfortunately, it does not let you chain waits. Due to this, we need to break our `Actions` chain into two parts and put a wait in between these two parts.

The reason behind using a wait is to make sure that the browser has had a chance to render the submenu before we move on and try to interact with it. If you don't do this, you will see intermittent errors occasionally. We don't want flakey tests. We want to be sure that the submenu has rendered before we try and interact with it. Hence, the wait is important.

Remember to code your tests defensively. If you have a modern, powerful machine and you are only testing on a modern browser, such as Chrome, things will generally work without adding waits to check whether they have happened. These same tests will probably not work so well on a VM that is running Internet Explorer 8 when you start doing some cross-browser compatibility checks.

Hopefully, this looks quite simple. So, are there any caveats? Unfortunately, yes. Browsers that do not have support for native events may not work.

As mentioned earlier, you cannot use JavaScript to trigger a CSS `:hover` event. This means that a driver that does not support native events cannot emulate the conditions required to trigger a CSS `:hover` event, and the test will not work. An example of a driver that does not support native events is Safari on OS X. This code will not work in Safari.

To get it working in Safari, you will need to write some code to start moving the mouse cursor around the screen, and once you start doing this, things start getting quite complicated. We will have a look at things that you can't do, and possible workarounds, in *Chapter 8, Keeping It Real*.

Working with drag and drop

Another HTML construct that is hard to work with is a page that allows you to drag and drop elements. For this example, we will create a simple HTML page that uses jQuery to allow us to drag some elements around the screen. We are also going to add an element that will destroy any of the draggable elements that we drop onto it so that these draggable elements can be removed from the page. Let's start off with the basic HTML:

```
<!DOCTYPE html>
<html lang="en">
<head>
    <meta charset=utf-8>
    <title>Drag and drop</title>
    <style type="text/css">${TBC}</style>
    <script src="https://ajax.googleapis.com/
ajax/libs/jquery/2.1.3/jquery.min.js"></script>
    <script src="https://ajax.googleapis.com/
ajax/libs/jqueryui/1.11.3/jquery-ui.min.js"></script>
```

```
    </head>
    <body>
    <header>
        <h1>Drag and drop</h1>
    </header>


    <div>
        <p>Drop items onto the red square to remove them</p>

        <div id="obliterate"></div>
        <ul>
            <li>
                <div id="one" href="#" class="draggable">one</div>
            </li>
            <li>
                <div id="two" href="#" class="draggable">two</div>
            </li>
            <li>
                <div id="three" href="#" class="draggable">three</div>
            </li>
            <li>
                <div id="four" href="#" class="draggable">four</div>
            </li>
            <li>
                <div id="five" href="#" class="draggable">five</div>
            </li>
        </ul>
    </div>
    </body>
    <script type="application/javascript">${TBC}</script>
    </html>
```

This HTML code has some links to the jQuery libraries that we are going to use and a couple of ${TBC} tags, where we are going to add in some styling and JavaScript. Let's add the styling.

This will transform our elements into some nice boxes that will be easy to interact with. As we did before, we can put this styling inline or link it to an external file. The choice is yours.

```
<style type="text/css">
        li {
            list-style: none;
```

```
    }

    li div {
        text-decoration: none;
        color: #000;
        margin: 10px;
        width: 150px;
        border: 2px groove black;
        background: #eee;
        padding: 10px;
        display: block;
        text-align: center;
    }

    ul {
        margin-left: 200px;
        min-height: 300px;
    }

    #obliterate {
        background-color: red;
        height: 250px;
        width: 166px;
        float: left;
        border: 5px solid #000;
        position: relative;
        margin-top: 0;
    }
</style>
```

Finally, we need to add the jQuery code to make the drag-and-drop parts actually work. It's simple code and should be quite easy to follow:

```
<script type="application/javascript">
    $(function () {
        $(".draggable").draggable();

        $('#obliterate').droppable({
            drop: function (event, ui) {
                ui.draggable.remove();
            }
        });
    });
</script>
```

We now have a page that has a big red box and five smaller boxes. The smaller boxes can be dragged around the screen, and if we drop one of the smaller boxes on the big red box, it will be destroyed. Give it a go to make sure that it's all working correctly.

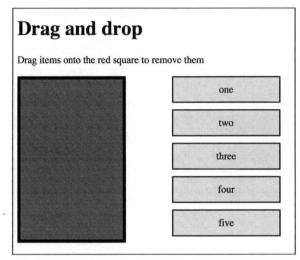

The **Drag and drop** web page

Now, we need to write our Selenium test. We are going to write a simple test that checks how many smaller boxes exist. This test will then check whether they are destroyed if we drag them over the big red box.

We will start by getting the test page, setting up the objects that we are going to need to interact with, and checking whether we have five draggable boxes to start with, as follows:

```
driver.get("http://ch6.masteringselenium.com/jsDragAndDrop.html");
Actions advancedActions = new Actions(driver);
final By destroyableBoxes = By.cssSelector("ul > li > div");
WebElement obliterator = driver.findElement(By.id("obliterate"));
WebElement firstBox = driver.findElement(By.id("one"));
WebElement secondBox = driver.findElement(By.id("two"));

assertThat(driver.findElements(destroyableBoxes).size(),
is(equalTo(5)));
```

We are now happy that everything is in place, and we are ready to start checking whether the drag-and-drop functionality that destroys the smaller boxes, works. We have already set up the `advancedActions` object and found all of the elements that we are going to interact with. So, the rest of the code should be clean, simple, and clear:

```
advancedActions.clickAndHold(firstBox)
        .moveToElement(obliterator)
        .release()
        .perform();

assertThat(driver.findElements(destroyableBoxes).size(),
is(equalTo(4)));
```

The preceding code performs three steps to drag an element over the red box. First of all, we find the element that we want to drag and click, and hold our left mouse button on it. Then, we move (or drag) the element over to the red box. Finally, we let go of the mouse, which will cause the element to be dropped.

After we have dragged our box onto the red box and destroyed it, we are counting the number of boxes available on the screen again to check whether we now have four instead of five. We can also check whether the element that we were dragging has become stale (that is, it is not in the DOM any more), but for the purposes of this example, the count is adequate.

It all works and it's quite clear what is going on, but we can make our code even simpler. Seeing that drag and drop is a reasonably common action, a shortcut was put in, which does all of the aforementioned commands for you.

Lets expand our test to destroy another box, but this time, we will use the `dragAndDrop()` method, as follows:

```
advancedActions.dragAndDrop(secondBox, obliterator).perform();

assertThat(driver.findElements(destroyableBoxes).size(),
is(equalTo(3)));
```

The `dragAndDrop()` method takes two parameters—the element that we want to drag and the element we are going to drag it to.

We now have a nice, small piece of code that has given us the ability to do very powerful things.

Working with offsets

Let's make the drag-and-drop code a little bit more complicated. We are going to change the main page markup and the JavaScript slightly to make it more challenging to automate.

First of all, we are going to change the HTML code by adding a `<span>` element in each draggable element. We are going to move the text for the element into this `<span>`, as follows:

```
<ul>
    <li>
        <div id="one" href="#" class="draggable">
            <span>one</span>
        </div>
    </li>
    <li>
        <div id="two" href="#" class="draggable">
            <span>two</span>
        </div>
    </li>
    <li>
        <div id="three" href="#" class="draggable">
            <span>three</span>
        </div>
    </li>
    <li>
        <div id="four" href="#" class="draggable">
            <span>four</span>
        </div>
    </li>
    <li>
        <div id="five" href="#" class="draggable">
            <span>five</span>
        </div>
    </li>
</ul>
```

Next, we are going to tweak the JavaScript and change it so that you cannot drag the `<div>` element by using the `<span>` element. Instead, we are going to force the user to move their mouse cursor towards the left or the right so that it is not hovering over the text, as follows:

```
<script type="application/javascript">
    $(function () {
```

```
$(".draggable").draggable({cancel: "span"});

$('#obliterate').droppable({
    drop: function (event, ui) {
        ui.draggable.remove();
    }
});
});
</script>
```

Once you have updated the code, reload the page in your browser and give it a try. It should still work as before, as long as you try to drag the element from the side of the box and not from where the text is displayed.

Now try and run the test script that you previously wrote to automate this page. You will see that it fails. The problem is that when you use the Advanced Interactions API to try and drag an element around the screen, the default point used to click and hold on the element is its center. We have now placed a <span> element over the center of the <div> element, and the <span> element is not draggable. To fix this, we need to find a way to click and hold our left mouse button down on the <div> element while avoiding the <span> element. Let's have a look at some code that can do this for us:

```
driver.get("http://ch6.masteringselenium.com/
jsDragAndDropWithHandle.html");
Actions advancedActions = new Actions(driver);
final By destroyableBoxes = By.cssSelector("ul > li > div");
WebElement obliterator = driver.findElement(By.id("obliterate"));
WebElement firstBox = driver.findElement(By.id("one"));
WebElement secondBox = driver.findElement(By.id("two"));

assertThat(driver.findElements(destroyableBoxes).size(),
        is(equalTo(5)));

advancedActions.moveToElement(firstBox)
        .moveByOffset(-40, 0)
        .clickAndHold()
        .moveToElement(obliterator)
        .release()
        .perform();

assertThat(driver.findElements(destroyableBoxes).size(),
        is(equalTo(4)));
```

This time, instead of using `clickAndHold(firstBox)` to move the mouse cursor to the element and perform the left click, we are breaking it down a bit more. First, we move our mouse to the element. Then, we shift the mouse to the left by 40 pixels. Finally, we hold down our left mouse button.

Why 40 pixels? Well, I had a look at the markup, and after visually inspecting the `<span>` elements, I saw that none of them were larger than 32 pixels in width. This meant that moving 40 pixels to the left should always ensure that I'm not hovering over the span, but I am still hovering over the button.

Let's run the test again. This time, it will drag the boxes as expected and everything will pass. Now, there is a potential gotcha in this test that you should be aware of. Let's tweak the test code again and make it look like this:

```
advancedActions.moveToElement(firstBox)
        .moveByOffset(-40, 0)
        .clickAndHold(firstBox)
        .moveToElement(obliterator)
        .release()
        .perform();
```

If you now run the test again, it will fail. Why did it fail? If you pass an element to the `clickAndHold()` method, it will move the mouse to the center of that element. So, what we have done in the preceding code is as follows:

- Moved the mouse to the center of our `<div>` element
- Moved it 40 pixels to the left
- Moved it back to the center of the `<div>` element
- Clicked and held down the left mouse button

It's a common mistake. The code looks correct, and you can spend hours trying to debug something that should work, but it just doesn't.

 Remember that if you are using offsets, don't pass elements into `clickAndHold()`.

So, can we simplify the preceding code? Let's change our code to set the offset in the `moveToElement()` command instead of breaking it into two pieces, as follows:

```
advancedActions.moveToElement(firstBox, -40, 0)
        .clickAndHold()
        .moveToElement(obliterator)
        .release()
        .perform();
```

If you now run this code, you will see that your test starts to fail. Our code refactor looks sensible. What's going on? Well, we have hit another quirk in the Advanced Interactions API. Offsets don't work in the same way for all commands. If you pass an offset into a `moveToElement()` command, the offset is based on the top-left corner of the element, not the center. What we have actually done with this code is:

- Moved the mouse to the top-left corner of the `<div>` element
- Moved it 40 pixels to the left
- Clicked and held down the left mouse button

Obviously, if we move 40 pixels to the left when we are at the top-left corner of the element, our mouse will no longer be over the element. Instead, we need to change the offset to something that takes into account the fact that the cursor is in a different place. Let's fix the code and get our test passing again, as follows:

```
advancedActions.moveToElement(firstBox, 1, 1)
        .clickAndHold()
        .moveToElement(obliterator)
        .release()
        .perform();
```

This time, we are doing the following:

- Moving the mouse to the top-left corner the `<div>` element
- Moving it 1 pixel to the right and 1 pixel down
- Clicking and holding down the left mouse button

If we run the test again, we will see that everything starts working and the test now passes once more.

 When working with offsets, check the method that you are working with to see whether the offset is based on the center of the element or the top-left corner of the element.

I mentioned earlier that I had set arbitrary offset values to make the tests pass. However, this is something that I should not have done. This is the offset equivalent of using `Thread.sleep()`, and this is something that you shouldn't ever do. Instead, we should write a function that can figure out where we can safely place the mouse cursor before performing a click action. Now, we also know that this function should take into account two different starting positions for our mouse cursor—the center of the element and the top-left corner of the element. Unfortunately, there is no real, generic function for this. It will all depend on how the elements are rendered.

Let's put together an example class to work out the cursor location with the current markup. Hopefully, this will give you something that you can build upon if you ever come across this problem in the real world. First of all, we need to make some assumptions. Here are our assumptions for this class:

- The `<div>` element is a quadrilateral
- The `<span>` element is a quadrilateral
- The `<span>` element is always centered within `<div>`

Now, we have our assumptions. Let's write some code and work through it, as follows:

```
package com.masteringselenium.tests;

import org.openqa.selenium.ElementNotVisibleException;
import org.openqa.selenium.WebElement;

import static com.masteringselenium.tests.CalculateOffsetPosition.
CursorPosition.CENTER;
import static com.masteringselenium.tests.CalculateOffsetPosition.
CursorPosition.TOP_LEFT;

public class CalculateOffsetPosition {

    public enum CursorPosition {
        TOP_LEFT,
        CENTER
    }

    final WebElement parentElement;
    final WebElement childElement;
    final CursorPosition cursorPosition;
    private int xOffset = 0;
    private int yOffset = 0;

    public CalculateOffsetPosition(WebElement parentElement,
    WebElement childElement, CursorPosition cursorPosition) {
        this.parentElement = parentElement;
        this.childElement = childElement;
        this.cursorPosition = cursorPosition;
        calculateOffset();
    }

    public int getXOffset() {
```

```
            return xOffset;
    }

    public int getYOffset() {
        return yOffset;
    }

    private void calculateOffset() throws
    ElementNotVisibleException {
        int elementOneHeight =
        parentElement.getSize().getHeight();
        int elementOneWidth = parentElement.getSize().getWidth();
        int elementTwoHeight = childElement.getSize().getHeight();
        int elementTwoWidth = childElement.getSize().getWidth();

        if (elementTwoHeight >= elementOneHeight &&
        elementTwoWidth >= elementOneWidth) {
            throw new ElementNotVisibleException("The child
            element is totally covering the parent element");
        }

        if (cursorPosition.equals(TOP_LEFT)) {
            xOffset = 1;
            yOffset = 1;
        }

        if (cursorPosition.equals(CENTER)) {
            if (elementTwoWidth < elementOneWidth) {
                xOffset = (elementTwoWidth / 2) + 1;
            }
            if (elementTwoHeight < elementOneHeight) {
                yOffset = (elementTwoHeight / 2) + 1;
            }
        }
    }
}
```

When working with offsets, we need to be able to return an *X* and a *Y* offset. So, rather than writing a method, we have a class. The class constructor reads in the parent element and the child element, and an enum value telling us whether the current mouse position is at the top-left or the center.

The first thing that we do is throw an ElementNotVisibleException if the child element is bigger than the parent element. In this situation, we are not going to be able to drag an element around. So, we may as well fail quickly.

Figuring out TOP_LEFT is simple. If the child element is not the same size as that of the parent element, an offset of 1,1 should always work, as this will put us in the top-left corner of the parent element.

Working our CENTER is a little more complicated. We need to take the existing height or width of the child element and then work out how far up, or towards the right, we need to go to move the mouse cursor off the child element. If one of the dimensions of the child element is the same as that of the parent element, we don't bother changing the offset for the dimension as there is no point.

We now have a couple of getters so that we can pull out the *X* and the *Y* offset and use them in our test. Let's plug this class into our test using a center offset and see it in action:

```
driver.get("http://ch6.masteringselenium.com/
jsDragAndDropWithHandle.html");
Actions advancedActions = new Actions(driver);
final By destroyableBoxes = By.cssSelector("ul > li > div");
WebElement obliterator = driver.findElement(By.id("obliterate"));
WebElement firstBox = driver.findElement(By.id("one"));
WebElement firstBoxText = driver.findElement(By.cssSelector
("#one > span"));

assertThat(driver.findElements(destroyableBoxes).size(),
        is(equalTo(5)));

CalculateOffsetPosition op = new CalculateOffsetPosition(firstBox,
firstBoxText, CalculateOffsetPosition.CursorPosition.CENTER);

advancedActions.moveToElement(firstBox)
        .moveByOffset(op.getXOffset(), op.getYOffset())
        .clickAndHold()
        .moveToElement(obliterator)
        .release()
        .perform();

assertThat(driver.findElements(destroyableBoxes).size(),
        is(equalTo(4)));
```

As you can see, we have made a couple of small changes. We need to find the text element so that we can correctly calculate the offset. Then, we just calculate the offset and plug it in. It all works, and it makes sure that when the text of the span element expands in the future or the <div> container shrinks, our test won't start failing for no obvious reason.

If you are going to put a hard-coded value into one of your tests, stop and think first. You may just be creating a future failure for no good reason.

It doesn't always work for me

The Advanced Interactions API is powerful, but it's not perfect. Sometimes, things just won't work.

Let's take our last example (the drag-and-drop page). The code works because we are using JavaScript to create the drag-and-drop functionality.

You can rewrite that example page by using the HTML5 draggable attribute and adding some event listeners. However, if you did this, the Advanced Interactions API will not be able to drag and drop the boxes any more because it doesn't yet (as of Selenium version 2.45.0) support this.

As new technologies come out, it takes time for the core Selenium bindings to support them. So, what do you do when something doesn't work for you and you need to write a script? Well, you have a couple of options, which are as follows:

- Write a patch for Selenium and submit it
- Work around the issue

One of the most common ways to work around limitations in Selenium is to start using a JavaScript executor. In the next chapter, we will have a look at how JavaScript executors work and what you can do with them to get around problems.

Summary

When you have finished reading this chapter, you should now be able to:

- Have a good general understanding of the Advanced Interactions API
- Utilize the Advanced Interactions API to automate CSS-only hover menus
- Drag and drop elements with the Advanced Interactions API
- Understand how to use offsets to make sure that you are hitting the correct trigger point in elements
- Know the limitations of the Advanced Interactions API

In the next chapter, we will have a look at how we can utilize the
`JavascriptExecutor` class. We will examine what it is capable of doing and
ask ourselves whether we should be doing these things. We will also see how
we can work around some of the limitations that we have come across so far.

7
JavaScript Execution with Selenium

In this chapter, we will look at how we can directly execute JavaScript snippets in Selenium. We will explore the sort of things that you can do and how they can help you work around some of the limitations that you will come across while writing your scripts. We will also have a look at some examples of things that you should avoid doing.

Introducing the JavaScript executor

Selenium has a mature API that caters to the majority of automation tasks that you may want to throw at it. That being said, you will occasionally come across problems that the API doesn't really seem to support. This was very much on the development team's mind when Selenium was written. So, they provided a way for you to easily inject and execute arbitrary blocks of JavaScript. Let's have a look at a basic example of using a JavaScript executor in Selenium:

```
JavascriptExecutor js = (JavascriptExecutor) driver;
js.executeScript("console.log('I logged something to the
Javascript console');");
```

Note that the first thing we do is cast a `WebDriver` object into a `JavascriptExecutor` object. The `JavascriptExecutor` interface is implemented through the `RemoteWebDriver` class. So, it's not a part of the core set of API functions. Since we normally pass around a `WebDriver` object, the `executeScript` functions will not be available unless we perform this cast.

If you are directly using an instance of `RemoteWebDriver` or something that extends it (most driver implementations now do this), you will have direct access to the `.executeScript()` function. Here's an example:

```
FirefoxDriver driver = new FirefoxDriver(new FirefoxProfile());
driver.executeScript("console.log('I logged something to the
Javascript console');");
```

The second line (in both the preceding examples) is just telling Selenium to execute an arbitrary piece of JavaScript. In this case, we are just going to print something to the JavaScript console in the browser.

We can also get the `.executeScript()` function to return things to us. For example, if we tweak the script of JavaScript in the first example, we can get Selenium to tell us whether it managed to write to the JavaScript console or not, as follows:

```
JavascriptExecutor js = (JavascriptExecutor) driver;
Object response = js.executeScript("return console.log('I
logged something to the Javascript console');");
```

In the preceding example, we will get a result of `true` coming back from the JavaScript executor.

Why does our JavaScript start with `return`? Well, the JavaScript executed by Selenium is executed as a body of an anonymous function. This means that if we did not add a `return` statement to the start of our JavaScript snippet, we would actually be running this JavaScript function using Selenium:

```
var anonymous = function () {
    console.log('I logged something to the Javascript console');
};
```

This function does log to the console, but it does not return anything. So, we can't access the result of the JavaScript snippet. If we prefix it with a `return`, it will execute this anonymous function:

```
var anonymous = function () {
    return console.log('I logged something to the Javascript
    console');
};
```

This does return something for us to work with. In this case, it will be the result of our attempt to write some text to the console. If we succeeded in writing some text to the console, we will get back a true value. If we failed, we will get back a false value.

Note that in our example, we saved the response as an object—not a string or a Boolean. This is because the JavaScript executor can return lots of different types of objects. What we get as a response can be one of the following:

- If the result is null or there is no return value, a null will be returned
- If the result is an HTML element, a `WebElement` will be returned
- If the result is a decimal, a double will be returned
- If the result is a nondecimal number, a long will be returned
- If the result is a Boolean, a Boolean will be returned
- If the result is an array, a `List` object with each object that it contains, along with all of these rules, will be returned (nested lists are supported)
- For all other cases, a string will be returned

It is an impressive list, and it makes you realize just how powerful this method is. There is more as well. You can also pass arguments into the `.executeScript()` function. The arguments that you pass in can be any one of the following:

- Number
- Boolean
- String
- WebElement
- List

They are then put into a magic variable called `arguments`, which can be accessed by the JavaScript. Let's extend our example a little bit to pass in some arguments, as follows:

```
String animal = "Lion";
int seen = 5;
JavascriptExecutor js = (JavascriptExecutor) driver;
js.executeScript("console.log('I have seen a ' + arguments[0]
+ ' ' + arguments[1] + ' times(s)');", animal, seen);
```

This time, you will see that we managed to print the following text into the console:

```
I have seen a Lion 5 times(s)
```

As you can see, there is a huge amount of flexibility with the JavaScript executor. You can write some complex bits of JavaScript code and pass in lots of different types of arguments from your Java code.

Think of all the things that you could do!

Let's not get carried away

We now know the basics of how one can execute JavaScript snippets in Selenium. This is where some people can start to get a bit carried away.

If you go through the mailing list of the users of Selenium, you will see many instances of people asking why they can't click on an element. Most of the time, this is due to the element that they are trying to interact with not being visible, which is blocking a click action. The real solution to this problem is to perform an action (the same one that they would perform if they were manually using the website) to make the element visible so that they can interact with it.

However, there is a shortcut offered by many, which is a very bad practice. You can use a JavaScript executor to trigger a click event on this element. Doing this will probably make your test pass. So why is it a bad solution?

The Selenium development team has spent quite a lot of time writing code that works out if a user can interact with an element. It's pretty reliable. So, if Selenium says that you cannot currently interact with an element, it's highly unlikely that it's wrong. When figuring out whether you can interact with an element, lots of things are taken into account, including the z-index of an element. For example, you may have a transparent element that is covering the element that you want to click on and blocking the click action so that you can't reach it. Visually, it will be visible to you, but Selenium will correctly see it as not visible.

If you now invoke a JavaScript executor to trigger a click event on this element, your test will pass, but users will not be able to interact with it when they try to manually use your website.

However, what if Selenium got it wrong and I can interact with the element that I want to click manually? Well, that's great, but there are two things that you need to think about.

First of all, does it work in all browsers? If Selenium thinks that it is something that you cannot interact with, it's probably for a good reason. Is the markup, or the CSS, overly complicated? Can it be simplified?

Secondly, if you invoke a JavaScript executor, you will never know whether the element that you want to interact with really does get blocked at some point in the future. Your test may as well keep passing when your application is broken. Tests that can't fail when something goes wrong are worse than no test at all!

If you think of Selenium as a toolbox, a JavaScript executor is a very powerful tool that is present in it. However, it really should be seen as a last resort when all other avenues have failed you. Too many people use it as a solution to any slightly sticky problem that they come across.

> If you are writing JavaScript code that attempts to mirror existing Selenium functions but are removing the restrictions, you are probably doing it wrong! Your code is unlikely to be better. The Selenium development team have been doing this for a long time with a lot of input from a lot of people, many of them being experts in their field.
>
> If you are thinking of writing methods to find elements on a page, don't! Use the `.findElement()` method provided by Selenium.

Occasionally, you may find a bug in Selenium that prevents you from interacting with an element in the way you would expect to. Many people first respond by reaching for the `JavascriptExecutor` to code around the problem in Selenium.

Hang on for just one moment though. Have you upgraded to the latest version of Selenium to see if that fixes your problem? Alternatively, did you just upgrade to the latest version of Selenium when you didn't need to? Using a slightly older version of Selenium that works correctly is perfectly acceptable. Don't feel forced to upgrade for no reason, especially if it means that you have to write your own hacks around problems that didn't exist before.

The correct thing to do is to use a stable version of Selenium that works for you. You can always raise bugs for functionality that doesn't work, or even code a fix and submit a pull request. Don't give yourself the additional work of writing a workaround that's probably not the ideal solution, unless you need to.

So, what should we do with it?

Let's have a look at some examples of the things that we can do with the JavaScript executor that aren't really possible using the base Selenium API.

First of all, we will start off by getting the element text.

Wait a minute, element text? But, that's easy! You can use the existing Selenium API with the following code:

```
WebElement myElement = driver.findElement(By.id("foo"));
String elementText = myElement.getText();
```

So why would we want to use a JavaScript executor to find the text of an element?

Getting text is easy using the Selenium API, but only under certain conditions. The element that you are collecting the text from needs to be displayed. If Selenium thinks that the element from which you are collecting the text is not displayed, it will return an empty string. If you want to collect some text from a hidden element, you are out of luck. You will need to implement a way to do it with a JavaScript executor.

Why would you want to do this? Well, maybe you have a responsive website that shows different elements based on different resolutions. You may want to check whether these two different elements are displaying the same text to the user. To do this, you will need to get the text of the visible and invisible elements so that you can compare them. Let's create a method to collect some hidden text for us:

```
private String getHiddenText(WebElement element) {

    JavascriptExecutor js = (JavascriptExecutor)
((RemoteWebElement) element).getWrappedDriver();

    return (String) js.executeScript("return
    arguments[0].text", element);

}
```

There is some cleverness in this method. First of all, we took the element that we wanted to interact with and then extracted the driver object associated with it. We did this by casting the `WebElement` into a `RemoteWebElement`, which allowed us to use the `getWrappedDriver()` method. This removes the need to pass a driver object around the place all the time (this is something that happens a lot in some code bases).

We then took the driver object and cast it into a `JavascriptExecutor` so that we would have the ability to invoke the `executeScript()` method. Next, we executed the JavaScript snippet and passed in the original element as an argument. Finally, we took the response of the `executeScript()` call and cast it into a string that we can return as a result of the method.

Generally, getting text is a code smell. Your tests should not rely on specific text being displayed on a website because content always changes. Maintaining tests that check the content of a site is a lot of work, and it makes your functional tests brittle. The best thing to do is test the mechanism that injects the content into the website. If you use a CMS that injects text into a specific template key, you can test whether each element has the correct template key associated with it.

I want to see a more complex example!

So you want to see something more complicated. Well, you may remember that we had a look at how we can use the Advanced User Interactions API to interact with a page that allowed you to drag and drop elements in *Chapter 6, Utilizing the Advanced User Interactions API*. The implementation that we used in that chapter was based on jQuery rather than the native HTML5 code. The Advanced User Interactions API cannot deal with HTML5 drag and drop. So, what happens if we come across an HTML5 drag-and-drop implementation that we want to automate? Well, we can use the `JavascriptExecutor`. Let's have a look at the markup for the HTML5 drag-and-drop page:

```
<!DOCTYPE html>
<html lang="en">
<head>
    <meta charset=utf-8>
    <title>Drag and drop</title>
    <style type="text/css">
        li {
            list-style: none;
        }

        li a {
            text-decoration: none;
            color: #000;
            margin: 10px;
            width: 150px;
            border-width: 2px;
            border-color: black;
            border-style: groove;
            background: #eee;
            padding: 10px;
            display: block;
        }

        *[draggable=true] {
            cursor: move;
        }

        ul {
            margin-left: 200px;
            min-height: 300px;
        }
```

```
        #obliterate {
            background-color: green;
            height: 250px;
            width: 166px;
            float: left;
            border: 5px solid #000;
            position: relative;
            margin-top: 0;
        }

        #obliterate.over {
            background-color: red;
        }
    </style>
</head>
<body>
<header>
    <h1>Drag and drop</h1>
</header>


<article>
    <p>Drag items over to the green square to remove them</p>

    <div id="obliterate"></div>
    <ul>
        <li><a id="one" href="#" draggable="true">one</a></li>
        <li><a id="two" href="#" draggable="true">two</a></li>
        <li><a id="three" href="#" draggable="true">three</a></li>
        <li><a id="four" href="#" draggable="true">four</a></li>
        <li><a id="five" href="#" draggable="true">five</a></li>
    </ul>
</article>
</body>
<script>
    var draggableElements = document.querySelectorAll('li > a'),
            obliterator = document.getElementById('obliterate');

    for (var i = 0; i < draggableElements.length; i++) {
        element = draggableElements[i];
        element.addEventListener('dragstart', function (event) {
            event.dataTransfer.effectAllowed = 'copy';
```

```
                 event.dataTransfer.setData('being-dragged', this.id);
            });
        }

        obliterator.addEventListener('dragover', function (event) {
            if (event.preventDefault) event.preventDefault();
            obliterator.className = 'over';
            event.dataTransfer.dropEffect = 'copy';
            return false;
        });

        obliterator.addEventListener('dragleave', function () {
            obliterator.className = '';
            return false;
        });

        obliterator.addEventListener('drop', function (event) {
            var elementToDelete = document.getElementById(
            event.dataTransfer.getData('being-dragged'));
            elementToDelete.parentNode.removeChild(elementToDelete);
            obliterator.className = '';
            return false;
        });
    </script>
    </html>
```

Note that the page looks pretty much identical to the one that we used in
Chapter 6, Utilizing the Advanced User Interactions API. However, the
implementation is different.

> Note that you need a browser that supports HTML5/CSS3 for this page
> to work. The latest versions of Google Chrome, Opera Blink, Safari,
> and Firefox will work. You may have issues with Internet Explorer
> (depending on the version that you are using). For an up-to-date list of
> HTML5/CSS3 support, have a look at http://caniuse.com.

If you try to use the Advanced User Interactions API to automate this page, you will
find that it just doesn't work. It looks like it's time to reach for JavascriptExecutor.

First of all, we need to write some JavaScript that can simulate the events that we need to trigger to perform the drag-and-drop action. To do this, we are going to create three JavaScript functions. The first function is going to create a JavaScript event:

```javascript
function createEvent(typeOfEvent) {
    var event = document.createEvent("CustomEvent");
    event.initCustomEvent(typeOfEvent, true, true, null);
    event.dataTransfer = {
        data: {},
        setData: function (key, value) {
            this.data[key] = value;
        },
        getData: function (key) {
            return this.data[key];
        }
    };
    return event;
}
```

We then need to write a function that will fire events that we have created. This also allows you to pass in the `dataTransfer` value set on an element. We need this to keep track of the element that we are dragging:

```javascript
function dispatchEvent(element, event, transferData) {
    if (transferData !== undefined) {
        event.dataTransfer = transferData;
    }
    if (element.dispatchEvent) {
        element.dispatchEvent(event);
    } else if (element.fireEvent) {
        element.fireEvent("on" + event.type, event);
    }
}
```

Finally, we need something that will use these two functions to simulate the drag-and-drop action:

```javascript
function simulateHTML5DragAndDrop(element, target) {
    var dragStartEvent = createEvent('dragstart');
    dispatchEvent(element, dragStartEvent);
    var dropEvent = createEvent('drop');
    dispatchEvent(target, dropEvent, dragStartEvent.dataTransfer);
    var dragEndEvent = createEvent('dragend');
    dispatchEvent(element, dragEndEvent, dropEvent.dataTransfer);
}
```

Note that the `simulateHTML5DragAndDrop` function needs us to pass in two elements—the element that we want to drag, and the element that we want to drag it to.

> It's always a good idea to try out your JavaScript in a browser first. You can copy the preceding functions into the JavaScript console in a modern browser and then try using them to make sure that they work as expected. If things go wrong in your Selenium test, you then know that it is most likely an error invoking it via the `JavascriptExecutor` rather than a bad piece of JavaScript.

We now need to take these scripts and put them into a `JavascriptExecutor` along with something that will call the `simulateHTML5DragAndDrop` function:

```
private void simulateDragAndDrop(WebElement elementToDrag,
WebElement target) throws Exception {
    WebDriver driver = getDriver();
    JavascriptExecutor js = (JavascriptExecutor) driver;
    js.executeScript("function createEvent(typeOfEvent) {\n" +
                "var event =
                document.createEvent(\"CustomEvent\");\n" +
                "event.initCustomEvent(typeOfEvent,
                true, true, null);\n" +
        "      event.dataTransfer = {\n" +
        "          data: {},\n" +
        "          setData: function (key, value) {\n" +
        "              this.data[key] = value;\n" +
        "          },\n" +
        "          getData: function (key) {\n" +
        "              return this.data[key];\n" +
        "          }\n" +
        "      };\n" +
        "      return event;\n" +
        "}\n" +
        "\n" +
        "function dispatchEvent(element, event,
        transferData) {\n" +
        "      if (transferData !== undefined) {\n" +
        "          event.dataTransfer = transferData;\n" +
        "      }\n" +
        "      if (element.dispatchEvent) {\n" +
        "          element.dispatchEvent(event);\n" +
        "      } else if (element.fireEvent) {\n" +
        "          element.fireEvent(\"on\" + event.type,
        event);\n" +
        "      }\n" +
        "}\n" +
```

```
               "\n" +
               "function simulateHTML5DragAndDrop(element,
                target) {\n" +
               "    var dragStartEvent =
                createEvent('dragstart');\n" +
               "    dispatchEvent(element, dragStartEvent);\n" +
               "    var dropEvent = createEvent('drop');\n" +
               "    dispatchEvent(target, dropEvent,
                dragStartEvent.dataTransfer);\n" +
               "    var dragEndEvent = createEvent('dragend');
                \n" +
               "    dispatchEvent(element, dragEndEvent,
                dropEvent.dataTransfer);\n" +
               "}\n" +
               "\n" +
               "var elementToDrag = arguments[0];\n" +
               "var target = arguments[1];\n" +
               "simulateHTML5DragAndDrop(elementToDrag,
                target);",
            elementToDrag, target);
    }
```

This method is really just a wrapper around the JavaScript code. We take a driver object and cast it into a `JavascriptExecutor`. We then pass the JavaScript code into the executor as a string. We have made a couple of additions to the JavaScript functions that we previously wrote. Firstly, we set a couple of variables (mainly for code clarity; they can quite easily be inlined) that take the `WebElements` that we have passed in as arguments. Finally, we invoke the `simulateHTML5DragAndDrop` function using these elements.

The final piece of the puzzle is to write a test that utilizes the `simulateDragAndDrop` method, as follows:

```
@Test
public void dragAndDropHTML5() throws Exception {
    WebDriver driver = getDriver();
    driver.get("http://ch6.masteringselenium.com/
    dragAndDrop.html");

    final By destroyableBoxes = By.cssSelector("ul > li > a");
    WebElement obliterator =
    driver.findElement(By.id("obliterate"));
    WebElement firstBox = driver.findElement(By.id("one"));
    WebElement secondBox = driver.findElement(By.id("two"));
```

```
        assertThat(driver.findElements(destroyableBoxes).size(),
        is(equalTo(5)));

        simulateDragAndDrop(firstBox, obliterator);

        assertThat(driver.findElements(destroyableBoxes).
        size(), is(equalTo(4)));

        simulateDragAndDrop(secondBox, obliterator);

        assertThat(driver.findElements(destroyableBoxes).
        size(), is(equalTo(3)));
    }
```

This test is very similar to the one that we wrote in *Chapter 6, Utilizing the Advanced User Interactions API*. It finds a couple of boxes and destroys them one by one using the simulated drag and drop. As you can see, the JavascriptExcutor is extremely powerful.

Can I use JavaScript libraries?

The logical progression is, of course, to write your own JavaScript libraries that you can import instead of sending everything over as a string. Alternatively, maybe you would just like to import an existing library.

Let's write some code that allows you to import a JavaScript library of your choice. It's not a particularly complex JavaScript. All that we are going to do is create a new <script> element in a page and then load our library into it, as follows:

```
    public void injectScript(String scriptURL) throws Exception {
        WebDriver driver = getDriver();
        JavascriptExecutor js = (JavascriptExecutor) driver;
        js.executeScript("function injectScript(url) {\n" +
                "    var script = document.createElement
                    ('script');\n" +
                "    script.src = url;\n" +
                "    var head = document.getElementsByTagName(
                    'head')[0];\n" +
                "    head.appendChild(script);\n" +
                "}\n" +
                "\n" +
                "var scriptURL = arguments[0];\n" +
                "injectScript(scriptURL);"
                , scriptURL);
    }
```

We have again set `arguments[0]` to a variable before injecting it for clarity, but you can inline this part if you want to. All that remains now is to inject this into a page and check whether it works. Let's write a test!

We are going to use this function to inject jQuery into the Google website. The first thing that we need to do is write a method that can tell us whether jQuery has been loaded or not, as follows:

```java
public Boolean isjQueryLoaded() throws Exception {
    WebDriver driver = getDriver();
    JavascriptExecutor js = (JavascriptExecutor) driver;
    return (Boolean) js.executeScript("return typeof jQuery
    != 'undefined';");
}
```

Now, we need to put all of this together in a test, as follows:

```java
@Test
public void injectjQueryIntoGoogle() throws Exception {

    WebDriver driver = DriverFactory.getDriver();

    driver.get("http://www.google.com");

    assertThat(isjQueryLoaded(), is(equalTo(false)));

    injectScript("https://code.jquery.com/jquery-latest.min.js");

    assertThat(isjQueryLoaded(), is(equalTo(true)));
}
```

It's a very simple test. We loaded the Google website. Then, we checked whether jQuery existed. Once we were sure that it didn't exist, we injected jQuery into the page. Finally, we again checked whether jQuery existed.

We have used jQuery in our example, but you don't have to use jQuery. You can inject any script that you desire.

Should I inject JavaScript libraries?

It's very easy to inject JavaScript into a page, but stop and think before you do it. Adding lots of different JavaScript libraries may affect the existing functionality of the site. You may have functions in your JavaScript that overwrite existing functions that are already on the page and break the core functionality.

If you are testing a site, it may make all of your tests invalid. Failures may arise because there is a clash between the scripts that you inject and the existing scripts used on the site. The flip side is also true—injecting a script may make the functionality that is broken, work.

If you are going to inject scripts into an existing site, be sure that you know what the consequences are.

> If you are going to regularly inject a script, it may be a good idea to add some assertions to ensure that the functions that you are injecting do not already exist before you inject the script. This way, your tests will fail if the developers add a JavaScript function with the same name at some point in the future without your knowledge.

What about asynchronous scripts?

Everything that we have looked at so far has been a synchronous piece of JavaScript. However, what if we wanted to perform some asynchronous JavaScript calls as a part of our test? Well, we can do this. The JavascriptExecutor also has a method called executeAsyncScript(). This will allow you to run some JavaScript that does not respond instantly. Let's have a look at some examples.

First of all, we are going to write a very simple bit of JavaScript that will wait for 25 seconds before triggering a callback, as follows:

```
@Test
private void javascriptExample() throws Exception {
    WebDriver driver = DriverFactory.getDriver();

    driver.manage().timeouts().setScriptTimeout(60,
    TimeUnit.SECONDS);
    JavascriptExecutor js = (JavascriptExecutor) driver;
    js.executeAsyncScript("var callback = arguments[
    arguments.length - 1]; window.setTimeout(callback, 25000);");

    driver.get("http://www.google.com");
}
```

Note that we defined a JavaScript variable named `callback`, which uses a script argument that we have not set. For asynchronous scripts, Selenium needs to have a callback defined, which is used to detect when the JavaScript that you are executing has finished. This callback object is automatically added to the end of your arguments array. This is what we have defined as the `callback` variable.

If we now run the script, it will load our browser and then sit there for 25 seconds as it waits for the JavaScript snippet to complete and call the callback. It will then load the Google website and finish.

We have also set a script timeout on the driver object that will wait for up to 60 seconds for our piece of JavaScript to execute.

Let's see what happens if our script takes longer to execute than the script timeout:

```
@Test
private void javascriptExample() throws Exception {
    WebDriver driver = DriverFactory.getDriver();

    driver.manage().timeouts().setScriptTimeout(5,
    TimeUnit.SECONDS);
    JavascriptExecutor js = (JavascriptExecutor) driver;
    js.executeAsyncScript("var callback = arguments[
    arguments.length - 1]; window.setTimeout(callback, 25000);");

    driver.get("http://www.google.com");
}
```

This time, when we run our test, it waits for 5 seconds and then throws a `TimoutException`. It is important to set a script timeout on the driver object when running asynchronous scripts, to give them enough time to execute.

What do you think will happen if we execute this as a normal script?

```
@Test
private void javascriptExample() throws Exception {
    WebDriver driver = DriverFactory.getDriver();
    driver.manage().timeouts().setScriptTimeout(
    5, TimeUnit.SECONDS);
    JavascriptExecutor js = (JavascriptExecutor) driver;
    js.executeScript("var callback = arguments[arguments.
    length - 1]; window.setTimeout(callback, 25000);");

    driver.get("http://www.google.com");
}
```

You may have been expecting an error, but that's not what you got. The script got executed as normal because Selenium was not waiting for a callback; it didn't wait for it to complete. Since Selenium did not wait for the script to complete, it didn't hit the script timeout. Hence, no error was thrown.

Wait a minute. What about the callback definition? There was no argument that was used to set the `callback` variable. Why didn't it blow up?

Well, JavaScript isn't as strict as Java. What it has done is try and work out what `arguments[arguments.length - 1]` would resolve and realized that it is not defined. Since it is not defined, it has set the `callback` variable to null. Our test then completed before `setTimeout()` had a chance to complete its call. So, you won't see any console errors.

As you can see, it's very easy to make a small error that stops things from working when working with asynchronous JavaScript. It's also very hard to find these errors because there can be very little user feedback. Always take extra care when using the `JavascriptExecutor` to execute asynchronous bits of JavaScript.

Summary

In this chapter, we:

- Learned how to use a JavaScript executor to execute JavaScript snippets in the browser through Selenium
- Learned about passing arguments into a JavaScript executor and the sort of arguments that are supported
- Learned what the possible return types are for a JavaScript executor
- Gained a good understanding of when we shouldn't use a JavaScript executor
- Worked through a series of examples that showed ways in which we can use a JavaScript executor to enhance our tests

In the next chapter, we are going to have a look at some of the limitations of Selenium. We will also have a look at the ways via which we can work around these limitations, and enhance Selenium by using additional tools.

8
Keeping It Real

In this chapter we will have a look at some of the things that you cannot do with Selenium, and some of the things that you should not do with Selenium. We will have a look at some solutions that will work around its limitations. The topics we will cover in this chapter are:

- Downloading files
- Checking network traffic
- Load testing

The first topic we are going to look at is something that I regularly end up talking about: downloading files with Selenium.

Downloading files with Selenium

At some point in your career, you are probably going to work with a website that allows the user to download something. There are many different types of things that may be downloadable and the most common are probably:

- PDF files
- Pictures (PNG, JPG, GIF)
- Archives
- Installers

When you are working on a site that allows you to download files of some type, you will be expected to test that this functionality works and, at some point, the idea of writing some automated checks for this functionality will probably come up.

The scenario

You are working in a small, agile team and are in a pre-planning session with your tech lead, business analyst, and product owner. The product owner has a story to give your users a new functionality that enables them to download PDFs from the website that you are working on. These PDFs are going to have legal terms and conditions in them to satisfy statutory requirements, so it is important that they are available. If they are not downloadable, your company may be liable for some fairly significant fines. In planning, your team agrees that this is a relatively trivial bit of functionality for the developers to implement. You also agree that it will be easy for you to run a quick manual test to check that the functionality works by clicking on the download link in your browser. We don't know what the content of these documents is going to be yet because the legal department hasn't got back to us.

The functionality is written, and the PDF download works fine; it's tested manually and looks good for sign off. The next day, you grab the product owner so that you can demo the new piece of functionality to them, but something has gone wrong. A new build was pushed to your test environment this morning and it seems that the PDFs are no longer there. A quick investigation shows that the files were accidently removed and the change has been reverted; however it still doesn't work when it hits your test environment! Further investigation shows that the links to the PDFs have also been changed in error; they are now linking to files that don't exist. That issue has now been fixed as well and eventually the new functionality is successfully demoed to your product owner. Overall this has been a messy day that nobody is very proud of, and it has highlighted the fact that this could very easily go wrong in the future.

The problem

Your product owner knows that the functionality works, but their faith has been shaken somewhat and they want you to find a way to ensure that this will not break again in the future. As a team, you all agree that the build should go red on the Linux CI server if changes the developers make break the new PDF download functionality.

So, what's next?

Writing the automated checks falls to you. You open up your development IDE and start writing Selenium code. Your plan is to replicate the actions that you would perform manually in an automated script:

- You load the page with the download link

- You find the `<a>` element on the page
- You click on it

Wait! It's a trap. As soon as you click on the download link your test stops because Selenium cannot interact with an OS-level dialog box.

You go and have a look at the Selenium mailing lists and see lots of posts talking about your problem. Most of them seem to be advocating the use of another tool called AutoIT and there is some talk about using a Java robot class. Almost everything you read talks about finding a way to interact with your OS-level dialog box…

STOP RIGHT THERE!

Now is the time to take a step backward and work out exactly what you want to test.

Do you really need to download that file?

When I ask people if they really need to download the file, they normally say, "Yes, I do! I need to make sure that the download functionality works, and continues to work, after a code change."

That sounds pretty reasonable so far. I then pose the following questions:

- How many files are you planning to download?
- How big are those files?
- Do you have enough disk space to hold all of those files?
- Do you have the network capacity to continually download those files?
- What are you planning to do with the files once you have downloaded them?

The answer to the last question is the most interesting one. People I talk to usually say something along the lines of, "Well, I don't know. Delete them? I just need to know that they download; I'm not actually planning to do anything with them."

So the real question is: do you really need to download a file to perform this test? What you are really saying is that when you click on the PDF download link, you want to be sure that you are getting a valid response from the server.

You are not really checking that you can download the file, you are checking for broken links.

This is a worthwhile test, but it doesn't actually require you to download anything. So let's forget about trying to interact with that OS-level dialog box for now and see how we can check to see if the link is valid.

Checking whether links are valid

It's actually pretty simple to check links. All you need to do is find the link on the page, extract a URL from its `href` attribute, and then check to see if sending an HTTP GET request to that URL results in a valid response.

Let's create some code to do this for us.

```
package com.masteringselenium;

import org.apache.http.client.methods.*;

public enum RequestType {
    OPTIONS(new HttpOptions()),
    GET(new HttpGet()),
    HEAD(new HttpHead()),
    PATCH(new HttpPatch()),
    POST(new HttpPost()),
    PUT(new HttpPut()),
    DELETE(new HttpDelete()),
    TRACE(new HttpTrace());

    private final HttpRequestBase requestMethod;

    RequestType(HttpRequestBase requestMethod) {
        this.requestMethod = requestMethod;
    }

    public HttpRequestBase getRequestMethod() {
        return this.requestMethod;
    }
}
```

First of all we have an enum that will define all of the various types of HTTP request that we could use to get content from our website. We are probably going to use GET most of the time, but you will come across the others at some point. Now on to the part that does the actual work. First of all we have our basic class:

```
package com.masteringselenium;

import org.apache.http.HttpResponse;
import org.apache.http.NameValuePair;
import org.apache.http.client.HttpClient;
import org.apache.http.client.config.RequestConfig;
```

```
import org.apache.http.client.entity.UrlEncodedFormEntity;
import org.apache.http.client.methods.
HttpEntityEnclosingRequestBase;
import org.apache.http.client.methods.HttpRequestBase;
import org.apache.http.impl.client.HttpClientBuilder;
import org.apache.http.protocol.BasicHttpContext;

import java.io.IOException;
import java.net.MalformedURLException;
import java.net.URI;
import java.util.List;

public class FileDownloader {

    private RequestType httpRequestMethod = RequestType.GET;
    private URI fileURI;
    List<NameValuePair> urlParameters;

    public void setHTTPRequestMethod(RequestType requestType) {
        httpRequestMethod = requestType;
    }

    public void setURLParameters(List<NameValuePair>
    urlParameters) {
        this.urlParameters = urlParameters;
    }

    public void setURI(URI linkToFile) throws
    MalformedURLException {
        fileURI = linkToFile;
    }
}
```

We have created an object that we can instantiate once, and then use multiple times to download different files. We have created some setters to allow you to set the URI you want to query, the type of request that you want to send, and some URL parameters if required for POST/PATCH/PUT requests. We have set our default request method to GET as it is probably the one you will use the most. The only thing you need to supply is the URI. The next step is to create the code that will negotiate with the remote server:

```
private HttpResponse makeHTTPConnection() throws IOException,
NullPointerException {
```

```
        if (fileURI == null) throw new
        NullPointerException("No file URI specified");

        HttpClient client = HttpClientBuilder.create().build();

        HttpRequestBase requestMethod =
        httpRequestMethod.getRequestMethod();
        requestMethod.setURI(fileURI);

        BasicHttpContext localContext = new BasicHttpContext();

        if (null != urlParameters && (
                httpRequestMethod.equals(RequestType.PATCH) ||
                httpRequestMethod.equals(RequestType.POST) ||
                httpRequestMethod.equals(RequestType.PUT)
                )) {
            ((HttpEntityEnclosingRequestBase) requestMethod)
                .setEntity(new UrlEncodedFormEntity(urlParameters));
        }

        return client.execute(requestMethod, localContext);
    }
```

If you forget to specify a URI, this code will quickly fail and throw a
NullPointerException. The only complexity in there at the moment would be
adding some urlParameters if you are using a request type that would normally
expect them.

Now that we can make a connection we need to do something with it:

```
    public int getLinkHTTPStatus() throws Exception {
        HttpResponse downloadableFile = makeHTTPConnection();
        int httpStatusCode;
        try {
            httpStatusCode = downloadableFile.
            getStatusLine().getStatusCode();
        } finally {
            if (null != downloadableFile.getEntity()) {
                downloadableFile.getEntity().getContent().close();
            }
        }

        return httpStatusCode;
    }
```

This code uses the previous method to negotiate a connection with a remote server, and then gets the HTTP status code for the file that we are interested in. We can then use this HTTP status code to work out whether the file is there or there is a problem. If the file is there I would expect a 200 (OK) or maybe even a 302 (Redirect). If it's not there, I would expect a 404 (Not found) or maybe, if things really went badly, a 500 (Internal Server Error).

It's up to you to define which HTTP status code is a pass or a fail; the preceding code will simply tell you what the HTTP status code is.

While this code is useful, it's not yet perfect. Lots of websites do not allow you to just download files; they have protected content that can only be downloaded by somebody who has a valid account on the website.

Now you should already have a Selenium script that is logging you into the website you are trying to test and allowing you to get the URI that you want to download. Let's use the information that Selenium has to trick the website into thinking that your Selenium session is actually performing the download. First of all we are going to add a constructor to our `FileDownloader` class and make it require a `WebDriver` object:

```
private WebDriver driver;

public FileDownloader(WebDriver driverObject) {
    this.driver = driverObject;
}
```

Then we need to use this driver object to get some information so that we can pretend our request is coming from the browser. First of all we will copy the user agent:

```
private String getWebDriverUserAgent() {
        JavascriptExecutor js = (JavascriptExecutor) driver;
        return js.executeScript("return
        navigator.userAgent").toString();
    }
```

Then, we need to copy the cookies:

```
private BasicCookieStore getWebDriverCookies(Set<Cookie>
seleniumCookieSet) {
        BasicCookieStore copyOfWebDriverCookieStore
        = new BasicCookieStore();
        for (Cookie seleniumCookie : seleniumCookieSet) {
            BasicClientCookie duplicateCookie =
            new BasicClientCookie(seleniumCookie.getName(),
            seleniumCookie.getValue());
            duplicateCookie.setDomain(seleniumCookie.getDomain());
            duplicateCookie.setSecure(seleniumCookie.isSecure());
```

```
                    duplicateCookie.setExpiryDate(
                    seleniumCookie.getExpiry());
                    duplicateCookie.setPath(seleniumCookie.getPath());
                    copyOfWebDriverCookieStore.addCookie(duplicateCookie);
            }

            return copyOfWebDriverCookieStore;
    }
```

We now have all the bits that we need to pretend to be the browser that Selenium is driving, so let's tweak our makeHTTPConnection() method to use this information:

```
    private HttpResponse makeHTTPConnection() throws
    IOException, NullPointerException {
        if (fileURI == null) throw new NullPointerException("No
        file URI specified");

        HttpClient client = HttpClientBuilder.create().build();

        HttpRequestBase requestMethod =
        httpRequestMethod.getRequestMethod();
        requestMethod.setURI(fileURI);

        BasicHttpContext localContext = new BasicHttpContext();

        localContext.setAttribute(HttpClientContext.COOKIE_STORE,
        getWebDriverCookies(driver.manage().getCookies()));
        requestMethod.setHeader("User-Agent", getWebDriverUserAgent());

        if (null != urlParameters && (
                httpRequestMethod.equals(RequestType.PATCH) ||
                    httpRequestMethod.equals(RequestType.POST) ||
                    httpRequestMethod.equals(RequestType.PUT))
                ) {
            ((HttpEntityEnclosingRequestBase)
            requestMethod).setEntity(new
            UrlEncodedFormEntity(urlParameters));
        }

        return client.execute(requestMethod, localContext);
    }
```

We are now duplicating the information set in the browser being driven by Selenium, so that our HTTP status checker code can use it when making our request. Now, if we use this code on a site that has protected content, the website will think that the Selenium session is making the call and present the file correctly.

This will work for most, but not all, sites. Some sites use HttpOnly cookies, which are not visible through JavaScript. If you are working with this type of cookie your mileage will vary. Some driver implementations make them visible, but others don't. You can't set HttpOnly cookies locally, so the best you can do is set a normal cookie and hope.

If you type document.cookies in your JavaScript console, you will see a list of cookies that Selenium can reliably collect.

Let's take this code and put it into an example test to show how it would be used. First of all we will need a very simple page for Selenium to read:

```html
<!DOCTYPE HTML PUBLIC "-//W3C//DTD HTML 4.01 Transitional//EN"
"http://www.w3.org/TR/html4/loose.dtd">
<html>
<head>
    <title>Download Test</title>
</head>
<body>
<h1>Download a Test PDF File!</h1>

<p>To download it click <a id="fileToDownload"
href="pdf/TestFile.pdf">Here</a>!</p>
<img id="anImage" src="images/myImage.png">
</body>
</html>
```

Notice that the href attribute in the example HTML isn't a fully qualified URI, but actually a relative path. This is fine, Selenium will convert relative paths into a fully qualified URI so we don't need to add any additional code to do this for us.

Now we will need to write a Selenium test that uses our FileDownloader class to parse the page, get a link, and check whether it exists:

```java
@Test
public void statusCodeFromEmbeddedFile() throws Exception {
    WebDriver driver = new HtmlUnitDriver(true);
    FileDownloader downloadHandler = new FileDownloader();
    driver.get("http://www.masteringselenium.com/
    downloadTest.html");
    WebElement fileThatShouldExist =
    driver.findElement(By.id("fileToDownload"));
    URI fileAsURI = new
    URI(fileThatShouldExist.getAttribute("href"));

    downloadHandler.setURI(fileAsURI);
```

```
        downloadHandler.setHTTPRequestMethod(RequestType.GET);

        assertThat(downloadHandler.getLinkHTTPStatus(),
        is(equalTo(200)));
    }
```

We now have a working test that will tell us whether our PDF exists on the server. You may have noticed that the example HTML also had an `<img>` tag in the markup. That's because you can also use this method to check that images on the website are actually there. It's exactly the same principle as working with an anchor; you just need to take the data in the `src` attribute instead of the data in the `href` attribute.

 Try to modify the preceding example so that it checks to see if the image on the page exists instead of the PDF. Think about what sort of attribute an image has that holds the URI.

Let's go back to our original scenario. We now have a test that is capable of checking that the PDF files that we added to our website are available with every new build. To do this, we are checking that the `href` attribute of our anchor links does indeed refer to the correct URI. We are then taking this URI and checking that, when we request the file that it refers to, we get a valid HTTP status code.

We now have a happy product owner and a team that has much more confidence that they will not break something when they work with the code around the download functionality.

What if I do need to download the file?

In our previous scenario we didn't actually need to download the file because we didn't know what the contents were supposed to be. Let's extend that scenario. Our product owner has now been provided with the PDFs that need to be downloaded from our website. The legal department has made it very clear to them that, if we serve up the wrong file, there will be legal implications, and that we need to be sure that the correct file is there for every release.

We now have a new requirement, we really do need to download the file and check that the contents are correct. So what do we do now? Well, we have a few options; let's take a look at them:

- Use AutoIt to click on the download dialog
- Write a Java Robot class to click on the download dialog
- Get our browser to automatically download files when we click on a link
- Extend our existing code

Well, we can extend our existing code, but are we going to be writing code for the sake of it? Let's have a look at the alternatives.

AutoIt

When we first started investigating the file download problem, everybody was raving about AutoIt on the Selenium users list, so that has got to be a good solution, right?

AutoIt is a scripting language that is only designed to automate a Windows GUI. This is great when you are working with Windows, but our CI server is running on Linux.

We could work around this problem by adding a build agent that runs Windows for our Selenium tests, but we would then have lost cross-browser compatibility. Dealing with downloads on Safari is going to be especially tricky since the only version worth supporting runs on OS X.

We also have to think about our developers. They are running a mixture of machines: Windows, Linux, and OS X. If we implement an AutoIt solution we are stopping a large percentage of our developers from running the build locally unless we start supplying them with VMs. Creating VMs so that we can run a single file download sounds a bit of an overkill.

It looks like AutoIt is not for us.

The Java Robot class

How about a Java Robot class, then?

From a compatibility point of view, this is much better; we can write cross platform code that will just work. However, we do still have some issues. The first problem that we will come across is that dialog boxes across operating systems differ so we will probably have to write code branches for each operating system.

Let's assume that we decide to do that; does everything work for us now? Initially yes, but when we run our test twice we find out that we have some new problems. When a file already exists we will be asked if we want to overwrite it, or save it using a new filename. This means we have to start adding more logic into our Java Robot implementation. What if we specify an alternative filename that already exists? Do we want to clobber that file?

We are coming across more and more problems that we need to code solutions for; this is not going to be a simple, or quick, bit of code.

Browser auto download

What about configuring the browser to automatically download the file, then?

This will get rid of the dialog box completely so we no longer have to write any complicated code to interact with a dialog, or deal with existing files that have the same name. If an existing file already exists, it will just append a number to the end of it.

This sounds great. We have removed all of the issues around dialog interaction and file naming; it sounds like we could have a winner.

Unfortunately we still have some problems. If you download a file that already exists, how do you know what the filename of the file you just downloaded is? Do we need to start checking file timestamps to see when it was downloaded?

Selenium is unaware of the download process because the browser controls it all. This injects some new problems into the mix. How do we know when the download has completed? Is our test going to finish and close the browser before the file download has completed?

It sounds like if we are going to implement a browser auto download, we are going to have to implement some reasonably advanced logic to work out what the file name is and whether we managed to download it.

Extending our existing code

Our existing code already does a lot of the work we want a file download solution to do. We are already mimicking the browser state and negotiating a connection to the content we want to download. It shouldn't be too hard to extend this slightly further, should it?

We have already negotiated a connection with the server to get the file that we want; it's just a case of using that connection to download the file instead of just checking the HTTP status code. We can then call our file anything we want and we will know when the download has completed because our code is controlling it.

Is this the perfect solution? Not necessarily. As noted before we may have some potential problems with HttpOnly cookies. However, it does seem to be the least complex solution so far.

Downloading a file with the help of Selenium

After looking at our available options, we are going to go with the least complex solution and extend our existing code. In our scenario, HttpOnly cookies are not a problem because we don't use them so we don't have to worry about any potential issues relating to them.

 If you are planning on using this solution, you should first spike it out and check that you can mimic HttpOnly cookies successfully if you are using them. You don't want to write code that is not fit for purpose.

We don't need to change any of our existing code, instead we are going to write a new method that will take the connection we have already negotiated with the server and use it to complete the file download:

```
public File downloadFile() throws Exception {
    File downloadedFile = File.createTempFile("download", ".pdf");
    HttpResponse fileToDownload = makeHTTPConnection();
    try {
        FileUtils.copyInputStreamToFile(fileToDownload.
        getEntity().getContent(), downloadedFile);
    } finally {
        fileToDownload.getEntity().getContent().close();
    }

    return downloadedFile;
}
```

This method will create a file in our temporary directory and then, using the connection we have already negotiated with the remote server, stream all the data from the remote file into it. We then close the connection to the remote server and return the file.

We are using a standard Java library to create a temporary file because this will guarantee that our file is unique. The other benefit is that, since we are putting this file in the `temp` directory, it will automatically get cleaned up by the operating system when required; we don't have to do the cleanup ourselves.

Let's plug it into a test to see how it works.

```
@Test
public void downloadAFile() throws Exception {
    FileDownloader downloadHandler = new FileDownloader(driver);
```

```
driver.get("http://www.masteringselenium.com/
downloadTest.html");
WebElement fileThatShouldExist =
driver.findElement(By.id("fileToDownload"));
URI fileAsURI = new
URI(fileThatShouldExist.getAttribute("href"));

downloadHandler.setURI(fileAsURI);
downloadHandler.setHTTPRequestMethod(RequestType.GET);

File downloadedFile = downloadHandler.downloadFile();

assertThat(downloadedFile.exists(), is(equalTo(true)));
assertThat(downloadHandler.getLinkHTTPStatus(),
is(equalTo(200)));
}
```

But that's not the same as clicking on a link and downloading the file…

Well, actually it is. When you click on the link your browser sends an HTTP GET request over to the web server and negotiates a connection. When it has negotiated a connection, it starts to download the file to a temporary location. It then tells your operating system that it's downloading a file, and asks what to do with it. This is the point where you will see an OS-level dialog box as the browser defers that request to the operating system and asks you what to do.

Once you have told the operating system the filename and download location, and then decided if you want to overwrite any existing files, the operating system will pass this information back to the browser. The browser then copies the file it has downloaded to a temporary location, the location specified by the operating system.

What you are actually doing by implementing this solution is taking the browser and the operating system out of the equation. A lot of people don't feel comfortable with this solution when they first see it. If you are one of those people, have another read of the last two paragraphs.

Notice that the only interaction with the website is the action of clicking on the download link (usually an anchor element with an `href` attribute, or maybe a form post if it's a little bit more complex). The code that your developers have written does not have any download functionality, they are just providing a link that the browser recognizes and processes accordingly.

By bypassing the browser and the operating system code, you are only bypassing code that your development team has no control over. Let's face it; if you click on a valid anchor to download a file and the browser has a bug that prevents it from working, there is not much you can do about it anyway. You could raise a bug with the browser vendor, but you can't force them to fix it. Even if you could force them to fix it, it's unlikely you will be able to force all of your users to download this updated version of the browser.

Secondly, what are the chances of a browser vendor releasing a browser version that cannot download a file when you click on a link? I would suspect they are pretty slim; browser manufacturers have a pretty good idea of what they are doing and I would be shocked if they didn't have at least one test that checked that file download functionality worked correctly.

So we have successfully downloaded the file, and our test has passed. Are we done? Not quite, we still haven't checked to see if the file that we downloaded is the correct one.

Checking whether we have downloaded the correct file

This is actually the most important part of our test. Being able to download a file, or even actually downloading one, does not prove that you have the correct file.

So how do we prove that we have the correct one? Well, the file that we have downloaded is a PDF file, so maybe we need to write some code that can read in a PDF file. We could then scan all of the text in the file and see if it is correct.

How do we know that the text is correct? Well we could put all of the text of a PDF file into our test, but that's a lot of text… It's going to be horrible updating this test every time the PDF file changes, and we don't know how often the legal department is going to ask us to make updates… This is starting to sound like a bad idea.

Always avoid hard-coding content into your tests wherever possible. This will make your tests high-maintenance, high-cost, and brittle by design. People often want to tweak the text displayed to a user. If this minor tweak causes all of your tests to fail you are doing it wrong. Focus on testing functionality and only check content where absolutely necessary!

The most simple and obvious way to check that the file is correct is to compare it to a known good copy of the file. This way we don't need to store any of the text from the file in our tests. If the file we have downloaded matches the original file, it must be the correct file.

So now we have two PDF files: a known good file and the file that we have downloaded. The next step is to compare them. This is where, as mentioned earlier, people usually look for libraries that read in PDF files. They then scan both files and try and compare the text in them to highlight errors.

What would we need in order to do this?

Well, we would need some PDF libraries because we don't want to write our own. Apache has a library called PDFBox that allows you to extract text. This could work, but once we have extracted the text from the PDF files, we would need to compare it to see if it is correct.

In our case, we want to check a PDF file. What if the file we want to compare isn't a PDF? What if it's a PNG, a JPG, or a Word document? We don't need to support any other files at the moment, but it's always worth keeping your code open-ended. A simple solution that can support multiple file types will always be good. So, when we look for our solution it's worth bearing in mind that we may need to start pulling in all sorts of different libraries to deal with all of these file formats.

The next question to answer is: do we want to try and show the differences between these two files? That's even more code and libraries since we need a way to calculate and display the difference between our downloaded file, and the known good file.

We also have another problem. That known good file could be quite large; where do we keep it? Source control? My personal view is that storing large files in source control is not ideal. I don't want to spend hours cloning a repository, and large files in source control have been known to cause problems if the server isn't configured correctly. You may not have to worry about this, whoever is administering your source control platform may have already thought about these problems, but it's something to keep in the back of your mind.

We are really just scratching the tip of the iceberg here. I'm sure you can think of many more questions and come up with many more problems that this generic solution needs to solve. It's starting to sound like we could have quite a lot of work here…

Let's stop right there and remember the KISS principle! We don't actually need to read in the file and compare the text line by line. We don't need to show diffs if our test fails. We just need to know if the file is correct or not. We can always save a copy of the file that we downloaded so that somebody can manually investigate any problems if the test fails.

You don't have to *automate* everything. Some things are much easier for humans to check. There is nothing wrong with using an automated solution to get some information that can be easily checked by a person. Don't spend hours trying to get a computer to do a job that a human brain can do in seconds. If your tests fail, a human with a brain is going to look at them anyway.

So how do I remove the complexity from this scenario and make my code simple? It's actually pretty easy because this problem has already been solved for us.

If you have downloaded files from the Internet before, you may have seen lots of sites publishing an MD5, or SHA1, hash of the file they are hosting. You can take an MD5, or SHA1, hash of the file you have downloaded and compare it to the one they have published. If the hashes match, you know that you have the correct file and it has downloaded correctly. This works because taking an unsalted MD5 or SHA1 hash of a file will always produce the same hash for the same file. So, if we take a hash of the file you have downloaded, and compare it to a known good hash of the file, we can instantly tell if it is correct or not. If the hash doesn't match, you can fail the test and save the file for manual examination later on.

By doing this, we are massively simplifying our code. There are also hundreds of utilities available that will perform file comparisons for you and that can be used to manually inspect bad files that have caused your test to fail. If things go wrong we can just pick up one of these utilities, which will quickly show us any differences.

This doesn't mean that you cannot write your own code to diff two files; this is not, however, something you need to write for the initial test. We generally wouldn't expect the wrong file to be downloaded so we don't want to spend lots of time writing code that will not be used. If this test fails regularly, that is when you may want to consider writing more complex code to help you diagnose the issue more easily.

So let's write a small bit of code that can check the file hash of a file, and give you a quick answer as to whether the file is the one you are expecting or not:

```
package com.masteringselenium.hash;

public enum HashType {
    MD5,
    SHA1
}
```

We have started off with an enum that we will use in our hash checking class to determine the type of hash that we are using. If you are only going to perform one type of hash check you probably won't need this extra bit of complexity, but for our example we are going to cater for both MD5 and SHA1. Next, we have the code that takes the file you have downloaded and generates a hash:

```
package com.masteringselenium.hash;

import org.apache.commons.codec.digest.DigestUtils;

import java.io.File;
import java.io.FileInputStream;
import java.io.FileNotFoundException;

public class CheckFileHash {

    public static String generateHashForFileOfType(File
    fileToCheck, HashType hashType) throws Exception {
        if (!fileToCheck.exists()) throw new
        FileNotFoundException(fileToCheck + " does not exist!");

        switch (hashType) {
            case MD5:
                return DigestUtils.md5Hex(new
                FileInputStream(fileToCheck));
            case SHA1:
                return DigestUtils.sha1Hex(new
                FileInputStream(fileToCheck));
            default:
                throw new UnsupportedOperationException(hashType.
                toString() + " hash type is not supported!");
        }
    }

}
```

This is again a very simple snippet of code; you just pass in a file and a hash type and it returns you the hash. You can then use it in your test, like so:

```
@Test
public void downloadAFileWhilstMimicingSeleniumCookies
AndCheckTheSHA1Hash() throws Exception {
    FileDownloader downloadHandler = new FileDownloader(driver);
    driver.get("http://www.masteringselenium.com
    /downloadTest.html");
```

```
    WebElement fileThatShouldExist =
    driver.findElement(By.id("fileToDownload"));
    URI fileAsURI = new URI(
    fileThatShouldExist.getAttribute("href"));

    downloadHandler.setURI(fileAsURI);
    downloadHandler.setHTTPRequestMethod(RequestType.GET);
    File downloadedFile = downloadHandler.downloadFile();

    assertThat(downloadedFile.exists(),
            is(equalTo(true)));
    assertThat(downloadHandler.getLinkHTTPStatus(),
            is(equalTo(200)));
    assertThat(generateHashForFileOfType(downloadedFile, SHA1),
            is(equalTo("
            8882e3d972be82e14a98c522745746a03b97997a")));
}
```

Using a different type of hash is as simple as changing the hash type and your expectation:

```
@Test
public void downloadAFileWhilstMimicingSeleniumCookies
AndCheckTheMD5Hash() throws Exception {
  FileDownloader downloadHandler = new FileDownloader(driver);
  driver.get("http://ch8.masteringselenium.com/
   downloadTest.html");
  WebElement fileThatShouldExist =
  driver.findElement(By.id("fileToDownload"));
  URI fileAsURI = new URI(
  fileThatShouldExist.getAttribute("href"));

  downloadHandler.setURI(fileAsURI);
  downloadHandler.setHTTPRequestMethod(RequestType.GET);
  File downloadedFile = downloadHandler.downloadFile();

  assertThat(downloadedFile.exists(),
      is(equalTo(true)));
  assertThat(downloadHandler.getLinkHTTPStatus(),
      is(equalTo(200)));
  assertThat(generateHashForFileOfType(downloadedFile, MD5),
      is(equalTo("d1f296f523b74462b31b912a5675a814")));
}
```

You now have some clean and simple code that will help you check that the file you have downloaded is correct.

You cannot track the network traffic with Selenium

A feature that Selenium does not support, and one that is requested time and again, is monitoring the browser network traffic. The Selenium development team has categorically stated that this will not be added to the WebDriver API, despite many cries of outrage. The reasons for not adding it are actually quite sensible.

Selenium drives the browser; it does not interact with the underlying mechanisms that the browser uses. As such, when Selenium loads a page, it is actually asking the browser to load a page. It does not interact with the remote server that is hosting the page, the browser does that, and as a result it doesn't know how the browser is interacting with the remote server. This interaction is not in-scope for WebDriver, and it never has been.

The issue is not completely straightforward however. The old Selenium 1 API did have some functionality that allowed it get network traffic, but only if you used Firefox. All involved agree that this was probably a bad idea because it relied on a vendor-specific implementation and it was never cross-browser compliant. The fact that this kludge used to exist in the old Selenium 1 API is normally held up as proof that Selenium 2 (and moving forward Selenium 3) should provide some support for tracking network traffic.

This does not however make sense. You have to remember that Selenium 2 was the result of merging Selenium with WebDriver. The Selenium 1 API was officially deprecated when this happened (although, due to communication problems, the decision was made to change the official position on that, it's now going to be officially deprecated with Selenium 3) and WebDriver was the new solution that everybody was supposed to use moving forward. One of the reasons that the Selenium 1 API was deprecated was because it was trying to be too many things to too many people and it was becoming bloated and unwieldy.

Holding up something that was deprecated because it had become bloated and unwieldy, and using it as a reason to make something bloated and unwieldy, really makes no sense.

But I really want to track my network traffic!

Well, it's not all bad news. Selenium doesn't explicitly provide support for network traffic; however, it does provide support for proxies. If you want to track your network traffic, what's the best way to do it? Why, a proxy, of course!

There are many proxies available, but we will focus on one in particular: the BrowserMob proxy. The BrowserMob proxy has been written with test automation in mind and integrates very easily with Selenium. Let's look at a basic implementation:

```
package com.masteringselenium;

import net.lightbody.bmp.BrowserMobProxy;
import net.lightbody.bmp.client.ClientUtil;
import net.lightbody.bmp.core.har.Har;
import net.lightbody.bmp.proxy.ProxyServer;
import org.openqa.selenium.Proxy;
import org.openqa.selenium.WebDriver;
import org.openqa.selenium.firefox.FirefoxDriver;
import org.openqa.selenium.remote.CapabilityType;
import org.openqa.selenium.remote.DesiredCapabilities;
import org.testng.annotations.AfterSuite;
import org.testng.annotations.Test;


public class ProxyBasedWD {


    private static WebDriver driver;

    @AfterSuite
    public static void cleanUpDriver() {
        driver.close();
    }

    @Test
    public void usingAProxyToTrackNetworkTraffic()
    throws Exception {
        BrowserMobProxy browserMobProxy = new
        BrowserMobProxyServer();
        browserMobProxy.start();
        Proxy seleniumProxyConfiguration =
        ClientUtil.createSeleniumProxy(browserMobProxy);

        DesiredCapabilities desiredCapabilities =
        DesiredCapabilities.firefox();
        desiredCapabilities.setCapability(CapabilityType.PROXY,
        seleniumProxyConfiguration);
```

```
driver = new FirefoxDriver(desiredCapabilities);

browserMobProxy.newHar();

driver.get("https://www.google.co.uk");

Har httpArchive = browserMobProxy.getHar();
        }
    }
```

Our basic implementation is really quite simple. We are creating an instance of `BrowserMobProxy`, starting it up and then creating a Selenium proxy configuration using the handy `ClientUtil` class provided by the `BrowserMobProxy` team. We then take this proxy configuration and use the `DesiredCapabilities` object to tell Selenium that we want to use it. When Selenium starts up, all network traffic will now be routed through `BrowserMobProxy`.

If we want to record the traffic, the first thing we need to do is to tell `BrowserMobProxy` to create an **HTTP archive (HAR)** of the network traffic. We then use Selenium to navigate to a website and perform some actions. When we are done, we retrieve the HTTP archive that has been created by `BrowserMobProxy`.

Earlier in the chapter we wrote some code to check the HTTP status code for specific resources; we could use a proxy to do the same thing. Let's extend our test to do that and see how usable a solution it is.

First of all we need to write some code to find a specific HTTP request and return the status code:

```
public int getHTTPStatusCode(String expectedURL,
Har httpArchive) {
    for (HarEntry entry : httpArchive.getLog().getEntries()) {
        if (entry.getRequest().getUrl().equals(expectedURL)) {
            return entry.getResponse().getStatus();
        }
    }

    return 0;
}
```

As you can see, parsing the HTTP archive is quite simple; we get a list of entries and then just iterate through them until we find the entry that we want.

However, this does expose a potential flaw. What if the archive is really big? With our example test here it's not really a problem because we are only making a single request, so it won't take long to parse the archive. It's worth noting that this single request generated 14 entries, though. Imagine how big the archive could get with just one standard user journey, or even a couple...

Now that we have our function to find a status code for a URL, we need to extend our test to use this additional code:

```
@Test
public void usingAProxyToTrackNetworkTraffic() throws Exception {
    BrowserMobProxy browserMobProxy = new BrowserMobProxyServer();
    browserMobProxy.start();
    Proxy seleniumProxyConfiguration =
    ClientUtil.createSeleniumProxy(browserMobProxy);

    DesiredCapabilities desiredCapabilities =
    DesiredCapabilities.firefox();
    desiredCapabilities.setCapability(CapabilityType.PROXY,
    seleniumProxyConfiguration);
    driver = new FirefoxDriver(desiredCapabilities);

    browserMobProxy.newHar();

    driver.get("https://www.google.co.uk");

    Har httpArchive = browserMobProxy.getHar();

    assertThat(getHTTPStatusCode("https:
//www.google.co.uk/", httpArchive),
        is(equalTo(200)));
}
```

This is where we see another potential flaw. If you look closely at the test, the URL that we are getting is not the same as the URL that we are asserting on. The one that we are asserting on has an extra slash. The simple solution is to make sure that you specify all base URLs with a trailing slash, but that can easily catch you out.

> Try comparing the two different implementations for finding HTTP status codes in this chapter. See how long it takes you to implement each one. When you have completed both of them, set up the same test, then time how long it takes for each one to complete. Which solution is faster? Which one would you prefer to have in your test code base?

It must be pointed out that collecting HTTP status codes is not the only thing you can do with network traffic. The fact that it's not a perfect solution for this use case does not mean that it isn't good for other things.

There are things that you can only do by tracking network traffic.

For example, if you were writing a checkout application and you wanted to be sure that any transactions in flight were explicitly cancelled when you navigated to a different URL, tracking the network traffic would be ideal. Similarly, if you wanted to check that a specific network request was formatted in a specific way, you would need to scan the network traffic.

There are also other avenues that open up to you if you are using a proxy.

Maybe you would like to simulate a bad network connection. Well, you can do this by configuring your proxy to limit upload and download speeds. How about blocking some content and then taking screenshots of every step of your user journey? You can then quickly, and easily, see what a flow would look like if the images were not available.

There are many interesting and unusual things you can do if you have access to, and can manipulate, the network traffic.

We have a very basic proxy implementation, but in its current form it doesn't really work well with the test framework that we created earlier in this book. Let's have a look at how we can extend that framework to support proxies.

First of all, we are going to need to tweak our POM a little bit to allow us to set proxy details on the command line. To do this, we first need to add in some additional properties:

```
<properties>
    <project.build.sourceEncoding>
    UTF-8</project.build.sourceEncoding>
    <project.reporting.outputEncoding>
    UTF-8</project.reporting.outputEncoding>
    <!-- Dependency versions -->
    <selenium.version>2.45.0</selenium.version>
    <!-- Configurable variables -->
    <threads>1</threads>
    <browser>firefox</browser>
    <overwrite.binaries>false</overwrite.binaries>
    <remote>false</remote>
    <seleniumGridURL/>
    <platform/>
    <browserVersion/>
```

```
        <proxyEnabled>false</proxyEnabled>
        <proxyHost/>
        <proxyPort/>
    </properties>
```

As you can see, I have not set any default values but, if you have a good idea what the proxy details will be, feel free to add them. I have also set the `proxyEnabled` property to false by default; you can change this to true if you always want to use a proxy. The next thing we need to do is set these as system properties, so that our test can read them in.

```
<plugin>
    <groupId>org.apache.maven.plugins</groupId>
    <artifactId>maven-failsafe-plugin</artifactId>
    <version>2.17</version>
    <configuration>
        <parallel>methods</parallel>
        <threadCount>${threads}</threadCount>
        <systemProperties>
            <browser>${browser}</browser>
            <screenshotDirectory>${project.build.directory}
            /screenshots</screenshotDirectory>
            <remoteDriver>${remote}</remoteDriver>
            <gridURL>${seleniumGridURL}</gridURL>
            <desiredPlatform>${platform}</desiredPlatform>
            <desiredBrowserVersion>${browserVersion}
            </desiredBrowserVersion>
            <proxyEnabled>${proxyEnabled}</proxyEnabled>
            <proxyHost>${proxyHost}</proxyHost>
            <proxyPort>${proxyPort}</proxyPort>
            <!--Set properties passed in by the
            driver binary downloader-->
            <phantomjs.binary.path>${phantomjs.binary.path}
            </phantomjs.binary.path>
            <webdriver.chrome.driver>${webdriver.chrome.driver}
            </webdriver.chrome.driver>
            <webdriver.ie.driver>${webdriver.ie.driver}
            </webdriver.ie.driver>
            <webdriver.opera.driver>${webdriver.opera.driver}
            </webdriver.opera.driver>
        </systemProperties>
        <includes>
            <include>**/*WD.java</include>
        </includes>
    </configuration>
```

```
<executions>
    <execution>
        <goals>
            <goal>integration-test</goal>
            <goal>verify</goal>
        </goals>
    </execution>
</executions>
</plugin>
```

We are now ready to start tweaking the rest of our code. The first thing we are going to do is update our `DriverSetup` interface. We want to add the ability to pass some proxy settings in when we generate our `DeisredCapabilities`:

```
package com.masteringselenium.config;

import org.openqa.selenium.Proxy;
import org.openqa.selenium.WebDriver;
import org.openqa.selenium.remote.DesiredCapabilities;

public interface DriverSetup {

    WebDriver getWebDriverObject(DesiredCapabilities
    desiredCapabilities);

    DesiredCapabilities getDesiredCapabilities(Proxy
    proxySettings);
}
```

We then need to update our `DriverType` enum to allow each `getDesiredCapabilities` method to support proxy details. The method for adding proxy settings should be the same for all drivers. So rather than add duplicated code into every `getDesiredCapabilities` method, we will add a new method that we can call to configure the proxy settings:

```
protected DesiredCapabilities addProxySettings(
DesiredCapabilities capabilities, Proxy proxySettings) {
    if (null != proxySettings) {
        capabilities.setCapability(PROXY, proxySettings);
    }

    return capabilities;
}
```

This method will take an existing `DesiredCapabilities` object, and a `proxySettings` object. First it will check to see if there are any proxy settings that need to be added. If there are, it will then add them to the `DesiredCapabilities` object that was passed in. Finally, it returns the `DesiredCapabilities` object, whether it was updated or not.

We now need to plug this into our `getDesiredCapabilities` methods. Let's start with our `FIREFOX` enum.

```
FIREFOX {
    public DesiredCapabilities getDesiredCapabilities(Proxy
    proxySettings) {
        DesiredCapabilities capabilities =
        DesiredCapabilities.firefox();
        return addProxySettings(capabilities, proxySettings);
    }

    public WebDriver getWebDriverObject(DesiredCapabilities
    capabilities) {
        return new FirefoxDriver(capabilities);
    }
}
```

The changes are actually very simple. The method now takes a `proxySettings` object. Then, instead of returning a capabilities object directly, it passes the `proxySettings` object and the capabilities object it has built to the `addProxySettings` method. It then passes the result of that method back as its return object.

The same modification can be applied to all of our `getDesiredCapabilities` methods, except for the PhantomJS one. PhantomJS is slightly awkward when it comes to proxies; they need to be set on the command line. It's fine, though, we will just write another method to set up our PhanomJS command line for us. Simple:

```
protected List<String> applyPhantomJSProxySettings(List<String>
cliArguments, Proxy proxySettings) {
    if (null == proxySettings) {
        cliArguments.add("--proxy-type=none");
    } else {
        cliArguments.add("--proxy-type=http");
        cliArguments.add("--proxy="
        +proxySettings.getHttpProxy());
    }
    return cliArguments;
}
```

This method will take our proxy settings and a list of command-line arguments and work out what we need to add. If proxySettings is not null, it will extract the required information and set the appropriate command line settings. If proxySettings is null, we explicitly set the proxy to none for good measure. We could probably get away with not doing this, but it's neat and tidy.

We now need to update our PHANTOMJS enum to use this method:

```
PHANTOMJS {
    public DesiredCapabilities getDesiredCapabilities(Proxy
    proxySettings) {
        DesiredCapabilities capabilities =
        DesiredCapabilities.phantomjs();
        final List<String> cliArguments = new ArrayList<String>();
        cliArguments.add("--web-security=false");
        cliArguments.add("--ssl-protocol=any");
        cliArguments.add("--ignore-ssl-errors=true");
        capabilities.setCapability("phantomjs.cli.args",
        applyPhantomJSProxySettings(cliArguments, proxySettings));
        capabilities.setCapability("takesScreenshot", true);

        return capabilities;
    }

    public WebDriver getWebDriverObject(DesiredCapabilities
    capabilities) {
        return new PhantomJSDriver(capabilities);
    }
}
```

As with the changes to our FIREFOX enum, the getDesiredCapabilities method now takes a proxySettings object. With PHANTOMJS, we still return the capabilities as before, though. The change here is where we set our command-line arguments. Instead of passing the cliArguments list into the setCapability method, we pass in the applyPhantomJSProxySettings method. The applyPhantomJSProxySettings method then updates the command-line arguments with the proxy settings and returns them to the setCapability method, ensuring our proxy settings are applied when PhantomJS starts up.

We are now expecting to pass proxy settings into our getDesiredCapabilities method. So, the final thing we need to do is modify WebDriverThread so that it can do this. The changes are relatively straightforward:

```
private final boolean proxyEnabled =
Boolean.getBoolean("proxyEnabled");
```

```
private final String proxyHostname =
System.getProperty("proxyHost");
private final Integer proxyPort =
Integer.getInteger("proxyPort");
private final String proxyDetails = String.format("%s:%d",
proxyHostname, proxyPort);

public WebDriver getDriver() throws Exception {
    if (null == webdriver) {
        Proxy proxy = null;
        if (proxyEnabled) {
            proxy = new Proxy();
            proxy.setProxyType(MANUAL);
            proxy.setHttpProxy(proxyDetails);
            proxy.setSslProxy(proxyDetails);
        }
        determineEffectiveDriverType();
        DesiredCapabilities desiredCapabilities =
        selectedDriverType.getDesiredCapabilities(proxy);
        instantiateWebDriver(desiredCapabilities);
    }

    return webdriver;
}
```

First of all, we have added some variables that will read in the proxy settings based upon the system properties that we set in our POM. Then we have updated our getDriver() method to use the proxy details to configure a proxy object, if proxyEnabled is equal to true. Finally, our call to getDesiredCapabilities has been updated to pass this proxy object.

You may have noticed in all the previous methods that we wrote, we performed a check on the proxy object to see if it was null before processing it. This enables us to send a null to getDesiredCapabilities without having to worry about it breaking anything later on.

We now have the ability to specify a proxy on the command line, and we can preconfigure one in our POM. This is great from the point of view of plugging corporate proxy details into your browser, however, it's not ideal if we want to use BrowserMobProxy. When we used BrowserMobProxy in our example test, you may have noticed that we were programmatically starting a BrowserMobProxy instance and interacting with it in our test. To do this, we really want to bake in support for BrowserMobProxy, and we also want to be able to forward on calls to our corporate proxy.

Let's extend our framework again to do exactly this. First of all, we will add a dependency to `browsermob-core` to our POM:

```
<dependency>
    <groupId>net.lightbody.bmp</groupId>
    <artifactId>browsermob-core-littleproxy</artifactId>
    <version>2.1.0-beta-2</version>
    <scope>test</scope>
</dependency>
```

This will make all of the `BrowserMobProxy` libraries available for our implementation.

> There are quite a few changes being made to `BrowserMobProxy` at the moment, and the new API that will be supported going forward is the 2.1.0 one. With this in mind, it seems prudent to use 2.1.0-beta-2 for examples in this section. See `http://bmp.lightbody.net` for more information.

Then we need to update `WebDriverThread` so that it can support `BrowserMobProxy`. We will start off by adding a couple of class variables:

```
private BrowserMobProxy browserMobProxy;
private boolean usingBrowserMobProxy = false;
```

We are going to use these later on to hold a reference to any `BrowserMobProxy` instance we start, and to track whether we are using it or not. The next step is to update our `getDriver()` method:

```
private WebDriver getDriver(boolean useBrowserMobProxy)
throws Exception {
    if (null != webdriver && usingBrowserMobProxy !=
    useBrowserMobProxy) {
        webdriver.quit();
        webdriver = null;
    }
    if (null == webdriver) {
        Proxy proxy = null;
        if (proxyEnabled || useBrowserMobProxy) {
            if (useBrowserMobProxy) {
                usingBrowserMobProxy = true;
                browserMobProxy = new BrowserMobProxyServer();
                browserMobProxy.start();
                if (proxyEnabled) {
                    browserMobProxy.setChainedProxy(new
                    InetSocketAddress(proxyHostname, proxyPort));
                }
```

```
                proxy = ClientUtil.createSeleniumProxy(
                browserMobProxy);
            } else {
                proxy = new Proxy();
                proxy.setProxyType(MANUAL);
                proxy.setHttpProxy(proxyDetails);
                proxy.setSslProxy(proxyDetails);
            }
        }
        determineEffectiveDriverType();
        DesiredCapabilities desiredCapabilities =
        selectedDriverType.getDesiredCapabilities(proxy);
        instantiateWebDriver(desiredCapabilities);
    }

    return webdriver;
}
```

We have started off by passing in a Boolean that tells us if we want to use `BrowserMobProxy` or not. We then check to see what the current state of our `WebDriver` object is. If it is not null, and not using a `BrowserMobProxy` instance when we want it to, we tell the `WebDriver` object to quit. We then set the `WebDriver` object to null, so that it is all ready to start up a new `WebDriver` instance that is using `BrowserMobProxy`.

Our next change is to the logic where we apply proxy settings. If we are using proxy settings as well as `BrowserMobProxy`, we apply those proxy settings to `BrowserMobProxy`. This ensures that we can still get to the website we are trying to test through our corporate proxy server. We then plug the `BrowserMobProxy` settings into Selenium. This means that Selenium will talk to `BrowserMobProxy`, which in turn will talk to the corporate proxy, which in turn will talk to the website we are trying to access. Notice that the `BrowserMobProxy` instance we create uses our class variable so that we can interact with it at a later date.

If we are not using a proxy, we just set Selenium up to use `BrowserMobProxy` as a proxy server so that we get access to our network traffic. If we haven't chosen to use `BrowserMobProxy` at all, the existing functionality will work as before.

Since we have changed the method to require a Boolean to tell us if we are using `BrowserMobProxy` or not, we need to now do some additional work. Instead of updating `DriverFactory`, we are going to wrap our `getDriver()` method with a couple of other methods that `DriverFactory` can call. This is why we changed `getDriver()` to private access.

The first method is another one called `getDriver()`; however, this one does not require a Boolean as an argument:

```
public WebDriver getDriver() throws Exception {
    return getDriver(usingBrowserMobProxy);
}
```

This can be used by the `DriverFactory` method without any changes so that our existing code continues to work. Notice that it uses the Boolean we are storing in our class to let our private `getDriver()` method know that it doesn't need to change anything.

Next we have the `getBrowserMobProxyEnabledDriver()` method:

```
public WebDriver getBrowserMobProxyEnabledDriver() throws
Exception {
    return getDriver(true);
}
```

This method will ensure that a `WebDriver` instance that uses `BrowserMobProxy` is started up (if the current instance is not already using one). This method can be called once at the start of your test, and then from that point onwards you can call `getDriver()` as normal.

Finally we have a `getBrowserMobProxy()` method:

```
public BrowserMobProxy getBrowserMobProxy() {
    if (usingBrowserMobProxy) {
        return browserMobProxy;
    }
    return null;
}
```

This is used to return the `BrowserMobProxy` instance so that you can give it commands. This is so that you can start collecting traffic, or examine traffic it has already collected.

The final step is to expose these new `getBrowserMobProxyEnabledDriver()` and `getBrowserMobProxy()` methods through `DriverFactory`.

```
public static WebDriver getBrowserMobProxyEnabledDriver()
throws Exception {
    return driverThread.get().getBrowserMobProxyEnabledDriver();
}

public static BrowserMobProxy getBrowserMobProxy() {
    return driverThread.get().getBrowserMobProxy();
}
```

Now everything is ready for you to use in your tests. Why don't you try writing a test that will check the network traffic (like the one we wrote earlier in this chapter) to try it out.

Writing performance tests with Selenium

It is theoretically possible to run performance tests with Selenium. You could start up a great big Selenium Grid and then point your grid at an application and run lots of tests against it.

So why don't people normally do this?

The sheer power that would be required to configure a grid that could actually hit your performance testing environment with enough traffic usually makes it a very expensive solution. You then also have the setup and maintenance costs of your grid. That being said, with the advent of cloud services, and tools such as:

- Ansible (`http://www.ansible.com`)
- Chef (`https://www.chef.io`)
- Puppet (`https://puppetlabs.com`)

It is much cheaper than it used to be. Once you have done the groundwork, it's also pretty easy to spin up slaves that can attach themselves to the grid as and when required. So, at the end of the day it is now something you could do.

The question is: should we do this?

Well, first of all you have to stop and think about what you are actually testing. When the server that hosts your website is under load, what is it actually doing? Well, it is taking a request from a browser over the network, performing some calculations on the server, and then sending a response to your browser.

None of this actually requires any interaction with what you, as a user, see on your screen (what is generally called the presentation layer). Selenium is a tool that explicitly interacts with the presentation layer. Why would we want to use a tool that is designed to interact with the presentation layer to try and send lots of network traffic to a server?

If the only tool that you have in your toolbox is a hammer, everything starts to look like a nail. You see that screw, it's sort of nail shaped and if you hit it hard enough with a hammer it will probably go into the wall. You will probably be able to successfully hang a picture from it as well…

This sort of scenario often happens with Selenium. You will find testers who have lots of Selenium experience but not much exposure to other tools. This is when Selenium starts to become their hammer. This is generally why people start to use a tool such as Selenium to do performance tests.

So, if it is a bad idea why are we even talking about it? Well, we can still use Selenium to help us create our performance tests and, thanks to the proxy implementation that we wrote earlier in this chapter, it's really easy!

What we are going to do is start JMeter up as a proxy server that records network traffic. We will then get Selenium to run a test while connecting through this proxy. As the Selenium test drives the browser, network requests will be made to our server and the JMeter proxy will collect them and build a basic test plan.

Obviously, creating a performance test plan is not quite as simple as just recoding the requests that have been captured and then playing them back. It does, however, give us a solid base to build upon. This will be useful where we have a series of user journeys already written in Selenium and we would like to take these user journeys and use them as the basis for our performance testing.

The focus here is on how to use Selenium to create that solid base that can be either built upon, or passed over to the people who are going to build the performance test scripts to get them started.

So first of all let's start up JMeter and set up the proxy that we are going to connect Selenium to. First of all we need to add an HTTP(S) test script recorder by performing the actions shown in the screenshot:

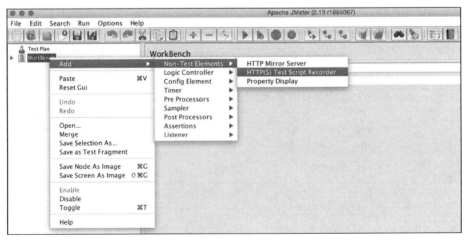

Creating a test script recorder

Then we just click on **Start**

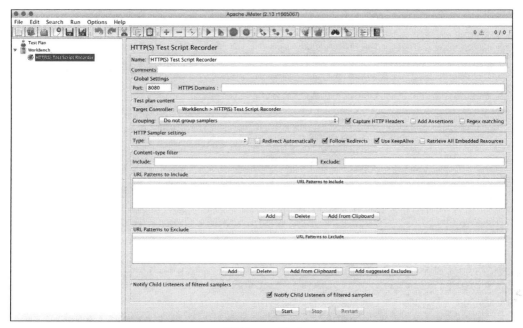

Clicking on **Start**

Our JMeter proxy is now up and running and ready to accept connections. So we now need to run our Selenium tests and tell them to connect to the JMeter proxy. Since we have already extended our Selenium framework to support proxies, all we need to do is provide the proxy details on the command line:

```
mvn clean install -DproxyEnabled=true -
DproxyHost=localhost -DproxyPort=8080
```

Now wait for your tests to run and you're done. Stop the JMeter proxy, save the test plan, and you have the start of a performance test plan in JMeter that is all ready to be built upon.

Don't use multiple threads when using a JMeter proxy to make things go faster. You want to capture user journeys that make sense and can be traced based upon the network requests. If you run more than one thread in parallel, you will get the network requests for all the tests running in parallel mixed up.

Penetration testing with Selenium

Penetration testing is one of those things that people don't often think about while they are building a product. It's usually seen as a phase of testing that is performed by a third party who has expertise in that area once a release has passed normal testing.

The problem with this view is that fixing security problems at this point may well be very expensive and require large amounts of refactoring, or even rewrites. Wouldn't it be good if we could do as much penetration testing as possible in the early development phases? This would give us a fast feedback loop that would allow us to make changes earlier in the development life cycle at a greatly reduced cost.

Selenium does not have any penetration testing functionality built in, but we can use other tools to supplement it. One excellent tool that can work well with Selenium is the **Zed Attack Proxy (ZAP)**. For more information about ZAP, have a look at `https://www.owasp.org/index.php/OWASP_Zed_Attack_Proxy_Project`.

ZAP is a penetration testing tool that searches for vulnerabilities in web applications. It is a proxy that sits between your browser and the website you are testing. As you use the website you are testing, ZAP logs all of the network calls and uses them to build up a series of attack profiles. The more functionality on your website you use, the more information ZAP has to build these attack profiles.

Once you have walked through the functionality of your site, you can tell ZAP to build a series of attack profiles based upon the information it has collected. ZAP then starts a series of attacks on your site and logs any potential vulnerability that it finds.

Obviously, the more functionality you use, the more information ZAP has and the better its attacks are. If you are testing your website with Selenium, it's probably a pretty safe bet that you cover a large percentage of functionality with your tests.

So what we are going to do is set ZAP up as a proxy and then use our proxy implementation to run our Selenium tests through ZAP so that it can generate an attack profile for our site.

Setting up ZAP is nice and simple:

1. First of all, open up ZAP.

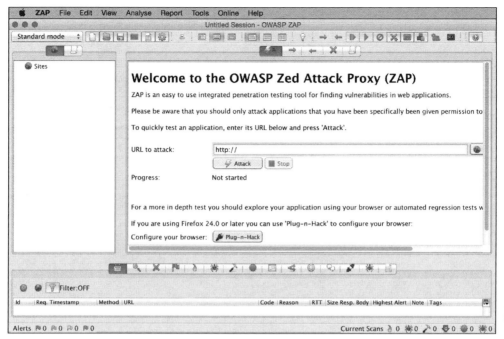

Starting up ZAP

2. Then go to **Tools | Options**.

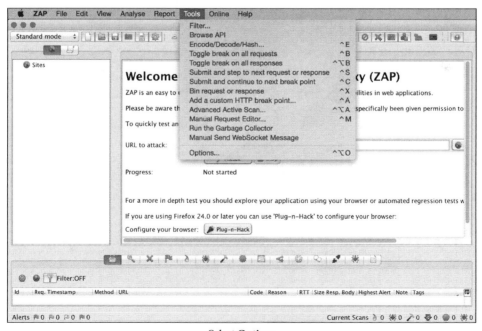

Select **Options**

3. Next, select **Local proxy**.

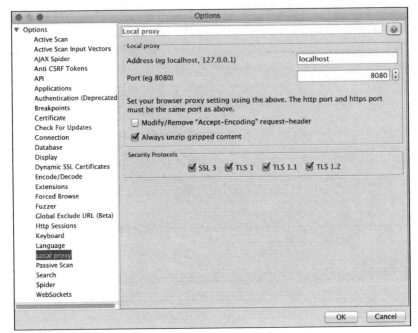

Select **Local proxy**

4. Finally, set the proxy address to localhost, and select a port; we will use 8080 for this example.

Now we need to run our Selenium tests using this proxy so that ZAP can monitor our network traffic and build attack profiles. Use the following command:

```
mvn clean install -DproxyEnabled=true -DproxyHost=localhost -
DproxyPort=8080
```

Now wait for your tests to complete and you're done. You can now tell ZAP to start attacking the site that you are testing. As it performs its attacks, it will highlight vulnerabilities and at the end will give you a list of things that need investigating.

ZAP can be very verbose and you should remember that it is reporting potential vulnerabilities. Not everything that it logs is a problem that needs a high-priority fix; some may be vulnerabilities in technologies that you aren't currently using. A lot of people get a nasty shock when they first run their website through ZAP.

Summary

In this chapter we have had a look at things that Selenium cannot do. We have also explored ways in which we can extend Selenium to work with other tools that can provide us with a more complete testing toolbox.

By the end of this chapter you should be able to:

- Check for dead links
- Download and validate files
- Use Selenium with various proxies (for example, for tracking network traffic)
- Use your Selenium tests as a base for performance tests in JMeter
- Use your Selenium tests to build attack profiles for penetration tests

In the next chapter, we are going to look at the how we can use Docker with Selenium. We will see how easy it is to start spinning up your own grid in Docker. We will also look at how we can integrate Docker into our build process.

9
Hooking Docker into Selenium

In this chapter, we will have a look at how we can get started with Docker and use it with Selenium. We will:

- Install Docker on our machines
- Set up Selenium Grid using Docker
- Learn how to start Docker containers as a part of our build

This will be a brief introduction to Docker and how it can be used with Selenium. It should give you an idea of the potential capabilities of Docker and get you thinking about ways in which you could integrate it into your current build process.

Introducing Docker

So, what is Docker?

Well, Docker is like a **VM (virtual machine)**, but it's not. In a traditional VM setup, you would take a machine, install an operating system on that machine, and then install a hypervisor such as VirtualBox (for more information, visit `https://www.virtualbox.org`) or VMware (for more information about VMware, check out `http://www.vmware.com`). You could then create a VM image on the hypervisor, which pretends to be a computer. This image would have its own BIOS and emulated hardware. You would then install an OS (operating system) on this image. This is generally referred to as the guest OS.

Once this is done, you would boot up the guest OS and treat it like any other computer. If you want to isolate your applications, you can create multiple guest operating systems, but this can be costly.

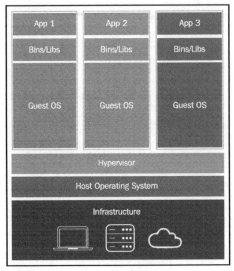

A traditional virtual machine

Docker is slightly different. It is a program that you install on the host machine instead of the hypervisor. Docker can then start up an application in what is known as a container. Containers are totally isolated, just like a virtual machine. However, Docker uses the host OS instead of a guest OS.

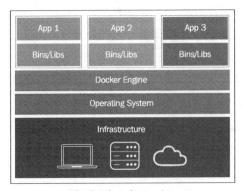

The Docker alternative

This gives you some advantages, which are as follows:

- Containers are not as resource-intensive as virtual machines
- Containers can start up much faster than virtual machines

So, how does Docker do this? Well, it uses a Linux technology called **namespaces**. The following are the Linux namespaces:

- `pid`: This is used for process isolation
- `net`: This is used to manage network interfaces
- `ipc`: This is used to manage interprocess communication
- `mnt`: This is used to manage mount points
- `uts`: This is used to isolate kernel and version identifiers

Docker uses these namespaces to isolate containers. This means that they are unaware of anything else that is running on the host OS. These containers have their own isolated process tree, their own isolated network stack, and so on.

The wonderful thing about Docker is that all of these containers can be made to interact with each other. This means that you can take lots of individual containers and stick them together to make something quite complex.

Let's use a basic **LNMP (Linux, Nginx, MySQL, and PHP)** setup as an example. Normally, you would create a Linux virtual machine and then install Nginx, PHP, and MySQL on it.

With Docker, you can split up this stack with multiple containers. The most common setup would be an Nginx container with added PHP support and a MySQL container. You can then link these two containers together to give you the LNMP stack.

For example, if you wanted to update MySQL, you would just delete the MySQL container and add a new one.

Wait a second! If I delete MySQL and start it up again, would I lose all my data?

Well, that's not a problem. Docker can also create data-only containers. So, you can create a data-only container that holds all the data that MySQL writes to the disk that is totally isolated from the MySQL install.

Docker can be extremely powerful. The hardest part is figuring out how to reduce your containers into single processes. People are so used to thinking along the lines of working systems with multiple components that it's hard to break out of this mindset.

All of this sounds great, but how do we use it?

Installing Docker

The easiest way to get Docker up and running depends on the operating system that you are using. Docker needs Linux. So, if you are running Linux, the process should be very simple. If you are using Windows or OS X, it's a little bit more complicated because you will need to use a virtual machine to run a Linux image that can run Docker. Let's start with Linux.

Linux

We are going to focus on an Ubuntu install in this section since it is one of the most popular Linux distributions. You don't need to run Ubuntu to be able to install Docker. Docker supports many different Linux distributions, and there are installation instructions for all of them available on the Docker website (for more information, visit `https://docs.docker.com/installation/`).

With Ubuntu, the first thing that you should do is check out the kernel version that you are running. You can do this with the help of the following command:

```
uname -r
```

If you are running a kernel version of 3.10 or higher, you should be fine.

> Some versions of Ubuntu are known to be problematic with a 3.10 kernel. If you are running one of these versions, you may need to upgrade your kernel to 3.13. Have a look at the installation documentation on the Docker website, `https://docs.docker.com/installation/ubuntulinux/`, for more information.

Our second dependency is a copy of `wget`. You probably already have this installed, but if you don't, installing it is nice and simple.

```
apt-get install wget
```

Finally, we need to download and install the Docker package (this command will ask you for your sudo password), as follows:

```
wget -qO- https://get.docker.com/ | sh
```

That's it. You should now have a shiny new Docker installation all ready for you to play with. You can check whether it worked by running the following command in your terminal:

```
sudo docker run hello-world
```

If everything is working, you should get something that looks like this:

```
Hello from Docker.
This message shows that your installation appears to be working correctly.

To generate this message, Docker took the following steps:
 1. The Docker client contacted the Docker daemon.
 2. The Docker daemon pulled the "hello-world" image from the Docker Hub.
    (Assuming it was not already locally available.)
 3. The Docker daemon created a new container from that image which runs the
    executable that produces the output you are currently reading.
 4. The Docker daemon streamed that output to the Docker client, which sent it
    to your terminal.

To try something more ambitious, you can run an Ubuntu container with:
 $ docker run -it ubuntu bash

For more examples and ideas, visit:
 http://docs.docker.com/userguide/
```

Hello world

Windows / OS X

The Windows and OS X installations are very similar to each other.

This information is for Windows 8.1 or lower. Windows 10 doesn't work yet (at the time of publishing this book), the next version of Windows Server is adding native Docker support. If this happens, the setup is going to be different. It may come bundled with Windows if we are lucky. If not, there will be a specific Docker install that doesn't require the use of a virtual machine.

First of all, you will need to go to `http://boot2docker.io` and download the appropriate installation package for your operating system. Then, you just need to run it:

Starting a boot2docker install

It is really just a case of making sure that you install everything and then wait for the installation to complete.

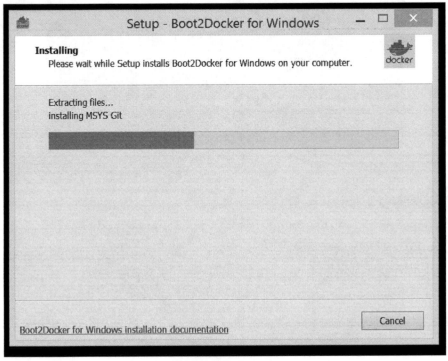

Installing boot2Docker

When it is finished, you will have an install of VirtualBox and Git as well as the all-important Docker VM. At this point, an icon will have been placed on your desktop, which you can use to perform an initial Docker run.

The boot2docker desktop icon

Now, if you run this, Docker will start up and a very basic Hello World container will be downloaded and spun up to let you know that everything is working as expected. That's it. Docker is now installed.

But it didn't work...

One common problem that usually affects Windows users who haven't run VMs on their machine before is a BIOS setting that prevents VirtualBox from working. Try starting the Docker VM by opening VirtualBox and running the VM manually. If you see a screen like this, it's a problem with your BIOS settings (or your hardware is just too old to run virtualization):

Virtualization turned off in your BIOS

If you are affected, you will need to go into your BIOS and find a setting related to virtualization and turn it on. It's usually got a slightly different name on every machine, and hence the slightly vague recommendation.

Once you have turned on the BIOS setting, reboot your machine and try starting up boot2docker again.

Getting started with boot2docker

You are now ready to open a terminal (or a Git Bash shell in Windows) and start using Docker. When you have opened your terminal, the first thing that you will need to do is execute this command:

```
boot2docker up
```

This will start up the Docker VM. You will be given three environmental variables that need to be configured to be able to enter the Docker commands directly into your terminal. Copying and pasting them should be sufficient.

Having problems on Windows? Don't forget to escape all \ characters. Still having problems? You can try setting up a System Environmental Variable. Use Windows key + *Pause* to get into the correct dialog.

In case you do have any problems, here is a quick cheat sheet that shows useful boot2docker commands:

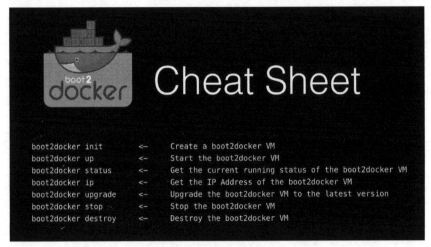

boot2docker cheat sheet

Now that we have Docker installed, let's use it to do something really useful.

Spinning up a Selenium Grid with Docker

At some point, most people who use Selenium have tried to get Selenium Grid up and running. As with getting any service up and running, it's normally a real pain. Some pain points that you may have come across are as follows:

- What software do I need to install to get Selenium Grid up and running?
- How do we keep Selenium up to date?
- How do we keep the browsers up to date?
- How do we deal with browsers becoming nonresponsive on the nodes?
- How do we deal with nonresponsive nodes in general?
- How do I ensure that the driver binaries (such as ChromeDriver) are kept up to date?

We can remove some of these pain points with Docker. Let's start off by spinning up Selenium Grid with Docker.

The general philosophy behind Docker is to have small containers that do only one thing. Unfortunately, the Selenium Docker images are a bit bigger than most images because they need to have access to some form of GUI as well as full-browser installs. The next step may take a while if you have a slow Internet connection.

First of all, we will need to pull down some containers from the Docker registry (for more information, visit `https://registry.hub.docker.com`). There are three images that we will need to get, which are as follows:

- The Selenium Grid hub
- The Firefox Selenium Grid node
- The Chrome Selenium Grid node

We can do this by using the pull command, as follows:

```
docker pull selenium/hub:2.45.0
docker pull node-firefox:2.45.0
docker pull node-chrome:2.45.0
```

This will download the three containers that we need to build Selenium Grid. Once we have downloaded these images, we can start them up. First of all, we will need to start up the Selenium Grid hub, as follows:

```
docker run -d -p 4444:4444 --name selenium-hub selenium/hub:2.45.0
```

Let's work through this command. The `-d` parameter will ensure that the `selenium-hub` container runs as a daemon. Docker containers are designed to start up, perform their intended function, and then shut down again. If you don't use `-d`, the container will instantly shut down. Next, we mapped a tunnel between the Docker container and the Docker host using port 4444 so that we can talk to the container using the host's IP address. Each Docker container has its own isolated network stack, and it will not be able to see anything that is not linked to it in some way. Then, we gave our container a name so that we can easily identify it. In this case, we called it `selenium-hub`. Finally, we specified the container identifier and the version that we want to spin up.

> If you try to run a container but you haven't pulled down the image, Docker will automatically try and pull it down for you.

Once the container has started, we can check whether it is there by using the following command:

```
docker ps
```

This will show us a list of all the containers that are currently running. Since we opened a tunnel to the Docker host, we will also be able to open a web browser and browse to the Selenium Grid console. To do this, we will need to use the IP address of the Docker host. If you are using Linux, it will be as follows:

```
http://127.0.0.1:4444/grid/console
```

If you are using boot2docker, you will need to get the IP address of the boot2docker VM and use it instead. To get the IP address, you will need to type the following in the terminal window:

```
boot2docker ip
```

You will then end up with a Selenium Grid console URL like this:

```
http://192.168.59.103:4444/grid/console
```

If you navigate to this URL in your browser, it should look like this:

The initial Selenium Grid console

We now need to spin up some nodes to connect these to Selenium Grid. Let's start with Firefox:

```
docker run -d --link selenium-hub:hub selenium/node-firefox:2.45.0
```

As we did before, we are running the container as a Daemon so that it does not shut down. However, we have not opened up a port between the container and the Docker host this time. Instead, we are linking this container to the container that we have already started—selenium-hub. We haven't specified a name for this node, but that's not a problem. If you don't specify a name, Docker will automatically allocate one for you. Finally, like the last command, we specify the container identifier and version.

If you refresh your browser, it should now look like this:

The Firefox node added

Next, we are going to add a Chrome node to give us an additional browser option, as follows:

```
docker run -d --link selenium-hub:hub selenium/node-chrome:2.45.0
```

The command is exactly the same as before. We just specified a different container ID this time. If you refresh your browser, it should now look like this:

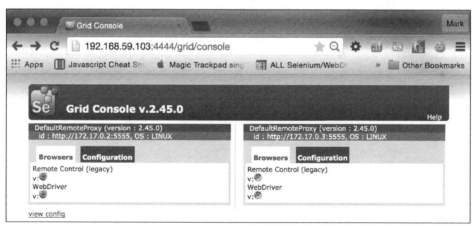

The Chrome node added

Now, in your terminal, try typing the following:

```
docker ps
```

This will show you a list of containers that are currently active, as follows:

CONTAINER ID	IMAGE	COMMAND	CREATED	STATUS	PORTS	NAMES
8b571c4bqbf9	selenium/node-chrome:2.45.0	"/opt/bin/entry_poin	2 hours ago	Up 2 hours		agitated_curie
d5136e55a100	selenium/node-firefox:2.45.0	"/opt/bin/entry_poin	2 hours ago	Up 2 hours		suspicious_jones
c1e265d60bcf	selenium/hub:2.45.0	"/opt/bin/entry_poin	2 hours ago	Up 2 hours	0.0.0.0:4444->4444/tcp	selenium-hub

The Docker process list

You will see that even though we didn't name the nodes that we started up, Docker has generated a unique name for them. Let's start up some more chrome nodes, as follows:

```
docker run -d --link selenium-hub:hub selenium/node-chrome:2.45.0

docker run -d --link selenium-hub:hub selenium/node-chrome:2.45.0

docker run -d --link selenium-hub:hub selenium/node-chrome:2.45.0

docker run -d --link selenium-hub:hub selenium/node-chrome:2.45.0
```

Note that we used exactly the same command as before, but we didn't have any errors. If you refresh your browser, you will now see all the additional nodes that we started:

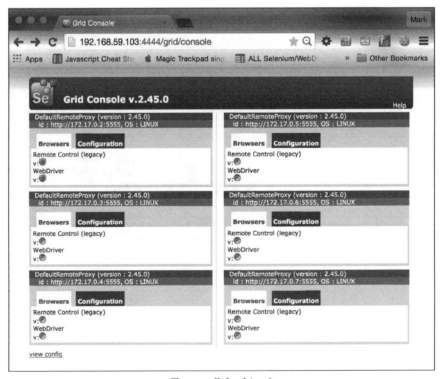

Chrome all the things!

Now, if you rerun the `docker ps` command, you will see the following additional nodes in your terminal:

All the container processes

You can spin up as many nodes as you like in this fashion. You are only limited by your computing power. If you decide that you don't need these many nodes, you can start shutting down some of them. Let's shut down one of the Chrome nodes because we have loads of them. The one that we are going to shut down has a container ID of `8f09bb8e2335`:

```
docker stop 8f09bb8e2335
```

 Different machines are capable of running a different number of containers. If your machine is struggling with five nodes, you may want to shut down some more. As a rule of thumb, figure out how many browsers you can open in parallel. Your machines should be able to handle the same number of nodes.

If you rerun the `docker ps` command, you will now see that we only have five nodes running:

One process has gone

However, try running the following command:

```
docker ps -a
```

In this case, we will see all six again, as follows:

Why do we see them all?

Docker doesn't remove your containers when you stop them so that you can do things such as look at the logs or copy the contents of the container into a tar file so that you can examine them. Once the container is stopped, it is dead though; you cannot restart it. Once you have finished with your stopped container, you can remove it with the following command:

```
docker rm 8f09bb8e2335
```

If you have stopped a container with a specific name (for example, the `selenium-hub` container), you will need to remove it before you can start another container with the same name.

If you have a lot of containers running, it can be very time-consuming to stop each one by container ID. However, there is a nice shortcut that we can use to stop all the containers:

```
docker stop $(docker ps -q)
```

> `$(docker ps -a)` is a BASH trick called command substitution. It takes the output of any command and replaces itself with the output. See `http://www.tldp.org/LDP/abs/html/commandsub.html` for more information.

This also works if you want to remove images:

```
docker rm $(docker ps -qa)
```

So, we now have a quick and easy way to start up Selenium Grid, and we can quickly tear it down again when we are finished with it.

Running tests against our new Selenium Grid

We now know how to quickly spin up Selenium Grid, but so far, we haven't seen it in action. Let's face it. It's not of much use if we can't use it to run some tests. If you have shut down Selenium Grid, you will need to start it up again:

```
docker run -d -p 4444:4444 --name selenium-hub selenium/hub:2.45.0
docker run -d --link selenium-hub:hub selenium/node-chrome:2.45.0
docker run -d --link selenium-hub:hub selenium/node-firefox:2.45.0
```

Next, we are going to reuse the Selenium framework that we built in *Chapter 1,* *Creating a Fast Feedback Loop,* and *Chapter 2, Producing the Right Feedback When Failing.* It already supports connections to Selenium Grid. So, we just need to specify the URL of the grid.

If you are using boot2docker on Windows or OS X, this is going to require a little bit of configuration because we can't connect to localhost to interact with Docker. Instead, we need to use a command to find out the IP address that the boot2docker VM is using so that we can connect to it. Don't worry. It is not difficult. You just need to type in the following:

```
boot2docker ip
```

In our case, the boot2docker IP address is 192.168.59.103, which means that we are going to need to run the following command:

```
mvn clean install -Dremote=true -Dbrowser=firefox -
DgridURL=http://192.168.59.103:4444/wd/hub
```

You can of course cheat when you are using a Bash shell and use the following command:

```
mvn clean install -Dremote=true -Dbrowser=firefox
-DgridURL=http://`boot2docker ip`:4444/wd/hub
```

Or finally, you can use the VirtualBox command line to set up port forwarding from your boot2docker VM to localhost, as follows:

```
VBoxManage controlvm boot2docker-vm natpf1 'seleniumgrid,t
cp,127.0.0.1,4444,,4444'
```

As you can see, you have a lot of options available. The one that you select will end up being your personal preference.

If you are using Linux, Docker is running natively. So, you don't need to worry about additional port forwarding.

Then, you can use the following command:

```
mvn clean install -Dremote=true -Dbrowser=firefox
-DgridURL=http://127.0.0.1:4444/wd/hub
```

This will run our tests against Selenium Grid, which has been set up in Docker. Refresh the grid console when you have started the tests and watch the status of the nodes change. You can try using multiple threads to use multiple nodes, as follows:

```
mvn clean install -Dremote=true -Dbrowser=chrome
-DgridURL=http://127.0.0.1:4444/wd/hub -Dthreads=2
```

Alternatively, you can even modify one of your tests to make them fail. If you do this, a screenshot will be taken to show you what was happening in the browser when the test failed.

This is a fully functional grid that can be used for real testing!

One final thing to note if you did set up port forwarding is that when you are done with your containers, you can remove it by running the following code:

```
VBoxManage controlvm boot2docker-vm natpf1 delete 'seleniumgrid'
```

Starting up Docker containers as part of the build

As we have seen, it's really easy to spin up and shut down the Docker containers. Wouldn't it be useful if we could do that as a part of a build?

In a perfect world, our build process would build our application and then install it in a Docker container. We would then be able to run tests against this container, and if everything worked as expected, we could publish the container in a private Docker registry. We could then take this Docker container and pass it through our promotional model until it hits live. We would then have something in live that is identical to the container that we originally built and tested. Thus, we would know that it works. If we have any problems with it in live, we can easily spin up another instance of this container in a test environment to reproduce the problem. Rather than passing around application installers, we can instead pass around preinstalled and working applications.

Let's have a look at how we can spin up containers as a part of our build. For this example, we are going to spin up the same Selenium Grid that we created earlier. Then, we are going to run a couple of tests against it to prove that it works. This process can of course be used to spin up any type of container for any purpose. This example is really just a quick exercise to get you up and running.

We are going to build a project structure that looks like this:

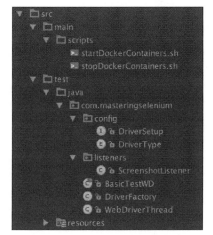

The project structure

As you can see from the preceding screenshot, the first thing that we need to do is write a couple of shell scripts to control Docker. Our first script is going to start up our containers and will be called startDockerContainers.sh.

```
#!/usr/bin/env bash
```

```
docker run -d -p 4444:4444 --name selenium-hub selenium/hub:2.45.0
docker run -d --link selenium-hub:hub selenium/node-chrome:2.45.0
docker run -d --link selenium-hub:hub selenium/node-firefox:2.45.0
```

Our second script is going to shut down the containers and remove them. It will be called stopDockerContainers.sh.

```
#!/usr/bin/env bash
```

```
docker stop $(docker ps -q)
docker rm $(docker ps -qa)
```

Since we are expanding upon the original Selenium implementation that we wrote in *Chapter 1, Creating a Fast Feedback Loop*, and *Chapter 2, Producing the Right Feedback When Failing*, we are using the `maven-failsafe-plugin`. This means that all the tests are executed in the integration phase. Due to this, we are going to start up the Docker containers in the pre-integration phase and then shut them down again in the post-integration phase. It's a Maven project. So, we are going to use a Maven plugin to execute these shell scripts in the relevant phases:

```xml
<plugin>
    <artifactId>exec-maven-plugin</artifactId>
    <groupId>org.codehaus.mojo</groupId>
    <executions>
        <execution>
            <id>Start Docker</id>
            <phase>pre-integration-test</phase>
            <goals>
                <goal>exec</goal>
            </goals>
            <configuration>
                <executable>${project.build.scriptSourceDirectory}
                /startDockerContainers.sh</executable>
            </configuration>
        </execution>
        <execution>
            <id>Stop Docker</id>
            <phase>post-integration-test</phase>
            <goals>
                <goal>exec</goal>
            </goals>
            <configuration>
                <executable>${project.build.scriptSourceDirectory}
                /stopDockerContainers.sh</executable>
            </configuration>
        </execution>
    </executions>
</plugin>
```

Don't forget to make your shell scripts executable. If you don't, the `exec-maven-plugin` will not be able to execute them!

We used a standard Maven project structure while creating our scripts. This means that we can use ${project.build.scriptSourceDirectory} Maven variable to locate our scripts easily in the POM.

We can now run our tests, and the containers will stop and start as part of the build. We haven't quite finished yet though. We need to know how to connect to Selenium Grid, which will be spun up as part of the build. Don't worry. It's not hard. It is exactly the same command that you used when Selenium Grid was not a part of the build. We are going to assume that you are either using Linux, or used the VirtualBox command to set up port forwarding for this section. You'll need to replace the localhost IP address with the actual IP address that you are using if this is not the case.

```
mvn clean install -Dremote=true -Dbrowser=firefox
-DgridURL=http://127.0.0.1:4444/wd/hub
```

Docker containers start up very quickly, but sometimes, you may need to make sure that the container has started before moving on to the next step of actually using it. We can do this by modifying the startDockerContainers.sh file, as follows:

```
#!/usr/bin/env bash


docker run -d -p 4444:4444 --name selenium-hub selenium/hub:2.45.0
docker run -d --link selenium-hub:hub selenium/node-chrome:2.45.0
docker run -d --link selenium-hub:hub selenium/node-firefox:2.45.0


echo -n "Waiting for grid to load."
while ! curl http://127.0.0.1:4444/grid/console > /dev/null 2>&1
do
  echo -n "."
  sleep 1
done
echo " "
echo "Connected to grid successfully"
```

What we have looked at so far is very much script-based. Maybe we should explore options that are more Maven-centric.

Using a Docker Maven plugin

There is `docker-maven` plugin available. In fact, there is more than one available.
I found seven when I went looking, and there are probably more now. At the time
of writing this book, all of the plugins suffered from one fatal flaw—they didn't
support Linux sockets. This means that they are only really useful if you are running
boot2docker at the moment. This really isn't ideal, but it's still worth investigating
how we can use them. The first one that I tried that really met my needs was the one
written by Wouter Danes (for more information, visit `https://github.com/wouterd/`
`docker-maven-plugin`). He also has Linux socket support on his list of intended
features. So, though it may not be good for Linux users right now, it hopefully will
be in the future.

We are going to base this Maven implementation off the shell scripts that we wrote
previously:

```xml
<plugin>
    <groupId>net.wouterdanes.docker</groupId>
    <artifactId>docker-maven-plugin</artifactId>
    <version>3.0</version>
    <executions>
        <execution>
            <id>start</id>
            <configuration>
                <containers>
                    <container>
                        <id>selenium-hub</id>
                        <image>selenium/hub:2.45.0</image>
                        <waitForStartup>Started SocketConnector
                        @0.0.0.0:4444</waitForStartup>
                    </container>
                    <container>
                        <id>selenium-chrome</id>
                        <image>selenium/node-chrome:2.45.0</image>
                        <links>
                            <link>
                                <containerId>selenium-hub
                                </containerId>
                                <containerAlias>hub
                                </containerAlias>
                            </link>
                        </links>
                    </container>
```

```
            <container>
                <id>selenium-firefox</id>
                <image>selenium/
                node-firefox:2.45.0</image>
                <links>
                    <link>
                        <containerId>selenium-hub
                        </containerId>
                        <containerAlias>hub
                        </containerAlias>
                    </link>
                </links>
            </container>
        </containers>
    </configuration>
    <goals>
        <goal>start-containers</goal>
    </goals>
</execution>
<execution>
    <id>stop</id>
    <goals>
        <goal>stop-containers</goal>
    </goals>
</execution>
        </executions>
    </plugin>
```

This can be broken down into three parts. First of all, we have the execution block where we define our containers. In this case, we have the same three containers that we had with our shell script. The first one is selenium-hub, which has a waitForStartup configuration element, where we can enter a regex that matches some content that will be displayed in the logs when the container has started up correctly. We then have the two Selenium Grid nodes, which are both linked to selenium-hub using the links configuration element.

Our second execution block is the one that starts up the containers and runs in the pre-integration-test phase. This mirrors what our exec-maven-plugin was doing in the pre-integration-test phase.

Finally, we have our last execution block that will shut down and remove our containers and is run in the post-integration-test phase. This, again, mirrors what the exec-maven-plugin was doing in the post-integration-test phase.

So far, the functionality looks identical to our previous implementation. We have one little extra piece that this Maven plugin gives us though. We are going to tweak the `seleniumGrilURL` property in the POM to let the plugin pass the Docker container IP address and port to the tests by default, as follows:

```
<seleniumGridURL>http://${docker.containers.
selenium-hub.ports.4444/tcp.host}:${docker.containers.
selenium-hub.ports.4444/tcp.port}/wd/hub</seleniumGridURL>
```

This is going to simplify what we run on the console because now, we no longer have to specify `seleniumGridUrl`. We are going to cheat a little bit more. We now know that we are going to run our tests by default against Selenium Grid, which is spun up by Docker, and we know that the Docker container host and port are going to automatically get passed into the test. So, we are going to change our remote property to default to `true`.

```
<remote>true</remote>
```

Now, we just need to run a test and see it in action:

```
mvn clean install
```

We haven't specified a browser, because we don't really mind which one is picked up. So, it will probably pick up Firefox by default. You will see that our test ran as before, but the output looks a lot more like the standard maven output this time.

The future with Docker

Right now, Docker does have some quite obvious limitations. It can only run Linux containers. This means that although it is easy to spin up Selenium Grid consisting of a Linux browser, we cannot create or start Windows containers. This means that running IE in a container is just not possible (unless you try to do something nasty with Wine).

However, all is not lost. Microsoft is currently working very closely with Docker, and they have already announced that The next release of Windows Server will have Docker support. Even better than that, you will be able to use Windows containers with Docker. So, in the future, we should be able to have IE running as a container. On the not-so-positive side, it's extremely unlikely that we will see older versions of IE running in containers. That being said, Microsoft is removing support for all of its old browsers and doing everything they can to get people to upgrade. So maybe it won't matter.

Summary

In this chapter, we had a look at Docker and how we can use it to start up Selenium Grid. Though this chapter was very much focused on running Selenium Grid, you should be able to see many more potential applications of Docker. New skills that you have gained will include:

- A good basic understanding of what Docker is and how it can help you
- Knowing how to install Docker or boot2docker on your machine
- Being able to quickly spin up Selenium Grid using Docker containers
- Be able to start and stop Docker containers as a part of your build process

In the next chapter, we are going to look at how you can help improve Selenium by fixing bugs and implementing new features. We will also examine what is in store for Selenium in the future as it becomes a W3C specification.

10
Selenium – the Future

In this chapter, we will have a look at what the upcoming Selenium W3C specification is and how it is going to affect the future of Selenium.

We will then have a look at how you can help Selenium meet its potential. To get involved with Selenium, you will need to have the following:

- A GitHub account
- A working Maven installation
- A working Python installation (at least version 2.7.9 to ensure that pip is bundled with it)

Selenium – the future of browser and device testing

The Selenium WebDriver API is becoming a W3C specification. It is still currently in the draft form, but work is in progress. So, how will the WebDriver API, which is becoming a W3C specification, affect the language bindings that I'm using? What does it mean to me?

Before we get into this, let's have a look at the basic architectural overview of Selenium. It will help us understand the scope of the specification.

First of all, we need to understand how Selenium works when it uses the WebDriver API (this is going to be the only API available for Selenium version 3.0 and higher). In Selenium, there are two main components. There is a local component with which the various language bindings interact. When you write your tests in the programming language of your choice, it is this local component that you are controlling. Then there is the remote component. This is the part of Selenium that receives commands from the local component and drives the browser.

An example of a remote component is ChromeDriver.

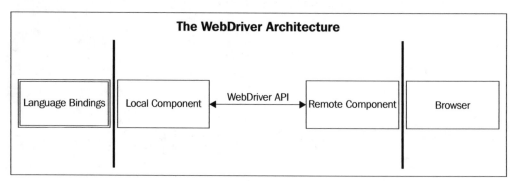

The WebDriver architecture

The local component and the remote component need to talk to each other so that your commands can be sent across to the browser. The communication between these two components is what the WebDriver W3C specification is documenting.

What this means is that the way the language bindings are written is not directly dependent on the W3C specification. They will continue to be idiomatic and should still feel natural to somebody who is used to using that language on a day-to-day basis. It is obvious that if we need to remove or add a functionality to be W3C-compliant, there will be changes at the language level, but they will be no different to the changes that are made to the language bindings that you would see if a functionality was added or removed.

So if it's just the interaction between the local and remote parts, it doesn't really affect me. Why should I care?

When the WebDriver API becomes a W3C specification (like HTML and CSS), it will be the standard way of automating browsers. This means that we are going to need people who know how to use Selenium because it is how browser automation will be done. All the skills that you have learned, or are learning, will be the skills that everybody is going to need to learn.

Everybody needs to learn Selenium, are you sure?

Well, all the big players are already writing their own driver implementations. Mozilla is hard at work on Marionette, which will drive Firefox. Google has already published ChromeDriver to drive Chrome. Opera has a blink-based OperaDriver, which can control the latest version of Opera. Even Microsoft is getting involved; there is already an IE WebDriver tool for IE11 developed by Microsoft that you can download and use today (for more information, visit `https://www.microsoft.com/en-us/download/details.aspx?id=44069`).

The other thing to note is that operating systems such as Chrome OS and Firefox OS are web-based. This means that you can drive them with the WebDriver API.

There is one notable omission in the previous line, and that is Apple. Currently (at the time of writing this book), Apple hasn't been involved in the WebDriver W3C specification. That being said, if the whole industry moves over to using the WebDriver W3C specification, it's really hard to test Safari. People will just start dropping support for Safari. It makes sense for Apple to implement it in some form in the future if they don't want Safari to become an obsolete browser.

It all sounds great so far, but is the WebDriver W3C specification going to add anything new?

The specification will clarify the implementation that the existing driver implementations should follow, and it will be adding more stuff as well. One of the really good things about moving forward will be a multi-touch API. Mobile devices are making up a greater percentage of the web market. Providing an automation API for web-enabled touch screen devices such as phones is going to be very important.

A more refined screenshot capability is currently planned to be a part of the specification. Wouldn't it be great if rather than taking a screenshot of a whole page, you could take a screenshot of a specific element? Breaking up a website into manageable chunks is one way to make image comparison useful. Sikuli has already demonstrated that this technology is usable. Now, Selenium is going to turn it into a standard.

The specification is still being worked on, and the current revision is available at `http://w3c.github.io/webdriver/webdriver-spec.html`. If you want to, you can still get involved. The specification is on GitHub. So, you can clone the repo and raise pull requests. For more information, visit `https://github.com/w3c/webdriver`.

If Selenium is the future, how can I help?

Well, there are lots of ways in which you can help the Selenium project. Believe it or not, it's not just hardcore coding skills that are required.

The first and the most important thing that you can do is find problems with Selenium and report them. The Selenium developers do an awesome job, but they are not infallible. They need your help with finding problems and raising defects so that they can fix them and make Selenium even better.

The problem with a lot of bugs that get raised against Selenium is that they are unclear and range from hard to impossible to replicate. One of the best things that you can supply when you raise a defect is a Selenium script that reproduces the problem. This gives the developers a way to see the issue firsthand, and it aids massively in regards debugging. It can also form the basis of a test to ensure that once fixed, the problem doesn't raise its ugly head again in the future.

That being said, you don't need to have a prewritten script that shows your problem. However, you do need to be very clear about what your problem is. Bugs that sound kind of valid but don't really have enough information so that they can be replicated are the worst. If a developer takes a day trying to make sense of a badly written bug report and gets so frustrated that they don't want to look at the Selenium codebase again for another week, we all lose out.

One of the biggest annoyances is people not providing the Selenium code. Your Selenium code is not special and secret. It's almost guaranteed that somebody else has done it before, and there is a good chance that they have made improvements in some areas. Share your code if you want to get it fixed.

When you raise bugs on Selenium, make sure that you do the following:

- Investigate the issue before you raise it! Don't waste people's time with a one-line bug saying that it doesn't work. What doesn't work?

- Write down the version of Selenium used, the language bindings, the browser, and the OS that you are using.

- Add as much information as possible. Stack traces, screenshots, and HTML code are great. They give people more information so that they are able to diagnose the issue.

- Try to create a Selenium script that reproduces the issue (the smaller the script, the better).

Great bugs mean issues that are easy to reproduce and which can be identified and fixed quickly. Everybody loves well-written bugs.

Getting set up to contribute to a Selenium repository

Selenium has quite a few repositories of code that you can check out, explore, and contribute to. The first thing that you will need to do, to be able to get a local copy, is to install Git (for more information, visit `https://git-scm.com`). Git is available on all the major operating systems. So, installing it should be a relatively pain-free process. If you don't just want to use the command line, you may want to have a look at the following additional clients. Some people like them, whereas others are fine with a terminal:

- TortoiseGit: `https://code.google.com/p/tortoisegit/`
- The GitHub Windows client: `https://windows.github.com`
- The GitHub Mac client: `https://mac.github.com`

Once you have installed Git, you can check out any of the Selenium codebases. When you first start looking at them, don't worry about forking local copies. You'll only need to do this if you want to raise pull requests. All Selenium code repositories are now held on GitHub (for more information, visit `https://github.com/SeleniumHQ`). First of all, the best thing to do is just check out an individual code base and have a play. Let's do this right now. We will start with the Selenium website, `https://github.com/SeleniumHQ/www.seleniumhq.org`.

```
git clone https://github.com/SeleniumHQ/www.seleniumhq.org.git
```

To get everything up and running, we are going to need to install a couple of things:

- Maven
- Python (at least Version 2.7.9 to ensure that pip is bundled with it)

Then, you will need to install Sphinx, as follows:

```
pip install -U Sphinx
```

Sphinx is a documentation generator that is used by the Selenium project to generate the Selenium website (visit `http://sphinx-doc.org` for more information). It will take `reStructuredText` files and convert them into other formats (in this case, HTML). Now, you are ready to build the project:

```
mvn clean install
```

After this, you can start up the site in exploded mode:

```
mvn jetty:run-exploded
```

You can now navigate to the Selenium website in your local browser by visiting `http://localhost:8080/`. If you make changes, they should be automatically updated since you are running the site in exploded mode. All that you will need to do is refresh the browser. Have a look around and see how easy it is to change things.

Aiding the documentation effort

Selenium is a very old project. The original work on it started in 2004. As a result, there have been many changes over the years and, as with all big and old projects, the documentation hasn't always stayed up to date or been as clear as it could be.

If you spend time going through the documentation, you will probably come up with the following:

- Minor errors (such as typos, grammar mistakes, and so on)
- Gaps where some available functionality has never been written about
- Documentation that is either no longer correct, or no longer relevant

Documentation always needs to be updated, and there are never enough people to do it. This is the perfect place to start contributing to the Selenium project. The documentation is roughly split into two areas. There is the existing Selenium HQ site, which contains the current documentation (for more information, visit `http://docs.seleniumhq.org/docs/`). There is also the new documentation project, which was created in 2013. The idea was to start writing the documentation from scratch (visit `http://seleniumhq.github.io/docs/` for additional information).

 The Selenium HQ site is more than just documentation. Don't think that you are limited to just enhancing the documentation. You are quite welcome to contribute a change to any aspect of the site.

Earlier in this chapter, we cloned a copy of the existing SeleniumHQ website. Hopefully, you have already examined and played around with it a bit. If we now want to take the next step and start contributing, we will need to turn our clone into a fork.

The process is very simple. First of all, go to the GitHub page for the documentation and then click on the fork button:

Ready to fork

GitHub will then do all the work for you. When it has finished, it will load the forked version of the site:

Fork complete

Note that on the right-hand side, you now have your own unique clone URL. There are two things that you can do at this point:

- Delete your existing local copy of the documentation and then clone your fork
- Change your remote to point at the new fork on GitHub

Deleting your local copy is easy. Just go to the parent directory that you originally ran your clone command in and use the following command:

```
rm -r www.seleniumhq.org

git clone <your personal clone url>
```

You will now have the forked version of the Selenium website cloned. You just need to set up an upstream remote, as shown in the following section.

 Be very careful whenever you use an `rm -r` or `rm -rf` command. The `-r` stands for recursive (that is, it will delete the directory that you have told it to delete along with the files and directories in the subdirectories of the original directory that you specified). The `-f` stands for force. It will do everything it can to delete the files. If you aren't paying attention and you run the command with elevated privileges, it's very easy to remove the wrong thing, or even everything on your hard drive by mistake!

Let's assume that you have some changes that you don't want to lose. The easiest thing to do in this situation is just change your remote.

We are going to do this in a couple of steps. First of all, we need to have a look at what we currently have set up in Git. We can do this by using the following command to list our remotes:

```
git remote -v
```

You will get something that looks like this:

```
Kezef:www.seleniumhq.org fyre$ git remote -v
origin  https://github.com/SeleniumHQ/www.seleniumhq.org.git (fetch)
origin  https://github.com/SeleniumHQ/www.seleniumhq.org.git (push)
```

The Git remotes

We are going to change the existing remote to an upstream. This will allow us to pull down any changes that are made in SeleniumHQ's copy of the code:

```
git remote set upstream https://github.com/SeleniumHQ/www.seleniumhq.org.git
```

If you check your remotes again, you will now have an upstream and an origin both pointing at the same thing:

```
Kezef:www.seleniumhq.org fyre$ git remote -v
origin  https://github.com/SeleniumHQ/www.seleniumhq.org.git (fetch)
origin  https://github.com/SeleniumHQ/www.seleniumhq.org.git (push)
upstream         https://github.com/SeleniumHQ/www.seleniumhq.org.git (fetch)
upstream         https://github.com/SeleniumHQ/www.seleniumhq.org.git (push)
```

Upstream added

Now, if you want to get your fork up to date with SeleniumHQ's copy of the code, all you need to do is use the following command:

```
git fetch upstream
```

```
git rebase upstream/master
```

This will pull down the latest code from the origin and then rebase it onto your current branch (in this case, origin/master). The final step is to now change our remote to point at the fork. First, copy the clone URL for your fork and then run the following command:

```
git remote set-url origin git@github.com:Ardesco/www.seleniumhq.org.git
```

Your remotes should now look like this:

```
Kezef:www.seleniumhq.org fyre$ git remote -v
origin  git@github.com:Ardesco/www.seleniumhq.org.git (fetch)
origin  git@github.com:Ardesco/www.seleniumhq.org.git (push)
upstream         https://github.com/SeleniumHQ/www.seleniumhq.org.git (fetch)
upstream         https://github.com/SeleniumHQ/www.seleniumhq.org.git (push)
```

Origin updated

You are now ready to make changes to the documentation. When you are happy with a change, you can create a pull request to submit it back to the Selenium developers.

 It's always useful to create a new branch for the changes you make. When you perform a pull request, it is not for a static piece of code. You are requesting that the branch that you are currently working on should be pulled in. This means that if you make any changes to the branch after making your pull request, they will also be added to the list of things that are being offered. Having a separate branch for each pull request allows you to easily isolate changes.

So far, we have been looking at the old site. Also, we did briefly mention earlier that there is a new documentation project. If you want to add documentation, this is probably the best place to start. To do this, you will need to clone the new documentation project (for more information, visit `https://github.com/SeleniumHQ/docs.git`).

The process is basically identical to the one that we followed to clone the Selenium website. Once you are done, you are ready to make changes to the document. Why not start updating the documentation and creating pull requests today?

Making changes to Selenium

We had a look at the various things that you can do to help the Selenium project. The big one is obviously adding code to Selenium itself. The first thing that you will need to do is fork the Selenium project and check it out locally. It's exactly the same process as before.

Once we have the code checked out, the first challenge is to build it. Selenium has lots of moving parts, and it's not always clear what you need to run. The two targets that will probably be useful for somebody working with Java are as follows:

```
./go test_java_webdriver -trace
```

```
./go test_firefox --trace
```

What you want to build will depend on which part of the code you are working on. There is a Rakefile in the root of the project, and if you look through this, you will see the various targets that are available to you.

> One thing that I always try to do is run a `./go` command and then expect everything to work. If it won't, there is code in Selenium for multiple operating systems, and you will not be able to run everything on your machine. Focus on the bits that you are changing, and trust CI to catch anything else.

If you get stuck and have any questions, the best way to get them answered is to go to the *#selenium IRC* channel on `irc.freenode.net` and have a chat with various people from the Selenium community. They are all very helpful and will probably have seen your problem before.

Now that we have got Selenium building projects locally, let's do something useful. Let's add something that is missing and then submit a pull request. The Selenium team has created a document to aid people who want to contribute towards the project. It's available at `https://github.com/SeleniumHQ/selenium/blob/master/CONTRIBUTING.md`. The most important thing to do is sign the **CLA** (**Contributor License Agreement**). If you don't sign this, your code cannot be accepted into the project. Once this has been signed, you can get on with making a pull request.

Selenium has a support class to convert colors from one format to another. It also has a predefined list of colors, as specified in `http://www.w3.org/TR/css3-color/#html4`. Since this list was created, an additional color has been added to the W3C spec, rebeccapurple. So, we are going to add this color to the `Colors` enum inside the support package.

The first thing that we are going to do is create a new local branch. This means that when we make changes and raise a pull request, we can switch to another branch and make more changes without affecting the pull request. Creating a branch is simple. You just use the following command:

```
git checkout -b rebeccapurple
```

Normally, when adding a change to the Selenium codebase, we would start off by writing a failing test that uses the functionality that we are about to implement. However, in this case, the change is just the addition of a constant to an enum. It's a simple code change. So. we don't expect it to have any side effects, and we don't really need to add any more tests. Let's start with the additional code that we are going to add:

```
POWDERBLUE(new Color(176, 224, 230, 1d)),
PURPLE(new Color(128, 0, 128, 1d)),
REBECCAPURPLE(new Color(102, 51, 153, 1d)),
RED(new Color(255, 0, 0, 1d)),
ROSYBROWN(new Color(188, 143, 143, 1d)),
```

Everything else is currently there. So, the only color that we are adding is rebeccapurple. Now that we have added our change, we need to run the tests to make sure that we didn't break anything. It would be a big surprise if our change did break anything, but always run the tests anyway:

```
./go test_java_webdriver -trace
```

Our tests pass

Now, we need to commit the change, as follows:

```
git commit -m "Add rebeccapurple to the Colors enum"
```

We are now ready to raise our pull request, but we have a bit more work to do. We need to make sure that our fork is up to date with the main Selenium repository. To do this, we need to add a remote and then pull in all the changes that have happened since we pulled down our copy of the Selenium repository. Let's add the remote first:

```
git remote add upstream https://github.com/SeleniumHQ/selenium.git
```

Then, pull down the latest code from the main Selenium repository and add it to our branch, as follows:

```
git fetch upstream
```

```
git rebase upstream/master
```

We now have the latest code on our local branch as well as the change. We need to push all of this up to our fork on GitHub, as follows:

```
git push origin rebeccapurple
```

We are now ready to make the pull request. Load your fork in GitHub with a browser, and you should see a big green button called **Compare & pull request**.

Compare and pull request

It's as simple as clicking the button. You will then be asked to confirm the branch that you want to generate the pull request with and the fork that you want to send it to.

Creating a pull request

When you are happy, click on **Create pull request**, and your pull request will be generated for you. You will get a summary that tells you the state of your pull request, and a Travis CI build will be triggered.

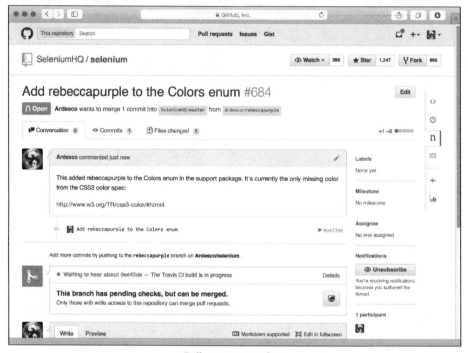

Pull request complete

When this is complete, it's all ready to be merged. You can sit back and wait, or jump into the *#selenium IRC* channel and check whether you can find a core committer.

Keeping your history clean

Selenium is a large project with lots of contributors. Due to this, there are lots of commits that are happening all the time. To keep the commit history clean, the developers try to ensure that each pull request that they merge into the main branch is just a single commit. We didn't have a problem with our change, because it was very simple. However, if you have made some quite far-reaching changes and have many commits, you will probably find out that you have some tidying up to do.

First of all, don't worry. It's not a big problem. Git has the ability to squash these multiple commits into one change. Let's have a look at how we can do this. We will start off with a project that has four commits that we want to squash into one.

```
commit 0eea1e81d8382d3add84e219b057c251b41d85fb
Author: Mark Collin <mark.collin@lazeryattack.com>
Date:    Thu Jun 18 20:45:51 2015 +0100

    Final bit of tidying, everything works and all the tests pass

commit dd3ccdf8cd9454dcee452ac0b27970fe290d7355
Author: Mark Collin <mark.collin@lazeryattack.com>
Date:    Thu Jun 18 20:45:17 2015 +0100

    Nearly done.

commit 498f31a372d1025e70da26556b4355fed0188fed
Author: Mark Collin <mark.collin@lazeryattack.com>
Date:    Thu Jun 18 20:45:01 2015 +0100

    It's all going well so far.

commit ad7ae7e6df169a323ad9995dc981e2db161afd1b
Author: Mark Collin <mark.collin@lazeryattack.com>
Date:    Thu Jun 18 20:44:16 2015 +0100

    Start of my great big change.

commit 0e67b7b688b505173264d4ba552b110a1985475b
Author: Daniel Davison <daniel.jj.davison@gmail.com>
Date:    Thu Jun 18 10:51:56 2015 -0400

    fix broken tests
```

Our four initial commits

We know that we have four commits. So, we are going to use the `rebase` command to interactively change these four commits and squash them into one, as follows:

```
git rebase -i HEAD~4
```

When you use the `rebase` command, Git will take the commits that you are interested in, show a screen that lists the commits, and ask what you want to do with them.

 You may want to get hold of a VI cheat sheet from the Internet at this point. If you are not used to VI, it can be quite frustrating. A reasonably good one is available at `http://www.viemu.com/vi-vim-cheat-sheet.gif`.

```
pick ad7ae7e Start of my great big change.
pick 498f31a It's all going well so far.
pick dd3ccdf Nearly done.
pick 0eea1e8 Final bit of tidying, everything works and all the tests pass

# Rebase 0e67b7b..0eea1e8 onto 0e67b7b (4 command(s))
#
# Commands:
# p, pick = use commit
# r, reword = use commit, but edit the commit message
# e, edit = use commit, but stop for amending
# s, squash = use commit, but meld into previous commit
# f, fixup = like "squash", but discard this commit's log message
# x, exec = run command (the rest of the line) using shell
#
# These lines can be re-ordered; they are executed from top to bottom.
#
# If you remove a line here THAT COMMIT WILL BE LOST.
#
# However, if you remove everything, the rebase will be aborted.
#
# Note that empty commits are commented out
```

Ready to change our commit history

We now need to tell Git to squash all the commits into just one commit. The commit at the top of the file was the original one. So, this is the one that we are going to leave as it is. The other commits will be squashed into this original commit.

```
pick ad7ae7e Start of my great big change.
squash 498f31a It's all going well so far.
squash dd3ccdf Nearly done.
squash 0eea1e8 Final bit of tidying, everything works and all the tests pass

# Rebase 0e67b7b..0eea1e8 onto 0e67b7b (4 command(s))
#
# Commands:
# p, pick = use commit
# r, reword = use commit, but edit the commit message
# e, edit = use commit, but stop for amending
# s, squash = use commit, but meld into previous commit
# f, fixup = like "squash", but discard this commit's log message
# x, exec = run command (the rest of the line) using shell
#
# These lines can be re-ordered; they are executed from top to bottom.
#
# If you remove a line here THAT COMMIT WILL BE LOST.
#
# However, if you remove everything, the rebase will be aborted.
#
# Note that empty commits are commented out
```

Selections made, ready to save

Now, we just need to save our changes. The easiest way to do this is by holding down *Shift* and pressing Z twice. You will then be presented with a screen asking you to specify a commit message for your newly squashed commit. You can either join together all the old commit messages, or you can use a completely new one.

```
# This is a combination of 4 commits.
My change squashed into one commit.

# Please enter the commit message for your changes. Lines starting
# with '#' will be ignored, and an empty message aborts the commit.
#
# Date:      Thu Jun 18 20:44:16 2015 +0100
#
# rebase in progress; onto 0e67b7b
# You are currently editing a commit while rebasing branch 'master' on '0e67b7b'.
#
# Changes to be committed:
#       modified:   .idea/compiler.xml
#       modified:   .idea/misc.xml
#
# Untracked files:
#       .idea/shelf/
#       android/
#       node_modules/
#
```

Our new commit message

Again, we need to save our changes. Hold down *Shift* and press *Z* twice again. We have now squashed all the changes into one commit. We can check whether the whole process worked by checking out `git log` again.

```
commit e6a1b1fa4e3b5aff87088ce240a1576d0c3dd0ab
Author: Mark Collin <mark.collin@lazeryattack.com>
Date:    Thu Jun 18 20:44:16 2015 +0100

    My change squashed into one commit.

commit 0e67b7b688b505173264d4ba552b110a1985475b
Author: Daniel Davison <daniel.jj.davison@gmail.com>
Date:    Thu Jun 18 10:51:56 2015 -0400

    fix broken tests
```

Just one commit now

Now that we have just the one change, let's push this to GitHub so that we can make our pull request, as follows:

```
git push
```

If you pushed the four commits to GitHub before you squashed your history, the push was probably rejected. It was rejected because rewriting the history for your codebase can cause problems if somebody else is also using your repository and they have already pulled the latest revision of code.

In our case, we don't have to worry about this problem because nobody else is using our branch. To get the code pushed up to GitHub, we will force the push, as follows:

```
git push -f
```

Now that our code has been pushed up to our fork on GitHub, we are ready to raise another pull request.

Now it's your turn

All in all, the commit process is quite simple. So, why don't you make some changes and submit a pull request right now? The Selenium developers have added a filter to the bug tracker on GitHub to identify the bugs that look like they may be quite simple.

These bugs are good candidates for people who want to work on the Selenium codebase but aren't sure where to start. Have a look at `https://github.com/SeleniumHQ/selenium/issues?q=is%3Aopen+is%3Aissue+label%3AE-easy`.

Summary

In this chapter, we had a look at what Selenium plans to be in the future and how you can help take it there. After reading this chapter, you should

- Know a bit about Selenium as a W3C specification
- Know the various routes that you can take to get involved and help make Selenium better
- Have a clear understanding of how to fork the Selenium code base
- Be able to raise pull requests to get the code that you added in the Selenium code base

Index

Symbol

$(docker ps -a) 226

A

Advanced User Interactions API
about 135, 136
drag and drop, working with 141-145
drawbacks 153
hover menus, working with 137-141
implementing 137
offsets, working with 146-152
AMI (Amazon Machines Image) 52
Ansible
URL 205
asynchronous scripts 169-171
AutoIt 183

B

boot2docker 219
browser auto download 184

C

Chef
URL 205
CLA (Contributor License Agreement) 247
CloudBees
URL 57
continuous integration
defining 50, 51
Jenkins 57-61
TeamCity 52-57

D

Docker
about 213-215
advantages 214
containers, starting up 228-231
future 234
installing 216
Linux installation 216
Linux namespaces, using 215
OS X installation 217-218
Windows installation 217, 218
Docker Maven plugin
URL 232
using 232-234
documentation
about 242-245
references 242
DriverFactory class 94
DRY (Don't Repeat Yourself)
about 105
applying, to page objects 106-111
DSL (domain-specific language) 126

E

exceptions
defining, as oracles 75
ElementNotVisibleException 78, 79
InvalidElementStateException 82
NoSuchElementException 75-77
NoSuchFrameException 77
NoSuchWindowException 78
SessionNotFoundException 85
StaleElementReferenceException 79-82

LNMP (Linux, Nginx, MySQL, and PHP) setup 215

M

Maven 2
multiple browser support
about 19-23
Chrome 24
Firefox 24
Internet Explorer 24
Opera 24-27
Safari 24

N

namespaces 215
network traffic
checking 192-204

P

page
loading, time 88
PageFactory annotations
proxied objects, initializing 118-120
using 117
page objects
about 112-114
DRY (Don't Repeat Yourself),
applying to 106-111
turning, into readable domain-specific
language 126-129
parallel tests
with TestNG 9-18
penetration testing
performing, with Selenium 208-210
performance tests
writing, with Selenium 205-207
prerequisites, for file downloads with
Selenium
about 182
AutoIt 183
browser auto download 184
existing code, extending 184
Java Robot class 183

Puppet
URL 205

R

readable domain-specific language
page objects, turning into 126-129

S

Sauce Labs
URL 61
SCM systems
about 48
Git 48
SVN 49, 50
Selenium
about 237-239
bugs, fixing 240
code base, forking 246-250
commit history, keeping clean 250-253
implicit wait timeout mechanism 92
page load timeout mechanism 91
script timeout mechanism 92
used, for performing penetration
testing 208-210
used, for writing performance tests 205-207
using 90
Selenium Grid
spinning up, with Docker 220-226
test, running against 226, 227
used, for extending capabilities 62-65
Selenium WebDriver API 237
Selenium repository
set up, contributing to 241
separation of concerns, with
page objects 114-116
source code management (SCM) 48
Sphinx
about 241
URL 241
stack traces
defining 70-72
SunSpider JavaScript benchmark
URL 89

Thank you for buying
Mastering Selenium WebDriver

About Packt Publishing

Packt, pronounced 'packed', published its first book, *Mastering phpMyAdmin for Effective MySQL Management*, in April 2004, and subsequently continued to specialize in publishing highly focused books on specific technologies and solutions.

Our books and publications share the experiences of your fellow IT professionals in adapting and customizing today's systems, applications, and frameworks. Our solution-based books give you the knowledge and power to customize the software and technologies you're using to get the job done. Packt books are more specific and less general than the IT books you have seen in the past. Our unique business model allows us to bring you more focused information, giving you more of what you need to know, and less of what you don't.

Packt is a modern yet unique publishing company that focuses on producing quality, cutting-edge books for communities of developers, administrators, and newbies alike. For more information, please visit our website at www.packtpub.com.

About Packt Open Source

In 2010, Packt launched two new brands, Packt Open Source and Packt Enterprise, in order to continue its focus on specialization. This book is part of the Packt Open Source brand, home to books published on software built around open source licenses, and offering information to anybody from advanced developers to budding web designers. The Open Source brand also runs Packt's Open Source Royalty Scheme, by which Packt gives a royalty to each open source project about whose software a book is sold.

Writing for Packt

We welcome all inquiries from people who are interested in authoring. Book proposals should be sent to author@packtpub.com. If your book idea is still at an early stage and you would like to discuss it first before writing a formal book proposal, then please contact us; one of our commissioning editors will get in touch with you.

We're not just looking for published authors; if you have strong technical skills but no writing experience, our experienced editors can help you develop a writing career, or simply get some additional reward for your expertise.

open source
community experience distilled

Selenium Design Patterns
and Best Practices

Build a powerful, stable, and automated test suite using Selenium WebDriver

Foreword by Jim Evans, core contributor to the WebDriver project

Dima Kovalenko

Selenium Design Patterns and Best Practices

ISBN: 978-1-78398-270-7   Paperback: 270 pages

Build a powerful, stable, and automated test suite using Selenium WebDriver

1. Keep up with the changing pace of your web application by creating an agile test suite.

2. Save time and money by making your Selenium tests 99% reliable.

3. Improve the stability of your test suite and your programing skills by following a step-by-step continuous improvement tutorial.

Selenium Essentials

Get to grips with automated web testing with the amazing power of Selenium WebDriver

Prashanth Sams

Selenium Essentials

ISBN: 978-1-78439-433-2   Paperback: 194 pages

Get to grips with automated web testing with the amazing power of Selenium WebDriver

1. Utilize Selenium WebDriver features for automation testing using outstanding techniques and strategies.

2. Learn how to build, customize, and maintain Selenium frameworks.

3. Packed with numerous practical examples, this book covers all the functions and commands that will help you grasp Selenium functions quickly.

Please check **www.PacktPub.com** for information on our titles

31646321R00157

Made in the USA
San Bernardino, CA
16 March 2016